The McCall's Book of HANDCRAFTS

Rooster is handsomely "feathered" with hardware — a variety of tacks, nails, and thin wire. See page 203.

The McCall's Book of HANDCRAFTS

a learn-and-make book

by Nanina Comstock
and The Editors of McCall's Needlework
& Crafts Publications

RANDOM HOUSE ● THE McCALL PATTERN CO.

Dedicated to

Elisabeth Blondel Gardner

Editor of McCall's Needlework 1935-1952

Library of Congress Cataloging in Publication Data

Comstock, Nanina
The McCall's book of handcrafts

I. Handicraft, I. McCall's needlework & crafts.
II. Title. III. Title: Handcrafts
TT145.C65   745.5   72-5753
ISBN 0-394-48300-6

Manufactured in the United States of America

98765432

Foreword

This book has many purposes: The beginner can learn a new craft by starting with an easy project and advancing to those more difficult — the explicit directions take no knowledge for granted. The expert craftsman can improve his skills by adding variety and new design ideas to his specialty. Many people who have become skilled in one craft soon find they are involved in learning others.

All are taught how to obtain professional results when producing even the simplest object. The same formula for directions is used throughout the book. For the convenience of the craftsman, all the equipment and materials needed are listed first. General directions are given wherever there are several items to be made in the same technique; then specific instructions follow for individual items. It is important to read all the directions through before starting work; then proceed step-by-step.

The variety of techniques encourages the craftsman to experiment in other areas — perhaps he will combine two or more crafts to produce a unique result; for example, see how candles are used with foil tooling, page 107.

One does not have to be an artist to be a successful craftsman — often untrained hands create original and beautifully designed folk-art heirlooms. What you yourself create today may be the treasured collector's item of tomorrow. All the handcrafts in this book came from creative, imaginative people. Let their exciting ideas inspire you to make your own craft into a creative art.

Acknowledgments

The contents of this book have been compiled from the McCall's Needlework & Crafts publications with the editorial aid of the following associates: Irma Bolley, Charlotte Brem, Betsy Emery, and Eleanor Spencer. The craftsmen who contributed the most are: Helen Andersen, Candles; Roslyn Cohen, Batik; Margaret Pennington, Macrame; Rosemary Taylor, Ceramics; Lee Lindeman, miscellaneous.

CONTENTS

Batik

Although the word batik originated in Java,
the beginning of this ancient folk art is not really
known for certain. Archeological evidence of batik
dates back 2,000 years and includes not only Central
and Southeast Asia, but also Japan and Africa.
In Indonesia, batik was originally done by the
women of the aristocracy who created many beautiful
and symbolic designs worn by both men and women
during the 16th and 17th centuries. Also, at this time,
batik was introduced to Europe from Java by the Dutch.
In recent years batik has become a very popular
craft technique in the United States, and the current
approach is fresh, free, individual, and unique.
This exciting craft is a simple wax-resist technique
for producing designs on white or light-colored fabric.
The wax is applied hot to the fabric following a
preconceived design or idea. Then the fabric is
dipped in a cooled solution of dye and water, where
only the unwaxed parts are dyed. However, the wax is
sometimes deliberately cracked to form fine lines of
color where the dye penetrates these cracks.
When wax is removed, the design appears. The process
may be repeated for number of colors desired; but in
this case, for the best results, it is a good idea for a
craftsman to have a knowledge of mixing colors.
Following is a sampling of what is being done today!

STEP-BY-STEP BATIK—EASY FOR BEGINNERS

1. Plan your design, then enlarge pattern on tracing paper. Lightly transfer the pattern lines to fabric.

2. Melt the wax in a double boiler. Place aluminum foil between the two pans to catch the wax drippings.

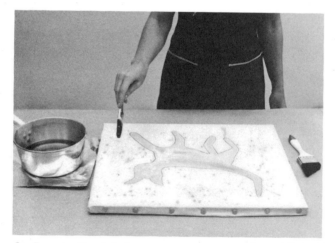

3. Secure the fabric to a canvas stretcher. "Paint" the wax on desired areas to retain the existing color.

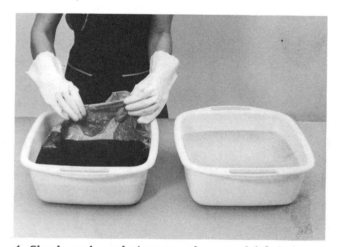

4. Slowly and gently immerse the waxed fabric into a dye bath. Leave the fabric in dye about 20 minutes.

5. Rinse the fabric in warm water (cold water causes excessive crackle). Then hang the fabric up to dry.

6. Iron the right and wrong sides of the fabric between paper towels until all of the wax is removed.

Cheerful cat dances across a speckled background of yellow, orange, and red. Starting with yellow fabric, the designer filled in the cat area with wax to protect it from the dye. To achieve background effect, wax was dribbled across area before each dyeing. Cracking of the wax caused red lines on body. Step-by-step directions for batik are illustrated at the left. Batik directions for Yellow Cat are on page 16.

HOW TO DO BATIK

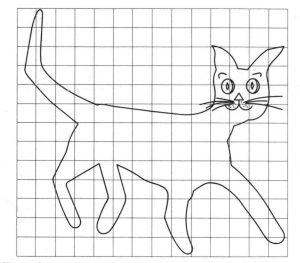

To enlarge Cat, copy on paper ruled in 1" squares.

EQUIPMENT: Large sheets of paper for planning designs. Large sheets of tracing paper. Soft pencil. Charcoal pencil or carbon paper. Ruler. Scissors. Thumbtacks. Wooden canvas stretchers (they come in various sizes) or other suitable frames. Waxed paper. Hot plate. Two saucepans. Aluminum foil. Sticks for stirring. Teaspoon. Immersible thermometer. Good quality flat and tapered stiff brushes in several widths for fine lines and large background areas, about ⅛" to 2" (see individual directions; make sure they will hold their shape and not get singed in hot wax). Dye bath containers: two large porcelain or plastic bowls or tubs. Rubber gloves. Apron. Iron. Ironing board. Paper toweling. Newspapers. Bleaching cleanser. Toothpick. Optional: cheesecloth.

MATERIALS: Fabric. Paraffin wax and beeswax. Dyes: ordinary household dyes may be used, but batik dyes are better; see individual directions for specific dyes. Uniodized salt. White vinegar.

GENERAL DIRECTIONS: See page 10 for step-by-step illustrations. **To Select Fabric:** Use smooth, finely woven fabric such as percale, fine silks, muslin, or cotton denim. Synthetic fabrics such as nylon, rayon, dacron, and drip-dry, permanent-press cottons are not as suitable because they do not dye as well. Fabrics such as heavy silks and satins can be used; however, they are not particularly suitable for the beginner.

Note: Since you cannot correct design after waxing and dyeing, you must decide upon the design before you begin and then work very carefully. However, because of the nature of batik, you can incorporate many mistakes into the general design of the project you have planned.

To Prepare Fabric: Work out your design on paper; make final version on tracing paper if transferring design to fabric. Go over lines of design on both sides of tracing. Cut the fabric the size of design, plus background desired, adding 2" all around. Wash fabric with soap or detergent and water to preshrink and remove sizing which may cause uneven coloring. Rinse well in clear water. If using colored fabric, boil for a few minutes and rinse well to remove any loose color dye. Let dry; iron smooth.

Place fabric on flat surface; with charcoal pencil, mark design on fabric freehand, using ruler or other equipment (see individual directions) to aid in spacing; or place tracing of design on fabric with carbon paper between and, with soft pencil, trace over lines to lightly transfer design to fabric (see Illus. 1). With thumbtacks, stretch fabric on canvas stretcher or frame and keep taut (see Illus. 3).

Cover working surface with aluminum foil, newspapers, or waxed paper. If design on fabric is too
continued on page 14

To enlarge Owl, copy on paper ruled in 1" squares.

A wise old owl sits on a branch, contemplating the world. The owl pattern is traced on yellow fabric and dyed orange, then brown. Before each dye bath, the areas to retain the existing color are "painted" with wax. The crest, eyes, nose, and feet are then outlined with an ink marker. Owl and Moon, page 16.

HOW TO DO BATIK
continued from page 12

continued from page 12

large for canvas stretcher, work directly on well-covered surface. Cover floor with newspapers.

To Prepare Wax: Generally for best results, use 60% beeswax and 40% paraffin wax or equal proportions. Where you do not wish crackle effect, use mostly beeswax.

Cut hole in sheet of aluminum foil to fit bottom of the top saucepan. Place the two saucepans on hot plate one atop the other with cut-out aluminum foil between to make double boiler (see illus. 2). Do not melt wax directly over flame! The foil is used to catch the wax drippings and avoid fire. Put water in bottom pan, wax in top. Heat wax to at least 170° F. and stir occasionally to hasten melting. Keep wax from overheating. After wax has melted, allow it to cool a little before applying to fabric. Turn heat off while working to keep wax from getting too hot; reheat if necessary. Take great precautions not to spill or get water even near the pot of hot wax. Water will cause splattering and you can be severely burned! If fire occurs, extinguish flame with salt, **not water.**

To Paint with Wax: Use smallest brush for delicate parts of design and use widest brush for background. If desired, you can use medium-size brush trimmed to a wedge (see lower left of Illus. 2). To do this, dip brush in hot wax; when cool, cut diagonally with scissors. Use the pointed end for fine lines and full area of brush for larger areas.

Work close to where the hot plate is. Make sure wax is at least 170° F. Dip brush in wax. Brush will fan out at first, so press out air and moisture against side of pan until brush is flat again. Test first on fabric scraps. If wax spot on fabric is dark, wax is ready for use; if not, wax needs to be heated more.

With full brush, apply wax to fabric with even strokes on areas not to be dyed with first color; use long strokes for large areas and short daubs for small areas (see Illus. 3). If fabric does not absorb wax immediately, then wax is not hot enough or you are working too slowly. Since hot wax will run somewhat, be sure to work within the outlines of your design. Be careful not to drip wax on fabric. If you are working with particularly heavy fabric, apply wax to both sides of fabric.

After waxing fabric, remove brush from pot of wax and leave on table edge with bristles extending over edge. Do not remove wax from brush.

To Dye Fabric: Put on apron and rubber gloves. Mix dye and water in plastic tub as indicated in package directions. Add teaspoon of uniodized salt to each quart of liquid (this will act as a color fixative; use vinegar if working with silk or wool fabric); stir to mix thoroughly. Paraffin wax must not be immersed in solution warmer than 90° F. Beeswax mixture will withstand dye bath up to 110° F. Some dyes need very hot water in which to dissolve; let solution cool before using. Start with lightest color dye first. If there are some particles of dye which have not dissolved, you can strain the dye through cheesecloth before using.

Before placing fabric in dye bath, lay it in lukewarm water to insure even penetration of dye. Slowly immerse waxed fabric into dye bath (see Illus. 4); be careful to avoid cracking wax if crackle effect is not desired. Leave fabric in dye bath for about 20 minutes; remove fabric from dye bath; rinse in clear, lukewarm water (see Illus. 5), remove excess water with paper towels, and hang up straight and smooth to dry. Remember that color will lighten as it dries. If color is too pale, dye again.

Clean tub with bleaching cleanser before preparing next color dye.

For second color, secure fabric to stretcher or frame. With wax, paint areas and lines which are not to be in second color dye (go over areas which have been previously waxed only if necessary). Soak fabric in lukewarm water. Immerse in dye bath, rinse, and hang to dry. Repeat for each additional color. If you desire crackled effect, you can rinse fabric in very cold water and crush it in your hands or scratch into wax with toothpick before last color bath. Dyes can be reused several times before they lose their strength. Store remaining solutions of dye in covered bottles or jars. Reheat when ready to use.

To Remove Wax: Cover ironing board with newspapers to protect it. Place fabric on ironing board between layers of paper towels. Iron (see Illus. 6). As the heat of the iron is applied, the wax will melt and be absorbed by the paper. As the paper becomes saturated, replace it with fresh paper toweling. Repeat until all wax is absorbed. Since the heat is a color fastening agent, iron entire fabric well. It may be necessary to have fabric dry-cleaned to remove all the wax. To care for batik fabric, it is usually best to dry-clean. However, you may wash wearing apparel as you would any fine fabric.

This charming coat vest is cut from white velveteen, using a long vest pattern. First, it is sewn up the sides, then the velveteen is dyed three times — pink, magenta, and purple—in a stunning batik design. Wax is brushed on for each dye bath to hold the previous coloring. Sewing details are completed after vest is dry-cleaned. Directions for Long Vest on page 16.

YELLOW CAT

See "How To Do Batik" on page 12. Enlarge cat pattern on page 12 by copying on paper ruled in 1" squares. Use yellow fabric 23" x 19½". Paint entire body with wax. With brush, sprinkle wax generously around background. Immerse in orange dye. When dry, sprinkle wax again around form. Immerse in red dye. After ironing, draw eyebrows, eyes, and whiskers, and outline nose in black ink marker. Draw mouth with red ink marker.

OWL AND MOON

See "How To Do Batik" on page 12. Enlarge owl pattern on page 12 by copying on paper ruled in 1" squares. Use yellow fabric 19½" x 23½". Paint moon, crest, eyes, nose, claws, and zigzag lines in stomach area with wax. Immerse in orange dye. When dry, paint lines on outer body and background (except branch) with wax. Scratch wax slightly on eye areas and crack wax lightly on moon. Immerse in brown dye. After ironing, draw eye circles and outline outer eyes, crest, nose, and claws with black ink marker. Outline chest area and sides of body with red ink marker.

LONG VEST

See "How To Do Batik" on page 12. Select one of McCall's vest patterns. Use white cotton velveteen and batik cotton dyes only. Wash fabric. Cut out fabric pieces according to pattern and sew side seams, but not shoulder seams. Lay fabric out flat. Use your own designs or see illustration for our designs. Our design is made up of simple straight, zigzag, and wavy lines and geometric forms such as triangles, rectangles, dots, and circles in various widths and arrangements. The design should be worked out before marking on the prepared fabric. Then, with charcoal pencil, lightly mark design on fabric, being careful to make design meet in front. Use ruler to mark straight lines and broad horizontal areas. You will need several size brushes for variety and a very fine tapered brush to make fine lines (use a Tjanting if you have one).

First, apply melted wax to areas that are to remain white. For velvet, you will need a lot of wax on brush. Always check wrong side of fabric to see whether wax has penetrated the fabric; if not, wax both sides. For all colors, mix one teaspoon of salt and one teaspoon of dye to quart of water.

Immerse fabric in bright pink dye bath for 20 minutes. Wax all areas that you wish to remain bright pink. Immerse in magenta dye bath for 20 minutes. Wax all areas that you wish to remain magenta. Immerse in purple dye bath for 20 minutes. When dry, iron off wax; dry-clean. Finish making vest.

NECKTIES

See "How To Do Batik" on page 12. You will need McCall's 40-minute tie pattern #2971 for regular ties and bow tie. Use batik silk dyes, paraffin wax, and three-quarters of a yard of white China silk for each tie. Wash fabric. Do not cut out fabric, but use the full ¾ yard and plan design on the bias across from corner to corner.

For each, mix one teaspoon of dye with one teaspoon of vinegar to a quart of water. Allow silk to remain in each dye bath for 20 minutes. When finished, iron off all wax and send to dry cleaners. Make ties, following pattern.

Pink and Blue Tie: Using any straight edge and ⅜" brush, draw horizontal and vertical lines with melted wax on silk, forming diamond areas with 1½" sides. Immerse silk into rose dye bath. When dry, place bottle cap about 1¼" diameter in center area. Apply melted wax around bottle cap, filling in entire remaining area. Repeat for each diamond. Immerse silk into mauve-purple dye bath.

Blue and Green Tie: Using a variety of different-size jar lids, place randomly around fabric; with ½" brush, apply melted wax around jar lids, forming rings. Immerse into light blue dye bath. Again place jar lids on fabric over blue-dyed areas and again draw rings around lids with melted wax. Immerse in yellow dye bath to get green shade. Repeat step with jar lids and wax. Immerse into mauve dye.

Yellow-Orange Tie: Place bottle cap in areas where you want flowers; apply melted wax in the form of petals around bottle caps. Immerse in yellow dye bath. Apply melted wax over all yellow except flower centers. Immerse in bright red dye.

Blue-Green Bow Tie: Spray melted wax on fabric by flicking waxed brush over fabric, covering most of fabric. Immerse in light blue dye bath. Repeat wax spraying sparsely. Immerse in dark blue dye bath. Remove all wax by ironing. Spray randomly again with wax to retain white and blue pattern in certain areas. Immerse in yellow dye bath.

These attractive ties are one-of-a-kind, high-style accessories. Using a variety of jar lids and bottle caps, a straight edge, and a free hand, the designs are drawn in wax on white silk. To dye the bow tie, the wax is spattered on. The silk is then dyed in two or more stages. Directions for Neckties, above.

The eye-catching totes pictured above make practical catchalls. Both styles are lined with clear plastic; the tall tote has an adjustable handle. Colorful sunset and flower designs are "painted" by applying wax on white cotton before each dye bath. See directions and repeat of designs on pages 20 and 21.

Amusing mushroom and fish designs are shown on the opposite page. Both are dyed twice on white cotton, using red, then blue dye for the mushroom motif and pink and sky-blue dyes for the fish designs. Directions start on page 20; the illustrations on page 21 show how designs are repeated or arranged on fabric.

TOTES AND FABRICS

EQUIPMENT: Straight pins. Sewing needle.

MATERIALS: One yard of white fabric, 48" wide for each bag (we recommend using 100% cotton denim). Batik dyes for cotton (see individual directions for colors, or use desired colors). Cotton fabric and clear plastic (same amount as for denim) for lining. Buckram for interlining, 40" wide. Matching sewing thread. For adjustable handle: 3 brass rings, 2¼" diameter.

DIRECTIONS: See "How To Do Batik" on page 12. Refer to illustrations on pages 18, 19, and 21.

Wash fabric. Dissolve one teaspoon of dye with one teaspoon of salt in hot water in a cup. Mix thoroughly. Pour into dye vat (tub or bowl). Add enough cold water to make one quart. Then double or triple amount so there is enough water to cover fabric. **Note:** If using a cotton-polyester blend denim, you should leave fabric in dye bath for 30 or more minutes.

Mushroom Design: You will need red dye and blue dye (½ teaspoon sky blue, ½ teaspoon royal blue). Enlarge mushroom patterns on page 22 by copying on paper ruled in 1" squares. Following illustration opposite or working out your own design, plan complete design for fabric and trace design onto tracing paper. Follow General Directions for transferring design to fabric. Apply melted wax to areas that are to remain white. Immerse into red dye bath for 20 to 30 minutes. Apply wax to areas to remain red. Immerse into blue dye bath for 20 to 30 minutes.

Fish Design: You will need pink and sky blue dyes. Enlarge patterns (page 22) by copying on paper ruled in 1" squares. Following illustration opposite or working out your own design, plan complete design for fabric; trace design onto tracing paper. Following General Directions, transfer complete design to fabric. With pencil, sketch in outlines of bubbles where you want them. Apply wax to areas that are to remain white (mouth, bubbles, eyes). Immerse into pink dye bath for 20 minutes. Apply wax to fish bodies so they will remain pink. Immerse into sky blue dye bath for 20 minutes.

Flower Design: You will need orange dye and purple dye (¾ teaspoon imperial blue and ¼ teaspoon red). Plan design and spacing of flowers. Use jar lid about 3" diameter as a guide for flower centers. Place lid on fabric where you want flower center to be and apply melted wax with brush in form of petals (see illustration) around jar lid. Repeat in all areas where you want flowers. Immerse in orange dye bath for 20 to 30 minutes. Apply dots of wax to centers of flowers and between flowers to retain orange color. Immerse in purple dye bath for 20 to 30 minutes. If flower center is not vivid enough, paint a concentrated amount of purple dye (¾ teaspoon imperial blue, ¼ teaspoon red, ¼ cup warm water) on flower centers around dots.

Sunset Design: You will need yellow, orange, and red dye. Plan placement of design. Using lid or paint can 4½" diameter as guide, pencil in circles on fabric for suns. Using wide and narrow brushes, apply melted wax in narrow and wide wavy bands across fabric along areas to remain white (see color illustration on page 18). Immerse into yellow dye bath for 20 to 30 minutes. Again apply melted wax in narrow and wide wavy bands across fabric along areas to remain yellow. Immerse into orange dye bath for 20 to 30 minutes. Cover remaining areas around suns with wax. Immerse into red dye bath for 20 to 30 minutes. If red suns are not deep enough when fabric is dry, paint on additional amount of concentrated dye (¼ teaspoon red dye, ¼ teaspoon cup hot water) to deepen.

To Make Tote: There are two styles. Make pattern first out of heavy brown paper following diagram 1 (see page 22) for short tote or diagram 2 for tall tote: Mark half crosswise as indicated by short dash line. Then cut out shaded areas at each side as indicated (seam allowances are included in dimensions given in diagrams). Pin pattern to fabric; cut out fabric. Fold fabric in half crosswise with right sides facing. Sew ½" seam at one side. Press seam open, and fold fabric following diagram 3; stitch across end where indicated by dotted line in diagram, making ½" seam. Repeat on other side. Turn bag right side out. To make permanent folds on front and back of sides, fold at each corner and stitch down from top to bottom on each side 1/16" from fold. Using pattern, cut cotton lining fabric and plastic (if desired); sew them together as one piece and make as for outer fabric; leave wrong side out and do not stitch side folds.

To stiffen sides and bottom, use buckram for interfacing before lining. For short tote, cut piece of buckram 38½" x 4"; fold up 11¼" at each end and insert into tote, glue at bottom and top of sides. For tall tote, cut piece of buckram 13" x 5" for bottom and two pieces each 17" x 5" for each side; insert into tote. Insert lining into tote, fitting it neatly in place. Fold top edges of tote down ¾" and fold top

continued on page 24

The four batik designs on opposite page show how to repeat the designs for the fabrics illustrated on pages 18 and 19. After enlarging the patterns given on page 22 for the fish and mushroom designs, follow these illustrations for placing them on the fabric.

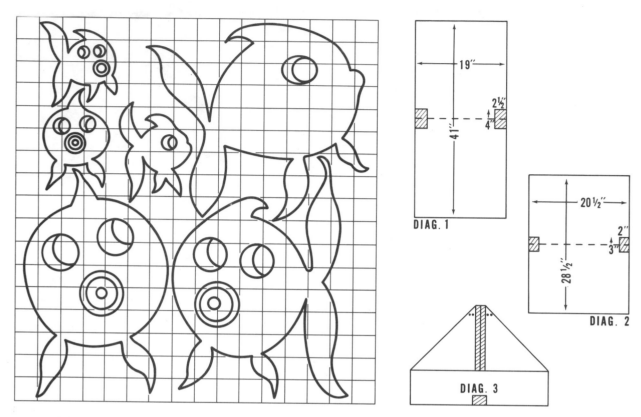

Copy fish patterns on paper ruled in 1″ squares.

Use diagrams above for the tote bags.

Enlarge mushroom patterns by copying on paper ruled in 1″ squares.

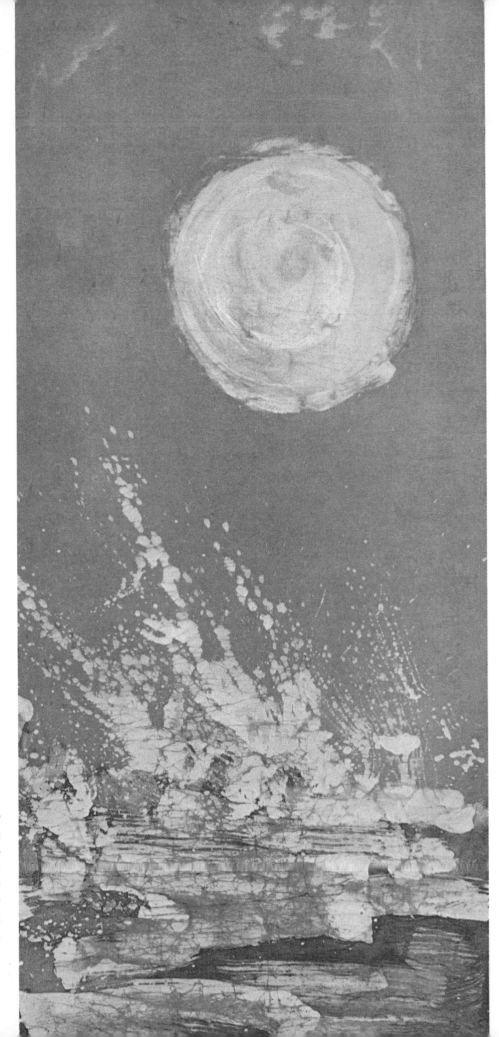

A sunlit ocean echoes mood and coloring of a Japanese screen painting. Spraying and crackling of wax make breaking wave, to contrast with the nearly solid hues of the blue sky and golden sun. Directions on page 24.

edges of lining down ¾" (top edges being between tote and lining); pin. Stitch around top ¼" from edge, stitching through all thicknesses including buckram.

If making the single adjustable style handle (on tall tote), make tabs first before sewing around top edge. To make tabs, cut two pieces of fabric, each 4" square. Fold each in half; turn edges in ½"; stitch along each side ¼" from edge. Fold each in half; place one 2¼" diameter brass ring on one tab and two on the other tab. Insert ¾" of raw ends of each tab inside top edge between tote and lining; then stitch around top edge. Cut fabric 28" x 4"; fold in half lengthwise; turn all raw edges in ½" and stitch along sides and ends ¼" from edges. Insert one end of handle through single brass ring at one side of tote; turn up end and sew to handle; at other end of handle, adjust length as desired through pair of rings.

For each double handle (on short tote), cut piece of fabric 19" x 3"; fold in half lengthwise; turn all edges in ½"; form point at each end as shown; pin to hold. Stitch all around ¼" from edges. Pin handle ends in place on each side of tote at a point 2½" below top edge; stitch in place.

SUNLIT OCEAN

See "How To Do Batik" on page 12. Use white fabric cut 24" x 50". Work general design out on tracing paper and transfer to fabric. Paint sun with wax. Spray areas for splashing waves freely with wax and brush wax on lower part of fabric unevenly for ocean. Immerse only lower part of fabric into green dye. When dry, crackle wax on lower part of fabric for ocean by wrinkling fabric. Immerse this part into aqua dye. When dry, paint part of aqua area with wax and immerse this part only into purple dye. When dry, paint ocean area with wax, leaving some areas free of wax. Immerse fabric into light blue dye. When dry, iron wax off sun. Excluding sun, paint entire sky lightly with wax in some areas for a streaked effect. Immerse fabric into yellow dye.

Candles

Little is known of the origins of candlemaking.
Candles were used by the Romans and in the middle ages;
although, at that time, the "candles" may have been
made by dipping sticks or cord into household fat.
Today, candles are popular as decorator accents and
for festive table decor as well as continuing to be used
for practical reasons and in religious ceremonies.
Craftsmen everywhere are updating this old craft
by making unusual candle designs and combining these
candles with other crafts to obtain new effects.
Further proof of the popularity of candlemaking
is demonstrated by the many candle shops throughout
the country. These shops not only sell a large
assortment of ready-made candles, but molds, wax,
wicks, and other materials for creating candles.
Some craftsmen prefer to make candles in the old
colonial molds, using bayberry and other traditional
materials, while many use kitchen utensils, blown
eggs, milk cartons, and all kinds of cans and
containers to obtain unusual shapes and new effects.
Candlemaking is a craft wide open for you to use your
own imagination! It can be almost a no-cost craft
— if old candles are melted down and their wax is
reused with bits of broken crayons for a variety of colors.

HOW TO MAKE CANDLES

EQUIPMENT: Newspapers. Waxed paper. Stick for stirring wax. Large and small cans or double boiler for melting wax. Cookie pans with sides for catching drippings. Sharp knife. Cooking oil. Additional equipment is listed in individual directions.

MATERIALS: Paraffin wax. Candle coloring dye: wax coloring cakes, disks, or wax crayons. Candlewicking.

GENERAL DIRECTIONS: Melting the Wax: Cover work area with newspapers and waxed paper to catch spilled wax. If any wax drips, it can be scraped up and reused. Melt wax in tin can set in pan of water or use double boiler. Use either large or small can depending upon amount of wax to be used. Never melt wax over direct heat or leave unattended on a lighted stove. Do not let temperature of wax go over 300° F. Take great precautions not to spill wax or splash water into the pot of hot wax. Water will cause splattering and you can be severely burned! If fire occurs, extinguish flame with salt, not water. Never allow wax to get into the plumbing system. Clean utensils in boiling water; do not pour this water down drain, throw away with other refuse.

Coloring the Wax: Use separate can for each color. Gradually add pieces of color cakes or crayon shavings (one crayon will color about one quart of wax) to melted wax until color is a shade or two darker than desired color; candle will lighten in color as it solidifies. To test for finished color, put a little wax in a small container and place in refrigerator until set. To pour wax into a mold, pinch one side of can to make a sharp lip. Be sure to stir the melted wax each time before you pour it to be sure the color is well mixed in. (Optional: Two tablespoons of stearine or stearic acid added to a quart of melted wax makes the candle more opaque, more durable, and intensifies the color.) Whatever coloring you use, do not try to mix batches of wax colored with different types of dye; if the bases are not the same, the colors will not fuse. Never use vegetable food coloring or any other water-base dyes, because they are not soluble in wax.

Wicking the Candles: Wicks from old candles may be used; new wicking may be bought at hobby stores (ordinary string may burn too quickly or smoke). If you wish to make your own candlewicking, take about ten ft. of medium-size soft cotton string or plumber's or carpenter's chalk line (at hardware stores). In one cup of water, dissolve one tablespoon salt, two tablespoons borax. Let string soak 12 hours, then hang it up for 24 hours to dry. When dry, coat string by dipping in melted wax. Place under cold running water to stiffen the wax. Directions for applying the wick are given in individual directions for each type of candle in this section.

MUSHROOM CANDLES

EQUIPMENT: Round half of an eggshell for each small mushroom cap; egg poacher pan for larger cap. Egg cup. Thick wire. Small flat paintbrush.

MATERIALS: Paraffin wax. Candle stubs 4″ long for stems. Candle coloring: Yellow, blue, red, white.

DIRECTIONS: See "How To Make Candles" above. Dry shell half in oven for 20 minutes at 300° F. Grease inside of shell with oil. With knife, taper one end of candle stub to blunted point, exposing 1½″ of fresh wick. Cut stubs different heights for variety.

Melt two slabs of wax. Support shell in egg cup. Fill shell to a depth of 1″; let set until cold. Peel of shell; this will give you small mushroom cap. With sharp knife, bore hole in underside of cap to fit point of stub. With wire, make hole through cap at center for wick. Dip top of stub in hot melted wax; push into cap from bottom, with wick going through hole to top of cap. Let set.

For large mushroom cap, use same procedure as for small cap, using the egg poacher pan for mold. Leave stub 4″ long.

Color remaining wax a light buff shade, using a tiny bit of yellow and just a touch of blue and a touch of red, plus a little white for toning. Immerse cap in wax. With brush, paint stem with this wax. Melt a small amount of wax in fresh can; mix in red, blue, and yellow coloring to get a rich brown. With brush, paint hot brown wax on underside of cap.

Mushroom candles nestle among ferns and gnarled wood, recreating a natural setting. Eggshells and an egg poacher are molds for mushroom caps; stems are candle stubs of various lengths. Mushrooms are dipped in brown wax. Directions on opposite page.

Egg candles are used as striking decorator accents. The candles are molded in eggshells, then dipped in wax for the desired colors. Florist's wire is used to mount the candles onto wood bases. Directions for making the Egg Candles are on page 30.

Candle balls in pastel fruit colors are a perfect complement to a sherbet dessert. Large and small Christmas balls are used as molds for these candles. The candles are put on a base of whipped wax. See the directions for Fruit Candles on page 30.

EGG CANDLES

EQUIPMENT: Raw eggs in a variety of sizes. Fine needle. Knitting needle. Clean wire. Poultry skewer or knitting needle. Small glass. Cardboard. Sandpaper. Brush. Hammer. Fine nail.

MATERIALS: Paraffin wax or old candle stubs. Candle coloring (see illustration for colors). Candlewicking. Optional: Four tablespoons of stearic acid per pound of wax to be added to melted wax to insure hardness, longer burning, and less dripping if desired. White pine wood cut into 2″ x 2″ x 1″ blocks. Heavy gauge florist's wire. Lacquer.

DIRECTIONS: See "How To Make Candles" on page 26. If using stubs in place of household wax, remove wicks. Melt wax in small can set in pan with 2″ of water. Using separate can for each color, color wax as desired, following General Directions. (Candle made of solid-colored wax will lack a transparency that one made of a central core of clear wax will have. You can add color later, when dipping, if desired.)

To prepare eggshell, poke ⅜″ hole in round end of egg with fine needle. Stir contents of egg with clean wire. Shake out contents of shell. Rinse shell in cold water; put in oven at 300° F. for 20 minutes to dry. This is to make membrane of shell adhere to shell rather than to candle. Coat inside of shell thoroughly with oil; drain. Place shell, hole side up, in glass set in pan to catch wax drippings. To determine amount of wax needed, fill shell with water; add one-eighth more to this amount for wax. For later dipping, triple this amount. Fill shell with clear or colored wax until overflowing. Wax will shrink as it cools. Keep filling shell (about five times). With each filling, poke down the center with knitting needle for easy flow of wax. A hole will remain in center. Keeping the shell on, run wire down through hole, through candle, and out the other end of eggshell. Remove wire, then run wick through hole. Cut ½″ diameter cardboard circle; make hole in center. Thread bottom end of wick through hole in cardboard; tie knot, leaving 1″ of wick below. Crack shell and remove. Remelt remaining wax to a temperature of 125° F. or just above the melting point. Holding candle by wick at top, slowly lower candle into remaining wax. When no more bubbles arise, withdraw candle slowly to insure an even coat. Let candle cool and dip again until desired color is obtained. Cool. Remove cardboard and cut off knot. Trim wick.

For mounting, sand wood smooth; coat with lacquer. Hammer nail into center of wood 1½″ deep; pull out. Cut 6″ length of florist's wire and insert into hole; heat and insert into candle along wick.

FRUIT CANDLES

EQUIPMENT: Large and small Christmas balls for molds. Small (jelly) glass. Knitting needle. Thick wire. Scissors. Paper toweling. Paper bag. Scrap of cardboard. Egg beater. Fork.

MATERIALS: Paraffin wax. Candlewicking. Red, yellow, and blue coloring. Cardboard. Aluminum foil.

DIRECTIONS: See "How To Make Candles" on page 26. Remove hanger from Christmas ball. To determine amount of wax needed, fill ball with water and pour it into can. Observe level and add one-eighth more. Melt wax in can to this level. Invert ball to dry thoroughly; then grease inside thoroughly with oil and drain.

Support ball in a small glass set in a cookie pan. Fill ball with melted hot wax until overflowing. Save the overflow wax to remelt. Wax in ball will shrink as it cools. After 20 minutes, poke knitting needle in ball and refill until overflowing; repeat, poking down the center with knitting needle each time for easy flow of wax. Allow ball to cool for several hours or until there is no feeling of warmth.

Holding ball in several thicknesses of paper toweling over a large paper bag, crack the glass with knife handle and slip off ball. Remove neck from wax ball.

Heat wire and run it through ball. Run wick through hole in ball. Leave 3″ of wick at top, 1″ at bottom. Cut ½″ diameter circle of cardboard; make small hole in center; run lower wick end through hole in center and tie knot just below cardboard.

To color ball, use melting can at least ½″ greater in diameter than ball. When clear wax has melted, add coloring for very pale tints: yellow and a little red for orange, a little red for pink, yellow and blue for green. Wax should be just barely melted. Test color by dipping end of a used white candle into melted wax. Dip ball repeatedly into colored wax until desired depth of tone is attained. When dipping, lower ball slowly and withdraw slowly for even coat. Hang by wick to cool between coats. Hang to set. Trim wick. Remove cardboard circle.

To make whipped base for small balls, cut a half-dollar size circle of cardboard and cover with aluminum foil. Melt a slab of wax. Let cool until it starts to congeal. With an egg beater, carefully beat wax until it forms a froth that stands in peaks. With fork, heap

continued on page 32

Brilliant candles are made with a variety of common "molds." Pagoda candles are shaped in plastic cookie trays. Hexagonal candle takes shape from parts of a plastic pin box. For rosette candles, wax is shaped in tartlet tins. Animal candles are formed with cookie cutters. Two braid-trimmed candles are made in gelatin molds. Multimold Candles, page 32.

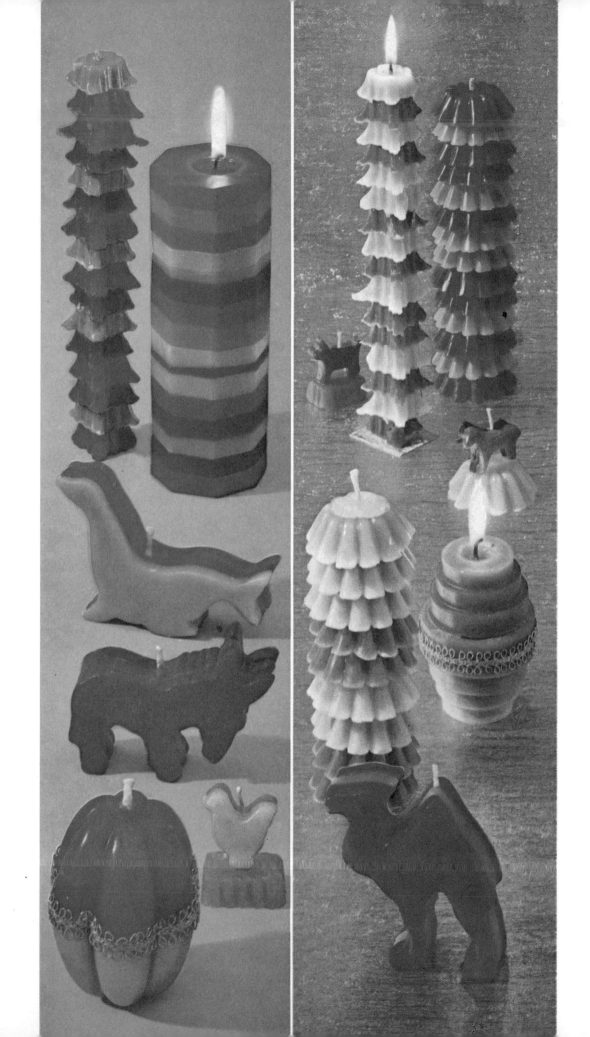

FRUIT CANDLES
continued from page 30

froth around cardboard circles. Set the candle ball in middle of froth and hold until it sets and stands securely upright.

MULTIMOLD CANDLES

EQUIPMENT: Large nail about diameter of candlewick. Molds: small tartlet tins, plastic cookie trays of various shapes in which store-bought cookies come; plastic trays from candy box; hexagonal plastic container for straight pins; large and small open animal cookie cutters; metal gelatin molds. Pie tin or cake pan. Optional: Candy thermometer, propane torch, stearic acid (available at hobby or drugstores).

MATERIALS: Paraffin wax. Candle coloring. Candlewicking. Trims: gold braid, sequin pins.

DIRECTIONS: See "How To Make Candles" on page 26. Thoroughly coat inside of mold with salad oil (makes candle smoother and unmolding easier). Wax should be about 150° F. for pouring or preferably a little less when you are using the thin, plastic cookie trays for molds; hotter wax will ruin this type of mold.

To set candle faster and allow easy release from mold, place in refrigerator (never in freezer). Candle is ready to come out of mold when wax feels cold; over-exposure to cold can cause cracks in the wax, so do not leave in refrigerator longer than necessary. When candle is ready it comes easily out of the mold, metal or plastic, and does not have to be pried out; just tap the side or bottom of mold. Assemble, finish as directed.

Assembling and Finishing: Melt wax for fastening pieces together, using either white or same color as candle. Any wax that spills over on candles when assembling can be easily removed when set by lifting off with knife. If using propane torch, have it on lowest possible setting. To use torch for assembling solidly fused pieces: Place shaved-off curls of wax in the depression in one piece; use the torch to melt it and also to go quickly over the next surface being added, so that the two surfaces will adhere more readily.

TWO-SECTION SQUAT CANDLES: Pour melted wax in each of two gelatin molds that are alike. Two different gelatin-mold candles are shown. Let cool in refrigerator; when wax has set some, but not hardened, use nail to make hole in center for wick. If candle has set hard before being pierced for wick, heat nail to make hole. Surfaces of candles to be fastened together may need a little leveling, which can be done by rotating them on heated flat piece of tin (or pie tin). Cut wick that will go through both halves and leave 1" to 2" extra at each end. Place wick in both candle pieces, then, with spoon, apply hot wax on one candle piece,

press other piece tight on it. Pull wick taut. Fill in center hole (around wick) with wax. Decorate by applying gold braid to center joint; fasten with sequin pins.

ROSETTE TIERED CANDLES: Fill the rosette-shaped tartlet molds with melted wax. Let cool in refrigerator; when wax has set some, but not hardened, use nail to make a hole in center for wick. Use a wick about 9" long for a candle made of 14 rosettes. Starting with top rosette, thread wick through hole, folding back about ½" at top and holding it tight with finger; spoon hot wax in depression in bottom of first rosette; slip second rosette on wick and press in place on hot wax, pulling wick taut. Add rosettes until candle is desired length, making sure that rosettes are being placed properly so that candle will stand straight when finished.

PAGODA CANDLES: Molds for the pieces in these candles are depressions on the bottom of the plastic cookie trays. Be sure the wax is no more than 150° F. or it will melt the mold. Let the wax cool in refrigerator; when wax has set some, but not hardened, use nail to make a hole in the center for wick, being careful not to puncture mold. Starting with the top pagoda piece, assemble these candles in the same manner as the Rosette Tiered candles above.

HEXAGONAL CANDLE: The mold for this candle is the bottom of the hexagonal plastic containers for straight pins. Separate the top and bottom. (The thinner slices are made in the lid of the container.) Any similar type of mold could be used to make this kind of candle. Line up the layers in the order you want them. Have a wick about two to three inches longer than the finished candle will be. Start with the top hexagon and assemble as for the Rosette Tiered Candles above, or use propane-torch method. After assembling, use torch to smooth off sides and fill in crevices, then shape sides with flat-bladed pocket or paring knife.

ANIMALS—LARGE: These animals can be poured two ways. If you have lots of wax, pour a layer the depth of the cookie cutter in pie tin or other container and let set until solid but still warm. Then
continued on page 34

The yellow tapers of the Fiesta Candles pictured on the opposite page are trimmed with layers of colorful shell shapes that create an illusion of flowers and leaves. A scallop shell is used as the mold to give texture, and the wax is then rolled into shape. The motifs are attached in a cluster at the bottom. Directions for the Fiesta Candles start on page 34.

cut out an animal with your cutter. If possible, cut all three pieces of the animal (from same or different colors) at the same time and fit them together while still warm. If you have a smaller amount of wax, hold the cookie cutter flat on a piece of waxed paper and pour the wax into the cutter until it is filled. Hold the cutter tightly for a little less than a minute, by which time it will have set sufficiently not to run out. Place on flat surface in refrigerator until cold, then remove cookie cutter. Assemble the pieces poured by either method; first, on the middle section use a heated nail to make a hole in which to insert the wick. Then heat the flat piece of tin; place one piece of animal on clean, flat surface (waxed paper-covered); holding second piece of animal in left hand and heated tin in right hand, place tin down on animal on table and at same time place animal in left hand on top of tin near edge, keeping hold on it; both pieces of the animal will have melted sides as you quickly slip out the piece of tin and position the two animals together. (The top animal should have the wick in it.) Then with this double-animal piece on the table, add the third animal in the same manner, being sure the part with the wick will be in the center. Even off the edges with a knife. If you have a propane torch, you can easily smooth off the outer edges and sides of the candle. These animals are shown all of one color (different shades), of two colors, and of three colors.

ANIMALS—SMALL: Pour a layer of wax about the depth of the small cookie cutter in small foil plate or container, and let set until solid but still warm. Then cut out an animal with the cutter. These animals are composed of two pieces. Cut a short wick; nick out a slight groove in one piece of candle and press wick in. Proceed to assemble animal as directed for large animal candles above.

Bases for small animals are poured in the rectangular and rosette-shaped trays. Any similar type of container would make an interesting base for these candles. Smooth edges of animals with knife or propane torch. Fasten the animal to the base by using the hot piece of tin to melt a little of the feet of the animal and the top of the base or use the propane torch to soften the wax, placing a tiny piece of extra wax (white or the same color) on the base at the point where the feet will be placed. Hold animal down tight until set on the base.

FIESTA CANDLES

EQUIPMENT: Scallop shell 3½″ wide. Round toothpick. Masking tape. Bottle about 6½″ tall with narrow mouth. Scissors.

MATERIALS: Yellow tapers 15″ tall. Paraffin wax, 4½ pounds for decorating four tapers. Wax coloring (one square per pound): red, yellow, blue.

DIRECTIONS: See "How To Make Candles" on page 26. To prepare taper for application, remove cellophane covering in which taper is packaged to a point 6″ up from base of taper. Secure the covering with masking tape. This covering is used to protect taper while it is being worked on. Stand taper upside down in bottle (size and shape suggested in Equipment). Taper should be supported but not restricted by bottle. In a soda pop can set in pan of water, melt wax over medium heat to ⅞ full. Work on one color at a time. For bright orange-red, add yellow coloring wax to get a bright lemon shade, then red coloring to get the orange-red; stir well. Pour orange-red wax into oil-greased cookie pan to depth of ⅛″. Let set until congealed but still warm. The wax should have an elastic quality for proper use. To test, lift a corner; if it breaks off and looks mushy, wait five minutes.

Lay the 3½″ scallop shell on the wax. Draw generous size square around it (you should get 12 squares; use extra for additional tapers). Peel off one square. Grease outside of scallop shell with oil. Place square on outside of shell; press wax to shell. Holding the wax-coated shell in one hand, start spreading the wax with the thumb and forefinger of the other hand; press and spread. Break off excess wax against edge of shell and return it to the melting can. When wax is so thin that you can see the ridges of the shell showing through white, peel wax off shell. Trim with scissors into a fan shape. With imprinted side of shape of shell on the outside, hold a round toothpick perpendicular to base; curl both sides of wax toward middle until they meet. You will have a shape which looks much like a flattened cornucopia, wider at one end than the other. Dip the narrower end of curled shell shape into hot wax to a depth of 1″ and apply flat side to the taper so that the wider end is 6½″ up from base of taper. Press the shape to taper and hold until set. Using sharp knife, trim edges of narrow end, rotating the motion of blade. Repeat with shell shapes until taper is surrounded (about six).

Using another can, melt more wax for light orange color; add yellow to wax, then add red slowly to get right shade. Stir; grease pan again; pour wax and repeat as with orange-red, placing the wider end of the shell shape ½″ above the previous row on the taper. Encircle taper with orange shapes (about nine). Drip hot wax across the joinings.

Melt wax in a third can; add yellow coloring until you get a clear shade. Make about 14 shell shapes as for others, and encircle taper with them, placed ½″ above previous row. Save yellow wax and add more fresh wax and a little blue coloring to get a chartreuse or light lime shade; make about nine shell shapes; from narrower end, cut them ½″ shorter than yellow shapes. With these shapes, encircle taper ½″ above yellow. Save the yellow-green wax, add more wax and add more blue coloring with a touch of red to get a

continued on page 36

Lovely, life-like white "roses" decorate a cake. To make rose candles, thin circles of wax in three sizes are shaped into pet-als, then are attached to the candle-stub base with hot wax. Directions for making Sculptured Roses are on the following page.

FIESTA CANDLES
continued from page 34

forest green color. Repeat as above, making seven shapes; cut these off ⅓ from narrower end. Add one more row of five dark green, cutting them off ⅔ from the narrower end.

SCULPTURED ROSES

EQUIPMENT: Small glass. Scissors. Coins: Penny, nickel, quarter. Round toothpick. Pastry trimmer.

MATERIALS: One pound paraffin wax. Stub of used candle 4″ tall. White, yellow, blue candle coloring.

DIRECTIONS: See "How To Make Candles" on page 26. Remove charred part of wick from candle stub and sharpen end to blunt point. Stand candle stub in small glass for ease in handling. In small can set in pan of water over medium heat, melt wax to ⅞ full. Add white coloring until wax looks like skimmed milk. Grease cookie pan with cooking oil. Pour hot wax into pan to a depth of ⅛″. Let set until congealed, but still warm. Gently press penny into wax five times to make five indentations. Do the same with nickel ten times, then with quarter 10 times. Cut out these circles with sharp knife. Peel away excess wax and put it in a low-sided can; remelt. You are going to put your fingers in this wax; wax should be just melted.

Meanwhile, in cookie pan you have 25 cutout disks. Pick up penny disk and, holding one edge with thumb and finger of one hand, start spreading melted wax with thumb and finger of other hand. A petal shape will result. Make sure wax is spread very thin so petal will look real. Trim sides to form a rounded top shape. Gently indent the top of this shape with a slight twist of the thumb and forefinger to make a broad heart shape as in a real rose petal. Curl the petal into a cylinder around a toothpick. Dip end into hot wax and press the hot end against the top-side of the candle stub so that the exposed wick is even with the top of the cylinder. Surround wick with five of these petals to form center of rose. Now work on shaping petals from the nickel-size disks. If wax has hardened, dip each disk into hot wax for a second or two before working with it. Spread as for smaller disk into a broad heart shape. Over the toothpick, curl back the edges of petal slightly. Redip petal into melted wax and apply the lower edge to candle. Repeat, overlapping the first petal. The redipping is to insure a dull sheen as in a real rose. Trim with sharp knife. Drip hot wax over joining to secure. Repeat with another row of nickel-size petals, curling these petals back a little more sharply. Repeat process with quarter-size petals, turning back the edges more sharply with each row. The last row of petals should be turned back enough so that point where petals are attached is not apparent.

To make leaves, color one slab of household wax green, using yellow and blue coloring tinged with red. Pour the hot wax into a greased cookie pan and, when congealed but still warm, cut three oval-leaf shapes for each rose (with a pastry trimmer) 2″ long, 1″ wide at center. Peel and lift up leaves; dip one end of each into hot wax and apply them equally spaced around bottom of rose. Dip hot wax across the joinings. Bend up leaves around rose so that leaves will conform to rose shape; let set. Cut candle off flat below leaves.

IMPRINTED CANDLES

EQUIPMENT: Ruler. Darning needle. Spoon or spatula. Pencil. Ice pick. Nail. Soup can 2½″ diameter, 3¾″ high. Square milk cartons, one-quart size. Masking tape. Smooth-textured dish towel. Medium-weight hammer. Implements obtainable at hardware or dime stores, such as: Two hex nuts ⅜″ and ¾″ diameters. Phillips head screw with ½″ diameter head. Bolt ⅛″ diameter. Two screw eyes ¾″ and 1⅜″ long. Skewer (or straight piece of wire coat hanger with one end bent into skewer-head shape ⅝″ diameter) 6″ long. Lamp switch knob ¼″ diameter (or use hollow rivet).

MATERIALS: Blocks of paraffin wax, about five to seven bars for each candle, or half of 11-lb. slab for all (do not use store-bought candles as they have an extra-hard outer coating of wax that makes them unsuitable for imprinting). Wax coloring. Candle-wicking.

DIRECTIONS: See "How To Make Candles" on page 26. Have soup can and cartons clean and ready. Cut milk carton to height of candles. Hammer ice pick or nail in center bottom of each container to make a hole no larger than wicking. Cut wicking about 4″ longer than needed to reach bottom of cartons or can. Dip the wick in melted wax (to melt, see below), thread it through a darning needle, and draw it through hole in bottom of cartons or can; tie knot at outside bottom end; tie top end to pencil; place it across container top to hold wicking taut.

Melt wax over low heat in top of double boiler and *continued on page 38*

These free-standing candles are incised in striking patterns made with common household tools. Melted paraffin can be colored with crayons, then molded in soup cans and milk cartons. The designs are created by tapping hardware — nuts, screws, knobs, skewers — against the sides of the candles. Directions for making the Imprinted Candles begin on this page.

IMPRINTED CANDLES
continued from page 36

keep over hot, but not boiling water. Using separate container for each color, color wax as desired, following General Directions. Remove wax from heat. Let wax cool a little, then fill cartons and can with wax. As the candles cool, hollows may form around wicks. Fill depressions with more melted wax. When wax in cartons has cooled and hardened, remove candles by tearing away cartons. Candle in can may be removed by placing it in warm water for a few minutes. Let candles harden for at least a day before imprinting.

To Imprint Designs: Make a pad to lay candle on while imprinting by folding dish towel or something similar. Practice your design and the use of imprinting implements on old candles or slabs of unmelted wax. To make design, place designing implement in position; imprint by tapping it firmly with hammer. **Note:** When working design near corner edge of candle top, be careful not to crack corner of candle. Work design on one side at a time; then repeat design on remaining sides. Always have lines on one side meeting lines on adjacent sides.

Small Green Candle (2¾″ x 4″): With skewer, imprint large X going from top corners to bottom corners of candle side. Make diagonal lines ½″ apart across candle, forming diamond-shaped areas. Within these areas, make double-circle imprint with lamp switch knob, leaving partial diamond shapes at edges empty.

Pink Candle (2¾″ x 3¾″): Lightly mark centers at outer edges of each side along top, bottom, and sides with nail. Lay skewer on candle, making first line at angle from center top to side center; repeat from side to bottom, bottom to side, and side to top. This leaves large diamond shape in center. Then make two more skewer lines ¼″ apart in each outer corner. Imprint Phillips head screw design in center and around inner edges of diamond.

Orange Candle (2¾″ x 3″): Lightly mark center of side; make an imprint with lamp switch knob. Make seven imprints, using ⅜″ screw eye, around this circle. Then make 14 imprints, using lamp switch knob, evenly spaced around screw eyes.

Purple Candle (2¾″ x 5″): With skewer, imprint head and line down center. Work two more skewer head-line designs on each side of first imprint; then two more designs between and ¼″ below the three. Finish each side with three slanted lines of varying lengths. Be sure these lines meet those on adjacent side for continuous design around candle. Imprint lamp switch knob design in center of skewer heads.

Large Red Candle (2¾″ x 6″): With skewer, make three vertical lines about ¾″ apart along length of candle, dividing it into four equal columns. Make horizonal line ¾″ from top and another ¾″ from bottom. In each top and bottom square, make imprint of round screw eye head only. Then make three full

imprints of screw eye in each of the four columns with heads up in first column; alternate position of head in remaining columns.

Large Green Candle (2¾″ x 6¼″): Center two columns of ¾″ hex nut imprints down length of candle, making six pairs. Then make lamp switch knob imprint in center of each hex nut imprint.

Round Small Red Candle (2½″ diameter, 3¾″ tall): Around top edge of candle, make small light markings, dividing it into six equal parts. Make two vertical skewer lines ¼″ apart down outside of candle on each side of six marked points to make six pairs of lines. Make a column of five ⅜″ hex nut imprints between each pair of lines. Imprint end (opposite head) of ⅛″ bolt in center of each hex nut imprint.

PEBBLED CANDLES

EQUIPMENT: Small cans. Pan. Teaspoon. Paper toweling. Sharp knife. Spatula. Pipe cleaners.

MATERIALS: Large white candles, 2″ diameter. Small, brightly colored candles for chunks (new or used).

DIRECTIONS: See "How To Make Candles" on page 26.

To make chunks (pebbles), fill small cans with water and place them in pan filled with water; place pan over medium-low heat. Cut colored candles into small chunky pieces. Put one small chunk in teaspoon and dip chunk into hot water in can for about two to four seconds. This will melt the outside surface of chunk. With spoon, immediately remove chunk from water and place it on sheet of paper toweling for one second (just to drain off excess water and for easier handling). While chunk is still soft, press it firmly on large white candle. Place another chunk in teaspoon and into hot water and repeat process above. Place warm chunk next to chunk on candle. Repeat to cover all around sides of candle.

Bear: Trace patterns for bear's bow tie, ear, arm,
continued on page 40

These rough-textured candles make interesting decorations for all occasions — just choose an appropriate color combination. The pebbled effect is created by pressing small chunks of soft, brightly colored wax (cut from other candles) onto plain white candles, 2″ in diameter. To make larger or smaller candles, change the center candle. Pebbled Candles, above.

PEBBLED CANDLES
continued from page 38

feet, and tail. Use 6″ candle for body. Use 2″ white candle for head; warm and shave it down to 1¼″ diameter. For nose, use a short white candle; warm and taper it to point for end of nose. Heat broad end and adhere to head. Heat broad end of head candle and adhere to body.

To make flat pieces, fill pan with wax about ¼″ deep. When solidified but still warm, place patterns on wax; cut out shapes with knife. Lift up shapes with spatula. Cut two arms, two ears, tail, and feet out of white wax in this manner. Dip part of each shape into hot wax and press into place on candle. Cut away any excess with knife. Feet go on bottom, extending out in front. Cover body, tail, head, arms, and feet with orange wax chunks, omitting the face, ears, and hands. For eyes, nose, and buttons, use black wax chunks. For ear centers, use pink wax chunks. Cut bow tie out of yellow wax and adhere.

For painting with wax (to outline areas), melt wax into thin liquid in can. Dip pipe cleaner into melted wax and quickly paint line or design with tip of pipe cleaner. Since wax on pipe cleaner cools quickly, dip pipe cleaner into melted wax frequently to complete design. Use separate pipe cleaner for each color. Paint eye centers with white wax. Paint outlines on arms, hands, tail, and feet, and dots on nose with black wax. Paint mouth with pink wax.

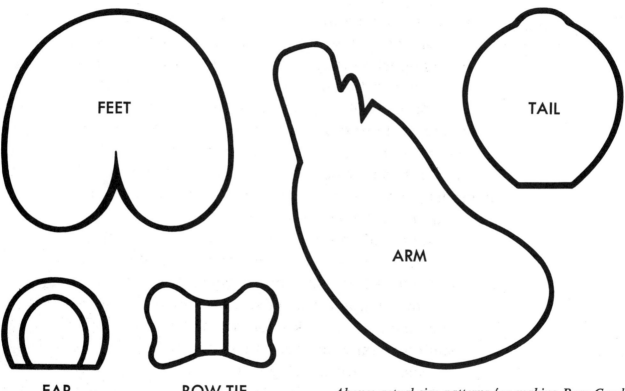

FEET

TAIL

ARM

EAR

BOW TIE

Above: actual-size patterns for making Bear Candle.

Ceramics

Traditionally, from prehistoric times, the potter
used the materials at hand — that is, the clay that
had been made from rocks decomposed through the
action of weathering and then carried by water
and deposited to form beds of clay. It is the action
of heat that changes natural clay into pottery.
Artifacts of fired clay have survived in all parts
of the world from ancient times to provide us with a
record of man's development, habits, and interests.
The words ceramics and pottery are commonly used
interchangeably by the layman. However, ceramics has
a broader meaning than pottery, as it includes a
variety of products such as porcelain, enamels,
glass, brick, or tiling, while pottery usually refers
to ware made from clay shaped while moist and soft,
then hardened by heat. Our first project gives
the beginner a recipe for making his own "clay"
from corn starch so that he can experiment at little
cost to see if working with clay appeals to him.
The relationship between the potter and his clay
is personal and intimate. Anyone can obtain pleasing
results from a lump of clay; but it is the physical
contact of the craftsman with his material that
makes him feel that he is a part of this good earth!

HOW TO MAKE CERAMICS*

(*from potter's clay; see instructions for homemade craft clay on page 44)

EQUIPMENT: Sturdy, flat working surface. Oil-cloth. Flat wooden boards or plaster bats. Sharp knife. Scissors. Rolling pin. Plastic wrap. Sandpaper, fine and coarse. Wooden modeler. Cutting wire (picture wire will do). Brushes for slips and glazes. Compass for marking bases. Ruler. Sponge. Wooden or metal spoon or scraper. Turntable (potter's wheel or lazy susan). Pottery kiln with firing temperature for clay or glaze used. Lightweight shelf props or insulating fire brick pieces. See individual directions for additional equipment.

MATERIALS: Moist clay as specified in individual directions. Slip made by mixing small amount of clay with water to get heavy cream consistency. Glazes and underglazes in desired colors (or those indicated in individual directions). See individual directions for additional materials.

GENERAL DIRECTIONS: Note: Red or brown clay shrinks about 17% to 20% in drying and firing. Our dimensions allow for shrinkage. If you are using a different type of clay, find out amount of shrinkage and adjust accordingly.

Cover working surface with oilcloth. Knead and wedge clay until it is free of air bubbles when cut with a wire. Work with just enough clay needed at a time. Keep all unused clay moist in plastic wrap. Slip is used to mend cracks and to join clay sections.

If you have the equipment and technique, you can throw shapes on wheel following dimensions given in individual directions. If not, build shape, using coil or slab method. When piece is shaped, set aside until it reaches leather-hard stage, i.e., is firm but not thoroughly dry. Then incise any decorative lines, if desired. If top edge is uneven, place on turntable. Hold cutting tool (knife or very long needle or hatpin) against edge of wall at desired height; turn; this will trim off top edge evenly.

Clay should dry very slowly to prevent warping.

Place a damp cloth over piece to help retard the drying process if atmospheric conditions make it necessary. When piece is dry, sand base to be sure it rests evenly on the table. Brush underglaze into any incised lines; sand off, leaving color in lines. Do not fire until bone dry; moisture left in clay may expand and cause piece to crack in firing. Bisque-fire natural clay to cone 05; fire oven-firing clay according to manufacturer's directions.

When piece has been fired, glazes may be added. To glaze natural clay, mix a glaze to the consistency of heavy cream. Lay glaze on with even brush strokes. Three coats are usually needed to insure the desired 1/64" thickness. Rub gently to eliminate pinholes between each application. Fire. For oven-fired pieces, follow manufacturer's directions for glazing.

Coil Method (for building bowl shapes if potter's wheel is not available): Cut appropriate template out of heavy cardboard for designated shape, if desired. If building piece on a flat base, roll out small slab of clay, mark with compass to size circle indicated in individual directions, and cut out with knife. Place clay circle on wooden board or bat. Make scratch marks around edge of clay circle with modeler. Brush edges of circle well with heavy slip. From supply of moist clay in plastic bag, break off balls of clay and roll with palms of hands into coils about ½" in diameter (coils may be larger or smaller, depending on size of piece). Keep coils as nearly uniform as possible. Lay a coil around slipped edge. Referring to template, put one hand around outside of bowl and, with fingertips of other hand, smooth inside of bowl. Now put one hand inside bowl and smooth outside with other hand, joining ends of coil evenly and blending completely with base circle. Roll another coil; scratch top of first coil with modeler, brush top with slip; then wedge (i.e., smooth) inside and out. Continue, check-
continued on page 44

Craft clay appliqués add color and whimsey to decorative and useful boxes. Flower-wreath box has posy-ringed mirror. Hearts-and-flowers decorate a trinket box. Imaginative tiles top a gold box for sundries. A "jeweled" pink cat stalks across a box containing cards. Glove box is topped with a bird and colorful tiles. Directions for Craft Clay Boxes on page 44.

HOW TO MAKE CERAMICS
continued from page 42

ing shape frequently with template held against outside edge. Use longer or shorter coils to increase or decrease diameter of bowl as you build. If shape is large or curves inward or outward very much, set it aside for several hours after several inches of building. When it dries slightly and strengthens, more coils can be added. Clay must never be allowed to become too hard, as coils will then separate as they dry. When bowl is shaped and leather-hard, template can be used to scrape off unevenness of coils on outside of piece, and a spoon can be used to smooth inside. For greater smoothness, use a damp sponge inside and out. When finished, decorate as indicated in individual directions.

Slab Method: You can start with a base as for coil method or leave bottom open. Roll out a large slab of clay ⅜" thick; following dimensions given in individual directions, cut out piece with knife. Lift up slab and gently bring the two end edges together, forming a cylinder. Place cylinder on base if one is required. If not, work directly on bat. Wet edges with a sponge; overlap and smooth joining with fingers to make wall uniform thickness all around; first smooth inside, then outside. If any cracking of wall occurs, smooth with fingers and modeler; sponge inside and outside smooth. Seal edges of base (if used) to bottom edges of cylinder with fingertips; small coils of soft clay may be worked into joining, inside and out. Smooth with modeler. To taper shapes, cut a few small wedges out around top edge (depth of cut will depend upon point of tapering); overlap cut edges; smooth out evenly with fingers and modeler. When finished, decorate as indicated in individual directions.

CRAFT CLAY BOXES

EQUIPMENT: Scissors. Pencil. Ruler. Sharp knife. Tracing paper. Lightweight cardboard. Two small paintbrushes, one with a fine point. Rolling pin. Pastry board. Damp cloth. Saucepan. Spoon. Aluminum foil.

MATERIALS: Craft clay (see recipe below). O-P Craft unfinished wooden boxes in desired sizes (available at hobby stores). Small mirror (optional). Spray paint in pastel color, gold, or a light color of wood stain. Tempera water color paints in colors desired. Clear plastic spray. Sequins and artificial pearl beads. Scraps of gold paper lace doilies. Velvet ribbons. Green metallic paper for leaves. All-purpose glue.

DIRECTIONS: Trace actual-size patterns on opposite page. Make separate patterns out of cardboard for each piece to be cut from clay (heavy lines on patterns): cat's head, body, and tail; bird head, body, and tail; leaf, watermelon, egg, large butterfly, large flowers, heart, and design rectangles. Other small designs and details are painted; these are indicated by the finer

lines in pattern.

Give boxes two coats of spray paint in color desired, or stain natural wood. Make craft clay as follows:

Craft Clay Recipe
1 cup Argo Corn Starch
2 cups baking soda (one-pound box)
1¼ cups water

Combine ingredients in a saucepan and cook over medium heat, stirring constantly, until thickened to dough-like consistency. Turn mixture out on board and knead slightly. Cover with damp cloth until cool. Keep unused portion in aluminum foil while you work, to keep pliable.

Roll out a piece of the clay to about ¼" thickness. Place cardboard patterns on clay and cut out with a sharp knife. Set aside to dry. For tile pieces, cut squares and rectangles from ½" to 2" long and in various widths. For cupped flowers (in flower wreath design) press a small piece of clay very thin and shape over fingertip, making scalloped edge.

When pieces are thoroughly dry, paint solid colors as desired. Then paint on designs in contrasting colors, following patterns. A few tile designs are given opposite. Others may be made as desired with circles, dots, diagonal and wavy lines.

Trace complete design for cat or flower bouquet onto box. Paint the details on box, indicated by finer lines on patterns, as shown in color illustration on page 43. Glue clay pieces on box, using glue liberally. Trim with sequins and beads.

For flower wreath box, a small mirror may be glued to top of box first. Then arrange and glue on flowers, clay leaves, and paper leaves in an oval design, over edges and around mirror.

For other boxes, glue bird pieces and tiles onto box tops as shown. Decorate fronts of the boxes with clay pieces, if desired. Add details of paint (such as bird's feet) and highlights of beads and sequins on box; cat has a gold paper lace collar and string of pearls at neck. Ribbon or paper lace motifs may be glued around box lids.

BEAD JEWELRY

See "How To Make Ceramics" on page 42.
EQUIPMENT: Nichrome wire. Toothpicks. Round object, such as pencil, to shape cylindrical beads.
MATERIALS: Natural or oven-firing clay. Slip. Engobes (colored clay slips used to decorate an object made of a contrasting color clay). Wax. Leather thong. Various other cords on which to string beads.
DIRECTIONS: Make beads as directed in "Descriptions of Beads," page 46. Be sure holes are big enough; make with a rounded toothpick, turning bead on toothpick several times until hole is larger than
continued on page 46

Trace actual-size patterns for the Craft Clay Boxes and arrange as illustrated on page 43.

BEAD JEWELRY
continued from page 44

toothpick.

Smooth off sharp edges made when toothpick is pushed through clay.

Bead may be left to dry on toothpick supported on each side so that bead dries evenly on all sides.

When glaze-firing, beads are supported in the kiln by 3 strands of nichrome wire (the kind used in the coils of toasters, electric kilns, etc.)—ordinary wire will not withstand the heat. The wire should be stretched between the supports in such a way that beads do not touch one another or other surfaces. Try to keep glaze away from hole to avoid glaze adhering to wire.

Never allow children to work with glazes that contain lead.

DESCRIPTONS OF BEADS: The following descriptions (of how necklaces shown were made) correspond to the numbered color illustrations on page 47. However, do not follow directions literally; use a free hand and play with shapes and colors.

1. Various sizes of cylinders were formed by rolling flattened clay over a round object such as a pencil. Self-glazing engobe was used for color contrast. The beads were strung on a leather thong.

2. White clay and red clay were kneaded together to make "marble" texture, rolled into a thick slab, cut into squares, the edges softened, the shape modified by gently pulling in opposite directions. Clear glaze was used for finish. When strung, beads were attractively spaced by separating with knots and small, wooden beads.

3. Flattened ovals. Designs were fired with soft, self-glazing engobes, rubbed with wax for finish. Ovals were strung with knots between beads.

4. After beads were shaped, "squiggles" of clay were pressed into them.

5. Different colors and sizes were unified by repetition of shape and "eye" design and repeat of wooden beads.

6. Beads of white clay were painted with blue engobe and finished with a transparent turquoise glaze. They were strung on a cord of twisted golden linen, each ceramic bead separated from the next by a small, dark wooden one.

7. Odd shapes, sizes, and colors were unified by black glaze. The underlying colors show through just enough to look mysterious.

8. Experiment with different textures and different-colored engobes; clear glaze.

9. Various-colored engobes and a clear glaze were used on red clay. The dots on the beads and dotlike wooden beads separating big beads give a gay effect.

10. Bottom bead was formed from a flat strip of clay. Design was painted with self-glazing engobe. Beads were finished with wax.

Shown at the left are the antique beads that were the inspiration for the colorful Bead Jewelry shown on the opposite page. The 2000-year-old Aggrey trading beads (top) originated in Egypt; the 600-year-old necklace is of Venetian origin.

Attractive bead jewelry, in symmetrical or free-form shapes, makes colorful accessories. The beads are made in various techniques with natural or oven-firing clay. Cylinders are formed by rolling flattened clay over a round object, such as a pencil. To make "marble" texture, white clay and red clay are kneaded together, rolled, and cut into squares. See directions for the Bead Jewelry on page 44.

Unusual pottery plaques, in a variety of shapes, are made with the easy slab method. Details are scooped out or scratched into clay. In some pieces, texture is shown by brushing on a white underglaze and then sanding lightly. Others are colored with glaze and refired — or bits of bright glass are fused to pottery for a brilliant contrast. The hanging plaques shown opposite can be grouped as a wind chime. The three round plaques at left are suspended in a simple arrangement. Directions for Hanging Plaques, page 50.

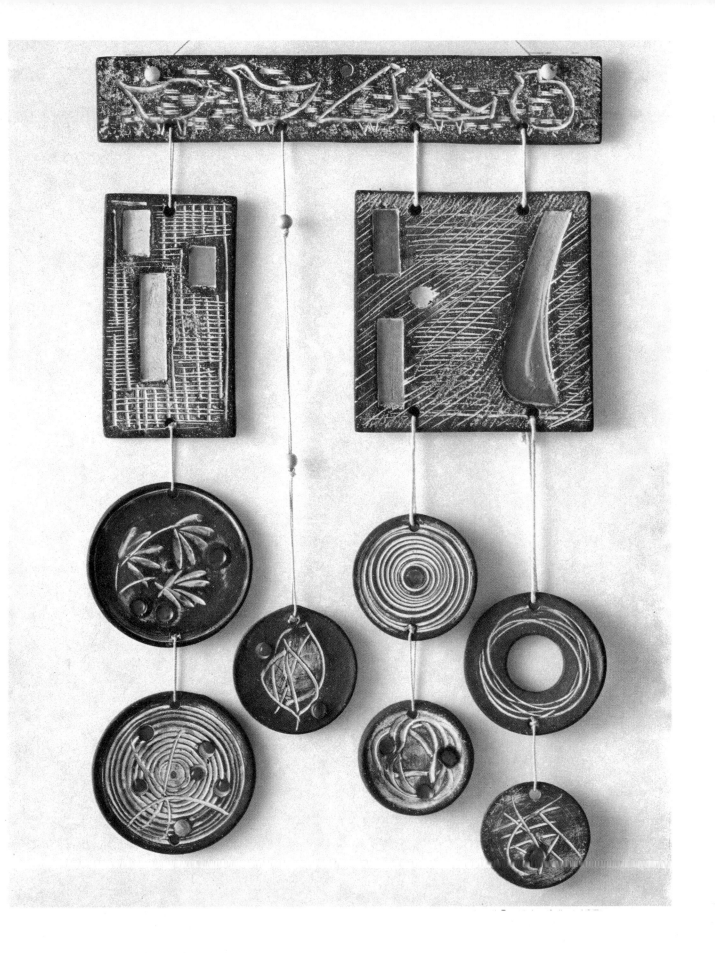

HANGING PLAQUES

See "How To Make Ceramics" on page 42.

EQUIPMENT: Pencil with good flat eraser tip. Paper for patterns. Metal skewer. Fine saw blade or fine-toothed comb. Dowel stick ½″ diameter.

MATERIALS: Clay. Slip. Glazes and underglazes. Leather lacing or nylon cord (fishing cord). Bits of colored glass (broken bottle glass). Scraps of foam rubber, felt. Household cement.

DIRECTIONS: Plan design on paper before working with clay. Using compass, ruler, and paper, make and cut out circles, squares, and rectangles in a variety of sizes (cut larger than desired finished size to allow for shrinkage in drying and firing). Roll well-wedged clay ⅜″ thick. Using paper pieces as patterns, cut desired number of clay shapes. With round edge of wooden modeler or pencil, freely draw circles, arcs, birds, flowers, etc., into surface of clay. Use end of ½″ dowel stick to impress circles at random, making them at least ⅛″ deep in clay. Cut out larger areas from clay. If a wheel or turntable is available, the lines can be cut into clay in pleasant patterns on a slowly spinning wheel head. Cut holes through center of circular pieces if desired and as shown. Cut holes ½″ from the edge of each shape and directly opposite each other for hanging later. Dry shapes slowly under weighted boards or bats.

There are several ways you can color shapes. Brush underglaze into incised lines and sand off the raised areas and fire; or fire first and then glaze as desired and refire. If you use a dark clay, a light underglaze can be brushed on and fired and then small pieces of broken glass carefully placed in indented areas and refired to 1500° to fuse glass to clay.

After final firing, arrange shapes into desired pattern. Cut leather lacing or cord into several lengths and attach pieces and make hangers. Knots can be slipped to back of shapes or left to show as part of the design. Plaques can be used for wind chimes.

UNICORNS

See "How To Make Ceramics" on page 42.

EQUIPMENT: Sharpened dowel, about ⅜″ in diameter, or round pencil.

MATERIALS: Clay: terra cotta, stoneware, or brown: 15 to 20 lbs. for large Unicorn, 3 to 5 lbs. for small Unicorn. Slip. **For Fountain:** "Little Giant" Pump; three ¼″ nipples; ⅜″ valve; ¼″ x ¾″ bushing; ¼″ coupling; hose. (**Note:** Consult hardware store for assembling, if necessary.)

DIRECTIONS: The size of unicorn depends upon size of pool. A good height for pool 4′ or 5′ in diameter is 15″ for larger unicorn. Use same method for building both large and small unicorns with variations if desired.

Coil-build a cylindrical shape, using Fig. 1 as a guide to general shape, about 13″ tall. (Do not make base; start with 6½″ diameter base coil.) Shape is built several inches taller than desired, because part of the top will be cut away to place head in position. Make coils heavier at base to add weight and stability. Exact roundness is not essential and the impression of coil and finger marks can add character to the piece. While base is still rather moist, indent two grooves with finger pressure in bottom quarter of body and curve piece inward to form leg areas. Add more clay if needed to give the feeling of legs. Roll a heavy coil and shape into simple hoof shape (Fig. 2). Attach hoof to base at each grooved area and wedge very well to bottom, keeping feet close to body.

For head, coil-build a second piece in vase shape, 2½″ at base, about 5½″ tall (Fig. 3). Allow both body and head to become firm enough to handle without deforming shapes. Cut top of body piece as indicated by dash line in Fig. 4 and place head on body as shown. It will be necessary to fit by trial and error, so start with shallow cut and continue fitting until desired angle is reached. When pieces fit to satisfaction, cut a good size hole in head where it overlaps top of body, if using unicorns as a fountain. Hole should not be noticeable from outside and is only to accommodate hose for water supply. Wedge head and body together very securely, using additional clay wherever needed to reinforce joint. Smooth well with finger to blend the two pieces together to a unified whole. Wedge some inside, if possible. When joint is firm, add the ears. To make ears, roll clay ¼″ thick and cut out triangular ear shape, using illustration as a guide. Curve at base and thin with finger pressure at the tip. Attach to head as shown and wedge very well, adding clay at base for strength, and blend in with head. For horn, make a 2½″ coil; taper at one end and wedge other end to head. For eyes, make indentations with dowel or pencil on each side of head; do not pierce clay. Make a "happy" mouth, if desired, by cutting slash at each side, as shown, with sharp knife. For mane, roll clay ¼″ thick and cut into several strips about ½″ wide and 3″ to 4″ long. Moisten one side with heavy slip and attach to head from horn and part way down neck by using fingers to form curve (Fig. 5) and then pressing firmly against body; then form another curve and attach to body in same manner; repeat to near bottom. Do not use one strip; short ones work better and can be joined where clay touches body. Cut a hole in base at exact center back large enough for water-supply hose to pass through easily, allowing for shrinkage in drying. Sponge piece thoroughly to smooth so it need not be scraped smooth when dry. Be sure base is level. Dry very slowly, keeping mane and ears under plastic wrap until body is almost dry. Set in protected area to prevent unnecessary handling. When completely dry, fire to maturing temperature of clay.

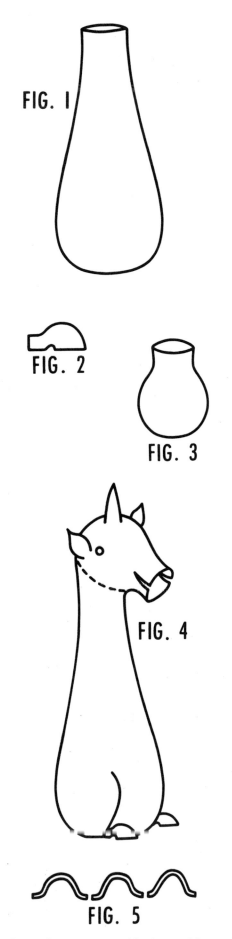

FIG. 1

FIG. 2

FIG. 3

FIG. 4

FIG. 5

Illustrations above are a guide for making unicorns.

FLOWER HOLDERS

See "How To Make Ceramics" on page 42.

EQUIPMENT: Rubber balls 4″ to 6″ in diameter. Skewer. Paper. Pencil. Unsharpened round pencil.

MATERIALS: Clay, any desired color. Slip. Glazes and underglazes in colors desired. Salad oil. Leather thongs or grosgrain ribbons for hanging.

DIRECTIONS: Girl's Head Flower Holder (page 55): Lightly oil rubber ball with salad oil and wipe off excess. Using fairly moist clay, cover oiled ball with pellets of clay to cover entirely, about ½″ thick. Roll ball lightly with palm of hand on hard, smooth area to smooth out surface of clay. Let dry several hours until firm to touch, but not dry. Cut through clay to form two halves; gently remove clay from ball with twisting motion. With ball removed, place two halves of clay together with slip and wedge seam until smooth and invisible. If shape is distorted it can be regained by rolling clay ball gently again on smooth surface. For neck, roll coil of clay about 2½″ thick; cut to about 3″ length and taper slightly at one end; flatten other end on table. Overlap ends and wedge together. With modeler, hollow out coil slightly to aid in drying. Attach neck to ball firmly with slip and soft clay; shape smoothly and flare out bottom a little. The neck should be fairly heavy to balance larger head. With soft clay, model a simple nose on head. Using modeler, cut lines in head to resemble hair and mouth. With pointed pencil, gently poke through clay for eyes. Using skewer and working in concentric circles, push holes through clay on top of head (be sure holes are large enough to hold flower stems and allow for shrinkage in firing). Dry thoroughly; sand or sponge to remove rough edges formed by modeler; fire to maturing temperature of clay.

Ball Flower Holder (page 56): Follow directions for making head part of Girl's Head Flower Holder, but use a larger ball. When rubber ball is removed and clay ball formed, gently push the ball against a smooth surface to flatten one side. Using modeler or pencil, freely cut design into clay to give a bark texture. Make a fairly large hole at top of flattened area (back) for hanging and for filling with water to hold fresh flowers. With sharply pointed pencil, poke holes at random on upper half of piece; poke them at angle at which you would insert flowers. Allow to dry; brush any color underglaze in lines cut with modeler. When dry, sand, leaving underglaze in grooves only. Fire. If piece is not watertight after firing, it is advisable to pour in heavy glaze, rotate it around, and pour out excess. Refire. String leather thong through large hole for hanging.

"Bacchus" Bowl Hanger (page 57): Use your favorite method of building: coil, wheel, or draping clay over mold. Make a bowl with diameter no greater than the width of your kiln when bowl is in the damp stage. *continued on page 54*

Mythical pottery unicorns, shown in gar-
den setting above and in close-up at the
left, can be made of terra cotta, stone-
ware, or a brown clay. Unicorns, formed
with the coil method, are hollow to hold
a water hose for a fountain effect. The
larger unicorn has a happy mouth—made
by cutting slashes at each side. Mane is
formed by using several strips of rolled
clay. Directions for Unicorns on page 50.

FLOWER HOLDERS
continued from page 51

When piece is firm enough to hold shape, but still moist, cut bowl in half with fine wire or knife. Place one half of cut bowl on piece of paper and draw a circle pattern large enough to permit a ¾" edge around bowl; bowl should fit almost entirely on the lower half of circle. With rolling pin and oilcloth, roll a slab of clay, and cut out circle. Place bowl half on circle; wedge in place with slip and soft clay, making a tight joint on the inside. Set aside until firmer. Roll another piece of clay ¼" thick and cut into ¼" strips. Draw face lightly on clay bowl with pencil, correcting as necessary by rubbing out lines with moistened finger. Liberally cover lines with slip and shape clay strips to follow lines of face. Press firmly in place and wedge lightly. Using pencil or modeler, cut hair lines, eye pupils, and any other design on bowl and circle. Cut hole in top of circle for hanging; cut another hole at bottom of bowl for drainage to use as outside planter (this hole can be plugged with florist's clay). Dry slowly and keep flat by using a light weight, such as a piece of wood or insulating brick, on upper half, to prevent warping as it dries. Brush underglaze freely over all decorated areas. Sand lightly, just enough to highlight the area. Fire flat with a light weight such as insulating brick on upper half. If piece is not watertight after firing, it is advisable to pour in heavy glaze, rotate it around and pour out excess. Refire. String leather thong through top hole for hanging.

Egg-Shaped Hanging Bowl (page 57): Follow directions for "Bacchus" Bowl Hanger, but make the greatest diameter of bowl a little below the top for a graceful shape. Cut rings around the damp piece, and cut flower design with modeler, before setting aside to firm; the flower center was made with an unsharpened end of a round pencil. Place the cut half of the bowl on paper and draw an oval pattern as for "Bacchus" Bowl Hanger, to conform to the shape of bowl; allow about five or more inches above bowl half. Finish as for "Bacchus."

PATIO PLANTERS, CANDLE HOLDER

See "How to Make Ceramics" on page 42.
EQUIPMENT: Pencil. Paper for patterns. Heavy cardboard. Skewer or blunt pencil. **For Patio Candle Holder:** Double boiler. Wooden paint-mixing stick.

MATERIALS: Slip. **For Patio Candle Holder:** Two lbs. red or brown clay, grogged or ungrogged. White underglaze; clear matt or gloss glaze, if desired. Two lbs. paraffin. One white and one colored crayon. Candlewicking. Oil of citronella. **For Small Round Planter and Broad-Top Planter** (each): Two lbs. brown clay. Leather shoelacing, 72" long. White underglaze (for
continued on page 58

A girl's-head flower holder "grows" flowers through tiny holes in the crown. Head is shaped by using a rubber ball covered with clay. After clay is cut — forming two halves — the rubber ball is removed and the two pieces are joined. Details of head are cut into the clay by using a modeler and pointed pencil. See the directions for Flower Holders on page 51.

These interesting flower holders can be made using clay, underglaze, and glazes of any desired colors. The thong-suspended Ball Flower Holder, at the left, is filled with flowers which are inserted into holes at the top half of the holder. The egg-shaped hanging pocket and the "Bacchus" Bowl Hanger, shown on the opposite page, are for planters or whimsical arrangements — for example, fireproof plastic grapes, sprayed copper leaves, and candles. See the directions for these Flower Holders on pages 51 and 54.

Broad-Top Planter); blue glaze (for Small Round Planter).

GENERAL DIRECTIONS: Enlarge patterns, page 60, for templates by copying on paper ruled in 1" squares.

Patio Candle Holder: If using a wheel, throw a simple shape similar to illustration and template #1. When dry take off wheel; decorate as indicated.

If coil building, cut template #1 of cardboard. Roll clay out and cut a 3½" diameter clay circle ¼" thick. Build up holder, following instructions for coil method and using template for shaping and size. Repeat double-leaf pattern one and one-half times for five leaves (vary each leaf if desired) on pattern paper. When holder is almost dry, place paper design around outside; with skewer or modeler, go over pattern to incise outside of holder. Be sure lines are clear and clean, but not too delicate. Make five equally spaced holes around holder about 1" from top edge. Dry thoroughly and sand lightly. Brush underglaze over entire outside; when dry, sand with coarse sandpaper, leaving color only in incised lines. Fire to maturing temperature of clay. Glaze if desired and fire again.

For candle, see "How To Make Candles" on page 26. Cut wicking about 6" longer than needed to reach bottom of holder. As wax for candle melts, add color by shaving white and colored crayons into wax. Stir with paint-mixing stick to mix well. As soon as wax is melted, dip wick into it; then pour a small amount of wax into bottom of holder, press wicking into wax; let wax cool and secure free end of wicking to a pencil placed across top of holder, so that wicking is held straight and taut up center of holder. If necessary, remelt wax in boiler; add one teaspoon of oil of citronella to wax just before pouring to make candle bug-repellent. Pour wax in holder, a little at a time. Be sure wax is not so hot that it will dislodge wicking. As wax cools, a depression may form in top center around wick; fill this with more melted wax. Allow wax to become firm before removing pencil support. When cool, cut wick so that about ¾" is above candle.

Small Round Planter: If using wheel, throw an almost-closed, squat shape similar to template #2; while turning at low speed, cut out a piece of clay to enlarge opening to desired size. When rather firm, cut from wheel and center upside down on wheel; with wire cutting tool, remove excess clay, forming rounded bottom.

If coil building, cut template #2 of cardboard; follow General Directions and make circle base, 4" diameter. When piece is firm, but not dry, cut three holes ¼" in diameter equally spaced around top edge of and about ⅜" below rim, using skewer or blunt pencil. Dry planter carefully; sand if necessary; fire to

continued on page 60

These decorative pottery accessories are perfect for indoor or outdoor settings. The planters are thrown on wheel for a bowl shape or built up with the coil method. Each is suspended by three leather thongs knotted through holes. The candle holder, decorated with leaf motifs, holds a homemade candle. Directions for Patio Planters, Candle Holder on page 54.

PATIO PLANTERS, CANDLE HOLDER
continued from page 58

maturing temperature of clay. Fill holes with soft clay to prevent glaze from running out and pour blue glaze inside planter, draining out excess. Push clay out of holes, then brush or spray glaze on outside. With damp sponge, remove band of glaze around outside top. Fire to maturing temperature of glaze. Cut 72″ lacing into three equal pieces, knot one end of each and thread through holes in planter, with knots inside or outside as desired. Tie lacings together at top and hang.

Broad-Top Planter: If using wheel, throw simple deep bowl shape, similar to template #3. When firm, invert; round bottom as for Small Round Planter. Decorate in inverted position. Use modeler, pencil, or knife to incise marks in clay. With wheel moving slowly, start at top of piece; hold hand steady with tool touching and marking piece and move down side of it without stopping. Stop about an inch from rim. Be sure groove is deep enough; repeat if necessary, following same lines. Quick vertical lines can be made with modeler while wheel still revolves.

If coil building, follow General Directions, cutting template #3 out of cardboard. Cut base circle 2½″ diameter.

After piece is leather-hard, decorate as above on wheel or lazy susan. Cut three holes, about ¼″ diameter, equally spaced around top edge, ⅜″ below rim. When dry, sand if necessary. Brush with underglaze, filling grooves. Then dry again, sand off excess, leaving color in grooves. Fire to maturing temperature of clay and underglaze. If using earthenware clay, it may be desirable to pour glaze inside piece to waterproof it and then refire. Cut 72″ lacing; knot and hang.

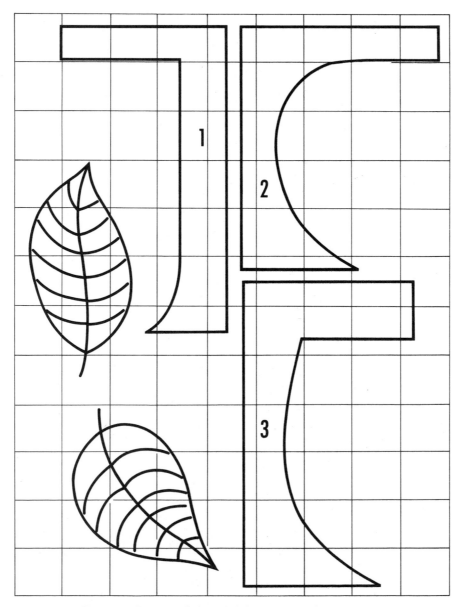

Patterns for templates and leaf design for the Patio Planters and Candle Holder; to enlarge on 1″ squares.

60

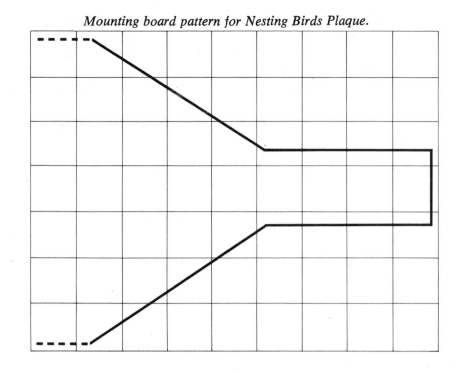

NESTING BIRDS PLAQUE

See "How To Make Ceramics" on page 42.

SIZE: Approximately 22″ long.

EQUIPMENT: Paper for patterns. Tracing paper. Skewer or blunt pencil. Kitchen sieve. Large sheet of plastic. Plywood panel ¾″. thick, 18″ x 30″. Saw. Weights, such as magazines. Medium steel wool. Clamps.

MATERIALS: Ten lbs. red or brown clay. Two lbs. grog. White underglaze or opaque white matt glaze. Slip. Orange and yellow waterproof, plastic-base (such as acrylic) paints or glazes. Plywood board ¼″ thick, 7″ x 21″. Two screw eyes 2½″. Picture wire. Epoxy glue. Shellac.

DIRECTIONS: Enlarge pattern for mounting board above by copying it on paper ruled in 1″ squares. complete pattern by continuing lines (indicated by dash lines) for 13⅜″ to make board 21″ long. Illustration of plaque is a little less than half-size, allowing for shrinkage; to make pattern, rule ⅜″ squares on tracing paper and place over illustration, then enlarge by copying on paper ruled in 1″ squares. Sift grog through kitchen sieve, eliminating all larger pieces. Add about one lb. finer grog to ten lbs. clay; knead and wedge well. Cover working surface with sheet of plastic, center clay on it, and, with palm, push clay down and out into long shape, approximately that of plaque. When roughly to shape, roll with rolling pin until about ½″ thick and longer and wider than needed. Check against pattern from time to time for size. Roll as evenly as possible. When rolled to size, allow to stand for several hours until firm, but not dry. Place pattern over clay; using blunt pencil or modeler, go over design firmly but not hard enough to pierce paper. Remove pattern; with sharp knife, cut off ex-cess clay from edges. Then deepen and widen your pattern imprint on clay. To be effective at a distance, lines must be clear and broad. Avoid going more than ⅛″ deep at any place. The firmer the clay, the cleaner a line can be cut, but do not allow clay to become dry at any time until design is complete. When entirely finished, allow to dry until quite firm, then cut into sections as indicated on plaque. Use a ruler or steel straight edge for good, clear cuts. Remove from plastic sheeting carefully and place on ¾″ plywood panel, in proper order, for drying. Cover with plastic and allow to dry slowly for several days. Check to be sure it is drying flat, weighting down with magazines if necessary.

When completely dry, sand each section lightly and round edges very slightly. Return to proper arrangement and cover with white underglaze. Do not work, at any time, on just one individual tile separately from the group, or piece will not have look of "wholeness" when completed. When dry again, sand with steel wool, leaving color in incised lines. Firing is very important: Place tiles flat on clean shelf and weight down edges with lightweight insulating brick or kiln shelf props. Do not stack two tiles together; try to fire in approximately the same position in kiln each time and at same temperature to avoid variation in shrinkage. Paint birds with paints or glaze. If glaze is desired, use a glaze with lower maturing temperature than first firing to prevent further shrinkage. Saw plywood to mounting board pattern shape. Insert screw eyes at sides, ¾″ from ends of board, for hanging with picture wire. Attach tiles in proper sequence to plywood with epoxy glue, using clamps overnight if possible. String picture wire through screw eyes and hang. If piece is to be used outdoors on patio wall, shellac back and all exposed areas of wooden mounting board.

BOWL-SHAPED LAMP

See "How To Make Ceramics" on page 42.
SIZE: 10″ high.
EQUIPMENT: Pointed dowels ⅝″, ½″, and ⅜″ diameters. **For Base:** Hammer. Coping saw (for cutting wood). Nail set. Drill with ⅜″ bit.
MATERIALS: Moist brown clay, about three lbs. Slip. Plywood ¼″ thick: one piece 4½″ square; two pieces 4½″ x 2¾″; two pieces 4″ x 2¾″. Finishing nails. Wooden disk 1¾″ diameter, ½″ thick with ⁷⁄₁₆″ hole in center. Flat black spray paint. Lamp pipe nipple ⅜″ outer diameter, 2″ long. Two lock nuts ⅜″ inner diameter. Check ring 1″ diameter or larger. Keyless socket, Leviton #12897 or equivalent. Canopy switch rotary type, Leviton #12326 or equivalent. Lamp cord and plug 6 ft. long. Duro Lite Globelite, 60 watt, 3″ diameter, with standard base.
DIRECTIONS: This shape is best built up by the coil method. Start with clay circle base about 5½″ diameter. Build shape out and up to 7½″ high and tapering to 5″ diameter at top (refer to illustration). Round off bottom edge with modeler. When firm but moist, decorate bottom ⅔ of shape with several rows of 12 equally spaced holes in each as shown, using ½″ and ⅜″ diameter dowels. Make holes alternate between holes of upper and lower rows as shown. Turn upside down and poke 12 equally spaced holes ¼″ diameter around base. With ⅝″ dowel, poke hole in bottom center of shape. Sand the holes especially well when dry so they will be clear and smooth. Fire. For base, nail together wood with butt joints to form a box 4½″ square and 3″ high with open bottom. Paint box and disk black. Drill hole in center top for pipe nipple; drill hole on one side near bottom for mounting canopy switch; drill hole in opposite side near bottom for lamp cord. Screw nipple into top hole with ⅛″ projecting through to inside of base; secure underneath with lock nut. Place disk over nipple on top of base. Place pottery lamp on disk and secure in place with lock nut and check ring. Attach socket to nipple, leaving a short length of cord to extend through nipple and connect in series to canopy switch and lamp cord. Screw in Globelite.

THREE KINGS

See "How To Make Ceramics" on page 42.
SIZE: About 8″ tall.
EQUIPMENT: Paper for pattern. 1 quart bottle, 3¾″ diameter with shape as illustrated.
MATERIALS: Air-drying (or regular) clay, dark brown or any desired color. Slip. White underglaze. Votive candles. Talcum powder.
DIRECTIONS: Enlarge pattern (p. 64) by copying on paper ruled in 1″ squares; make sides the same by reversing pattern to make either a large opening (left
continued on page 64

The unusual nesting birds plaque is cut from red or brown rolled clay. White underglaze outlines tree and nest. Waterproof paints or glazes color birds a brilliant orange and yellow. The finished tiles are mounted on a plywood board with glue; board is shellacked on back if plaque is to be used outdoors. See directions for the Nesting Birds Plaque on page 61.

side) or a smaller opening (right side). Cutout "V" shape is a dart to make pattern fit around neck of bottle. With rolling pin, roll out slab of clay, on oil-cloth, about ¼″ thick and large enough to place paper pattern over it. Place pattern down on clay; with knife, cut clay, following outline of pattern. Dust the clay and bottle lightly with talcum powder. Wrap clay around bottle (head goes around lower part of bottle neck); join head to opposite side (see illustration on page 66). Wedge edges of "V" together at back with slip and soft clay. Join ends of bottom strips, wedging together with slip and soft clay.

With modeler, model lines along each side of face (see illustration, page 66); model lines of beard. To give dimension to beards (one is shown flat), cut along each lower side of beard, curve beard outward and press sides flat against bottle underneath beard. Make holes for eyes with end of small dowel. For nose, wedge a small dab of clay to face or poke holes as for eyes. With modeler, mark designs and lines on robe as shown or as desired. Leave clay body on bottle only until reaches a leather-hard stage (after a few hours); then remove from bottle to dry. For base pattern, place bottle flat on pattern paper, mark around bottle; cut out pattern. Roll out clay to ¼″ thickness, place pattern on clay and, with knife, cut base; when body has been removed from bottle, center it over base; secure with slip and clay, wedging securely inside as well as outside. For each crown, roll out strip of clay ¼″ thick and long enough to fit around head. With knife, cut out points as shown or with end of small dowel poke holes all around for different design. Shape into a circle, wedge at seam, and secure to top of head, using heavy slip and modeler. Curve crown points outward as shown on pages 66 and 67.

Brush underglaze over entire piece; then remove glaze by sanding lightly; this gives color to modeled areas. Set aside to dry thoroughly (drying time depends upon humidity in the air); if not using air-drying clay, fire piece to maturing temperature of clay. Put votive candles inside Three Kings when finished.

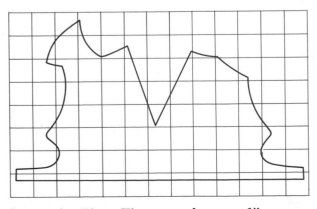

Pattern for Three Kings, to enlarge on 1″ squares.

Interesting glowing lights are cast through the holes encircling the side of an unusual bowl-shaped lamp. After shaping the lamp with the coil method, rows of equally spaced holes are formed with pointed wooden dowels in two diameters. The pottery lamp encasing a globe is attached to a wooden base. See the directions for making the Bowl-Shaped Lamp on page 62.

Three Kings candle holders are made with a brown clay, rolled flat, then cut to a pattern. Clay is shaped around a bottle, then etched with a modeler. Form is removed when the clay reaches a leather-like state; base is added. A white glaze is brushed over clay, then is sanded to reveal a texture and design details. Votive lights stay sheltered from the breeze. See directions for Three Kings on page 62.

Eight bells, suspended from a redwood frame, chime merrily when stirred by indoor or outdoor breezes. Bells in various shapes and sizes may be thrown on a wheel, slip-poured, or coil-built. Some bells are incised with free-hand line designs or cut in a circular pattern while revolving on a decorator's wheel. To make Wind Bell Hanging, see the directions below.

WIND BELL HANGING

See "How To Make Ceramics" on page 42.
SIZE: 12½" x 32".
EQUIPMENT: Paper for patterns. Heavy cardboard. Waxed paper. Steel wool. Dowels, butter molds, etc. to imprint designs. Skewer. Potter's decorating wheel. Small round cookie or biscuit cutter. Hammer.

MATERIALS: Moist clay in desired color, 10 lbs. Underglaze in contrasting color. Wooden beads ⅜" in diameter, about 24. Redwood lumber (or other wood, if using indoors): two pieces 32" x 1½" x ¾"; four pieces 9½" x 1½" x ¾". Cherry or redwood stain-wax. Nails, galvanized for outdoor use. Metal screw eyes, five. Surf-casting line, 45-lb. test, nylon twisted.

DIRECTIONS: Enlarge template pattern on page 70 by copying on paper ruled in ½" squares. Cut template of cardboard. For screen you will need to make eight bells ranging in size from 2¾" to 3½" in height and diameter when finished. Since clay shrinks in drying, start out with circles for bases at least ½" larger in diameter and work up to ½" taller than desired height. (These bells can also be easily thrown on wheel or slip-poured; ceramic supply stores have molds for bells if slip-pouring.) Allow bells to have

some variation in size and shape. Coil-built bells have the most interesting shapes, although their tone may not be as clear as the others. Build bells using template and coil method. While bells are still moist, but rather firm, apply decorations. Small pieces of moist clay can be applied with slip and pressed firmly to attach, then imprinted with dowel ends, butter molds, modeler, etc. to create design. Some bells can be incised with free-hand line designs or placed on a slowly revolving decorator's wheel and lines incised into them in circular pattern. Pierce each bell at the top with a pointed dowel to make hole for hanging. When decorated, put aside to dry thoroughly. Slight warpage will not affect the sound and often adds interest to the shape.

Each bell needs a clapper. For each clapper, make small clay bead by rolling small ball of clay; pierce hole through center with skewer. Make disks for decoration by rolling clay about ⅜″ thick; cut out with cookie or biscuit cutter. Poke hole through center

while still damp with skewer. Incise and decorate disks as desired.

When all pieces are thoroughly dry, sand lightly, if necessary. Brush with underglaze on raised or incised areas; rub off lightly with steel wool, leaving color in patterned area; fire. (The higher the firing, the clearer the bell tone.)

To make frame, nail pieces of wood together with simple right-angle joints, spacing evenly as illustrated. Sand wood smooth; stain. Divide each end section into three equal parts; divide center section into two equal parts. Screw eyes in marked areas. Using casting line, fit bells with beads, clapper, and disk as in Fig. 1 on page 70. Attach to frame by threading line through screw eyes, adjusting for length as desired and tying firmly with square knot. Avoid having bells touch each other, and try to have disks take the shock when ringing. Suspend frame from outside beam or support with two side stakes driven into the ground.

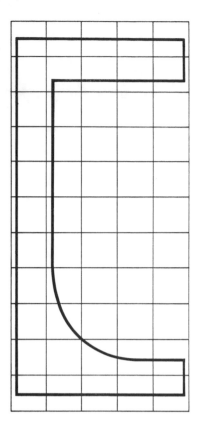

BELL

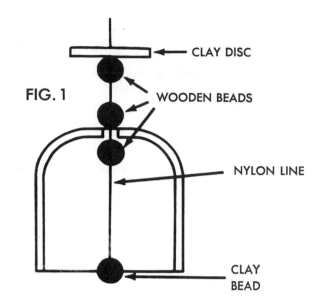

FIG. 1

CLAY DISC

WOODEN BEADS

NYLON LINE

CLAY
BEAD

Wind Bell Hanging: Enlarge pattern for bell template on ½" squares; Fig. 1 shows how bells are assembled.

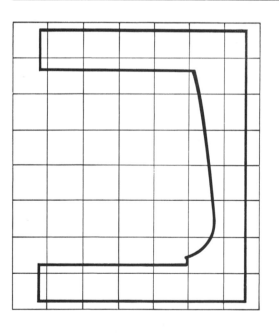

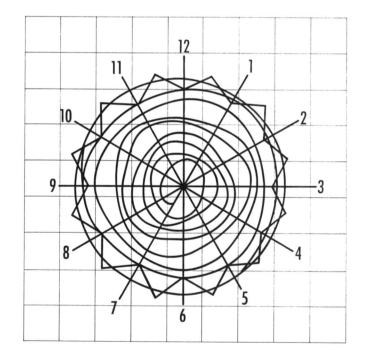

9   3

12
11   1
10   2
8   4
7   5
6

Sundial: Enlarge patterns for face of sundial and for base template on squares; Fig. 2 illustrates style.

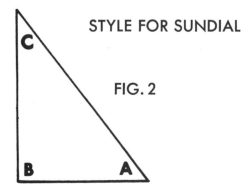

STYLE FOR SUNDIAL

FIG. 2

C

B   A

Sundial, shown in profile and from above, is a unique accessory for a garden or patio. The face of sundial is divided exactly as a clock. The triangular style will cast a shadow to indicate the time. When the sundial is mounted, it should have a southerly exposure and be free of shadows. See directions for Sundial on the following page.

SUNDIAL

See "How To Make Ceramics" on page 42.

SIZE: About 10½″ diameter.

EQUIPMENT: Paper for patterns. Heavy cardboard. Waxed paper. Steel wool. Protractor. Carpenter's level. Two small blocks of wood or two small bricks.

MATERIALS: Moist clay in desired color, 4 lbs. Underglaze in contrasting color. Waterproof cement.

DIRECTIONS: Enlarge pattern for base template (page 70) by copying on paper ruled in ½″ squares; enlarge pattern for face of sundial by copying on paper ruled in 1″ squares.

Roll out a large slab of clay as even as possible about ½″ thick; mark and cut out an 11″ circle. Place circle on bat or board. With pattern, divide circle into twelve equal parts and number them. Cut ¼″ wide and ¼″ deep groove from center to number 6 for holding the style. It is the shadow of the style that indicates the time of day. With pointed end of dowel or modeler and ruler, draw lines connecting numbers as shown. Incise remaining design lines at this time. To make base, coil build, starting with 3½″ base circle; work up to 2½″ in height, using template.

To make style, roll small slab of clay ¼″ thick; place between two bats or boards to keep perfectly flat. Allow to dry several hours; then cut a 4″ square. Following Fig. 2, mark an angle at A the same degree as the latitude in which you live, then mark and cut line from A to C. Continue to dry between bats or boards. When all pieces are completely dry, sand style to fit into groove. Rub underglaze into incised lines; sand off lightly with steel wool; fire. It is advisable to weight pieces down lightly with insulating brick during firing to insure their remaining flat.

Mounting of sundial is very important. Place it where it will be free of shadows from buildings and trees and have a southerly exposure. Use carpenter's level to be sure it is exactly level on base and compass is placed to determine that 12 o'clock faces true north. Place style in groove, A at 6, B at center. Attach style with cement and support with blocks of wood or bricks for 24 hours.

Macrame

One of the most enjoyable ways to spend random
hours and obtain dramatic results is to practice the
old art of macrame — a very popular craft today!
Only two simple knots are used — the square knot and
the half hitch. However, since ancient man started
tying vines together, hundreds of different knots
have been developed and some of the knots can be used
in macrame to add variety and interesting effects.
Macrame probably originated in the Middle East
hundreds of years ago. It spread into Europe during
the middle ages; but it became especially popular in
the nineteenth century with American and British
sailors, who created all kinds of intricate designs
and unusual objects. In the early twentieth century
practical items were made, such as purses and belts.
Then there was a lull in the popularity of macrame
until it started a comeback about five years ago.
Now it is one of the most popular handcrafts for men,
women, and children of all ages. Almost overnight, a
variety of materials became available to craftsmen —
from strong fine thread to rope and leather strips.
Is the popularity of this ancient craft a revolt
against our machine age of mass production? The only
tools you need to knot are your very own fingers!

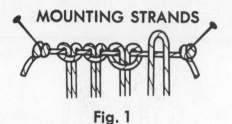

MOUNTING STRANDS

Fig. 1

HORIZONTAL BAR TO LEFT

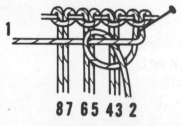

8 7 6 5 4 3 2

Fig. 2A — Half Hitch

Fig. 2B — Double Half Hitch

HORIZONTAL BAR TO RIGHT

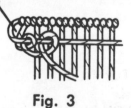

Fig. 3

DIAGONAL BAR — LEFT AND RIGHT

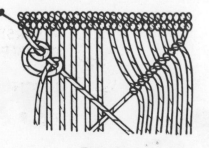

Fig. 4

HOW TO MACRAME

EQUIPMENT: Glass-headed pins. Scissors. Working surface such as a foam rubber pillow form. Rubber bands. Tape measure. Crochet hook size 1 or 0. Needle and thread.

MATERIALS: Heavy or medium-weight tightly twisted yarn or cord is most suitable. See Materials in the individual directions for each item.

MACRAME GENERAL DIRECTIONS: Practice making the knots on a sample first to become familiar with the technique. The working surface, such as a foam rubber pillow form, may be placed on a table or held in the lap. Some pieces may be easier to work on if suspended from a hook.

Mounting: A mounting cord to start the macrame piece is pinned horizontally across working surface. To do this, cut a strand of the yarn being used, about 6″ longer than the width of planned macrame piece. Knot both ends with an overhand knot (Fig. 12 on page 76) and pin knots to working surface to hold strand taut; place pins along length of cord if necessary. The working strands of yarn are tied onto the mounting cord, and the macrame knots are tied with these strands to form the design. To figure the length to cut required working strands, allow about 8 times the length of the finished macrame piece for each strand. Fold each strand in half and tie doubled strand on mounting cord as shown in Fig. 1. Hold doubled strand in front of mounting cord, fold over to back and pull ends through loop, tightening knot (Fig. 1). Mount required working strands close together. (For other methods, see Picot Mounting.)

To make working with long strands easier, wind each strand up, leaving about 15″ free below work; fasten each strand with a rubber band. As work progresses, unfasten rubber band and release more yarn.

Knots: The macrame designs are formed using two knots—the half hitch and the square knot—in various ways.

Half Hitch Bars: The half hitch is used to make

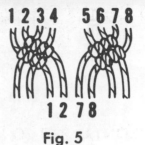

1 2 3 4 5 6 7 8

1 2 7 8

Fig. 5

VERTICAL
DOUBLE
HALF
HITCH

Fig. 6

ALTERNATE
HALF
HITCHES
2-STRANDS

Fig. 7

ALTERNATE
HALF
HITCHES
4-STRANDS

Fig. 8

REVERSED
DOUBLE
HALF
HITCH

Fig. 9

bars as in Fig. 2A and Fig. 2B and for mounting strands with a picot edge (see Picot Mounting). Bars are made over an end working strand, called a knot bearer. Always keep the knot bearer taut, and form the knot with another working strand over the knot bearer. Use pins to hold knot bearer in place whenever necessary (see Fig. 2A). With each working strand, make a half hitch as shown in Fig. 2A, then repeat, making a double half hitch as shown in Fig. 2B. Work bars from right to left or from left to right (Fig. 3). Fig. 3 shows a double bar being made. Work second bar close to first.

Diagonal Bars: These are made in same manner as horizontal bars with double half hitches, but the knot bearer is held diagonally downward to either right or left (Fig. 4). For double diagonal bars, use two end strands as knot bearers. Work double half hitches over outside strand for each bar, making second bar directly below first diagonal bar.

Instead of always using the outside strand as knot bearer when making double diagonal bars, work as in Fig. 5. For first bar, use second strand as knot bearer working to right; then use first strand as knot bearer for second bar. Going to the left, use seventh strand as first knot bearer and outside eighth strand as knot bearer for second bar.

Vertical Double Half Hitch: Use one working strand, held vertically, as knot bearer. Work double half hitches over vertical knot bearer as shown in Fig. 6. Knot is made the same as for horizontal bar.

Alternate Half Hitches: Work first double half hitch as for Fig. 6. Then, using second strand as knot bearer, make another double half hitch with first strand, Fig. 7. Four strands may also be used, Fig. 8. Work a double half hitch first with fourth strand over two center strands, then with first strand, again over the two center strands.

Reversed Double Half Hitch: Make first half hitch by bringing working strand under knot bearer, around and over knot bearer, then under itself, Fig. 9. Make second half hitch as in Fig. 6.

SQUARE KNOT

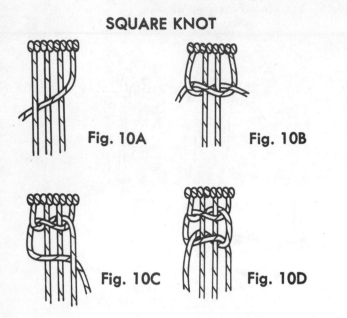

Fig. 10A   Fig. 10B

Fig. 10C   Fig. 10D

ALTERNATE ROWS OF SQUARE KNOTS

Fig. 11

OVERHAND KNOT

Fig. 12

Square Knot: This knot is made with four strands. Keeping the two center strands straight, tie knot with the two outer strands as shown in Figs. 10A, 10B, 10C, and 10D. Always hold center strands taut and tighten knot by pulling the two outer strands up into place. A simple square knot may also be made with just two strands, eliminating the center strands.

Alternate Rows of Square Knots: Make first row of square knots using four strands for each. For second row, leave two strands at each side free and redivide strands into groups of four, using two strands from adjacent knots of first row. Tie square knots across row, spacing row evenly across below first row. For third row, use all strands and make the same as first row. To form a pointed shape, make one square knot with center four strands. Divide strands from center knot and tie two square knots, using two more strands on each side, Fig. 11. Continue making each row wider than last in same manner. Rows may be decreased by leaving two more strands free on each side.

Overhand Knot: A small knot is sometimes used to bring strands together (Fig. 12). Mounting cord is also knotted at both ends with an overhand knot.

Finishing Edges: Ends may be finished off by making a bar at end of macrame. Turn work over and pull each strand through back of bar, using crochet hook. Cut off strands, leaving about 1″ ends; tack ends to back to secure.

To finish edge with picots, after making bar, turn work over. Starting from left, draw first strand end through back of second knot; pull down tightly. Draw second strand through back of first knot; pull down to lie loosely over first strand, thus making a picot. Repeat with each pair of strands.

To make tassels or fringe, gather a number of strands together and tie together with an overhand knot close to bottom.

Sinnets: Long lines called sinnets can be made by repeating the first half of the square knot on four strands, which will twist the line as it grows.

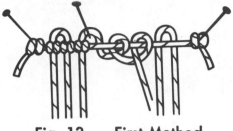

Fig. 13 — First Method

By repeating the complete square knot on four strands, you will get a flat sinnet. Sinnets can also be made with half-hitch knots.

Picot Mounting: First Method: To mount working strands with a picot edge, Fig. 13, fold each strand in half and place loop behind mounting cord. With first strand, make a double half hitch on mounting cord; then make a double half hitch with second strand, leaving a slight slack between knots (Fig. 13). When half hitches are pushed together, the slack forms the picot between knots. Repeat with each double strand. **Second Method:** Fold working strands in half and pin on top of mounting cord. Follow Fig. 14 to form picot, tightening knots close to pins. Place picot knots in back of mounting cord and tie each strand over mounting cord with a double half hitch.

Fig. 14 — Second Method

Circular Macrame: To work in a circle, a mounting cord is not used. Cut half the number of working strands required and tie them all together at center with another strand of yarn about 4″ long. All strands at both sides of center are used as working strands. Pin strands through center tie to working surface (knot down) and arrange strands out from center as shown in Fig. 15. Tie knots with all working strands around center in a circle. To make a circular bar, a separate strand is used as the knot bearer. Pin one end of knot bearer to working surface so that you can hold it taut while tying knots. Tie double half hitches with each working strand, over knot bearer, keeping the knot bearer the same distance from center all around; tie ends of knot bearer together and clip ends.

To increase the number of working strands in circular macrame, strands may be added between groups. To add two working strands, cut a length of yarn, fold in half and pin loop of strand between groups. Then proceed to make knots using the two extra strands.

To add four strands between groups, cut two lengths of yarn, fold in half and pin in place, Fig. 15. Tie a square knot with the four strands. Then proceed to make knots, using the four extra strands from the square knot.

CIRCULAR MACRAME

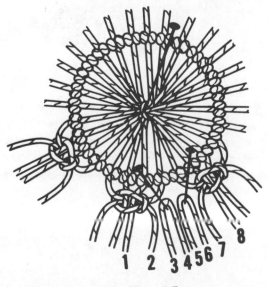

Fig. 15

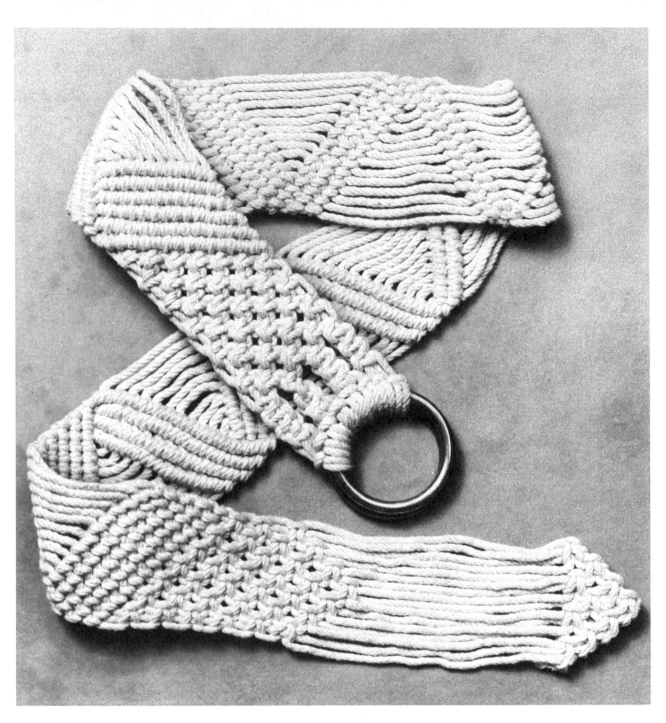

The bold geometric design of the belt, above, will appeal to men. The belt, 40" long (including the 2" brass-plated solid rings), is made of cotton cable cord. Pattern is a combination of square knots and diagonal bars. If desired, belt can be dyed beige color by dipping it into a strong solution of tea or coffee. See directions for Man's Belt on page 80.

The eye-catching belt (opposite page) worn at hips, ties at side; or at waist, ties at center. Belt, of heavy rug yarn, is worked from center to each end in a pattern of diagonal bars, square knots, vertical half-hitch sinnets, and horizontal bars. Three 2-¾" wooden drapery rings are worked into the design at the center and sides. Three-Ring Belt is on page 80.

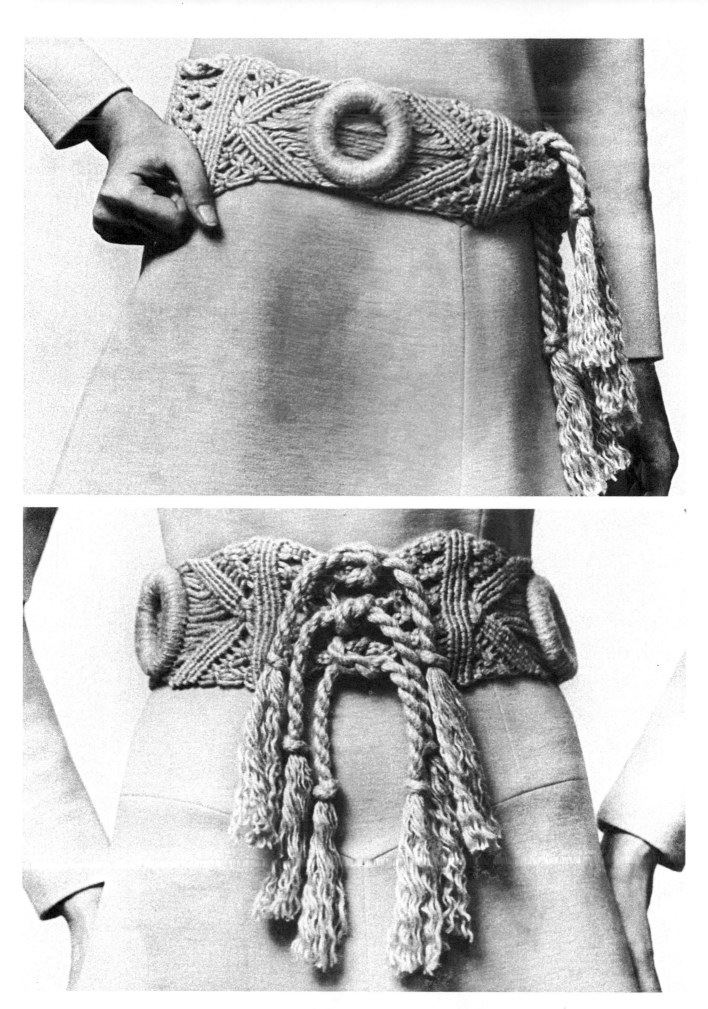

MAN'S BELT

SIZE: 40″, including rings.
EQUIPMENT: See page 74.
MATERIALS: Tytite Cotton Cable Cord #60, two (138 ft.) balls. Tandy brass plated solid rings 2″ diameter, two. All-purpose glue. Coffee or tea for dyeing (optional).

DIRECTIONS: See ''How to Macrame'' on pages 74-77. Cut eight 9½-yard long cords; fold in half and mount as in Fig. 1, on both rings. Divide strands into four groups of four strands each. Tie a flat sinnet of three square knots (Figs. 10A, 10B, 10C, 10D) with each group. Regroup strands into alternate groups of four and tie seven alternate rows of square knots (Fig. 11); begin and end with a row of three knots. Tie five more alternate rows of square knots, omitting two strands more at left each time.

Using first strand at left as knot bearer, tie a diagonal bar to right (Fig.4) with remaining strands. Tie five more bars to right, using first strand at left as knot bearer and omitting one more strand at right (knot bearer of last bar) as working strand each time. Tie five decreasing diagonal bars to left in same manner, using first strand at right as knot bearer each time. Tie four decreasing diagonal bars to right in same manner, using first strands at left as knot bearers. Tie three decreasing diagonal bars to left. Tie two decreasing diagonal bars to right. Tie one diagonal bar to left. Tie two decreasing diagonal bars to right, then three to left, then four to right, four to left, five to right, and five to left.

Beginning with first four strands at right, tie 12 alternate rows of square knots, using two more strands at left each time; begin with row of one knot and end with row of three knots. Tie alternate row of two square knots with eight center strands. Tie square knot with four center strands. Turn work to wrong side. Leave strands free for 4″. Divide strands into four groups of four strands. Tie three alternate rows of square knots, omitting two more strands at right and left each time, making a point. Turn ends to back and trim so they are even with first row of square knots of point. Glue ends to point. If desired, dye belt with strong solution of tea or coffee.

THREE-RING BELT

EQUIPMENT: See page 74.
MATERIALS: Aunt Lydia's Heavy Rug yarn, two 70-yard skeins tan. Unfinished wooden drapery rod rings, three 2¾″ in diameter.
DIRECTIONS: See ''How To Macrame'' on pages 74-77. Belt is worked in two halves, from center ring to one end, then from center ring to other end. For first half, cut 12 pieces of rug yarn
continued on page 82

Dainty evening bag, reminiscent of the old-fashioned reticule, is an easy beginner's project. A rectangular macrame piece is knotted with light-brown fine cord in diagonal bars and square-knot sinnets, both twisted and flat. The macrame (8″ deep, plus long, glass-beaded fringe) is attached to a velvet drawstring bag in deeper brown. Evening bag, page 84.

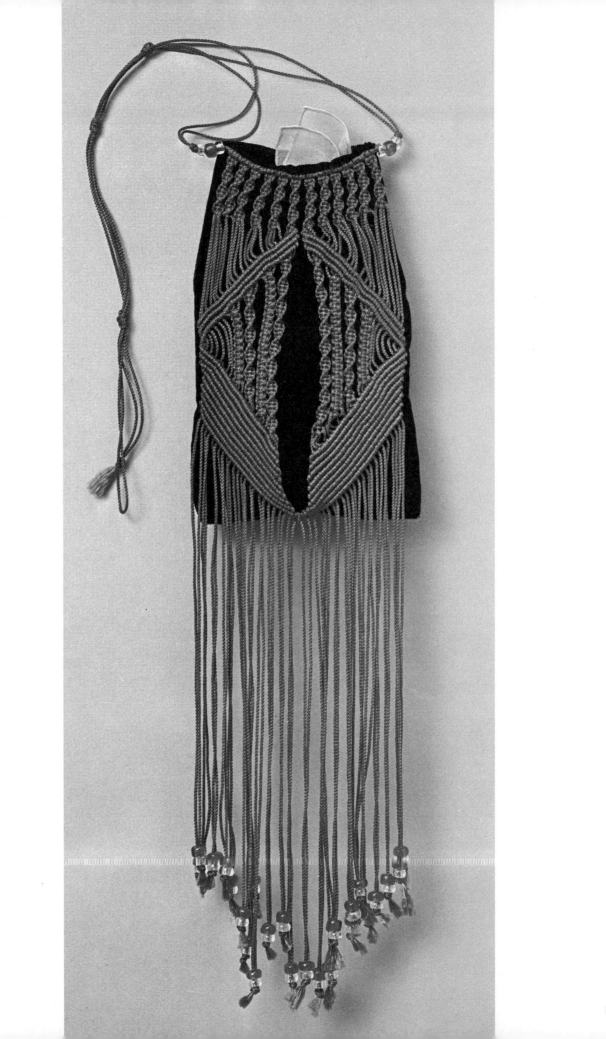

THREE-RING BELT

continued from page 80

each 5½ yards long. Fold each in half and mount on one side of a wooden ring as in Fig. 1; push strands close together on ring. You may find it easier to work the macrame belt by suspending the ring from a hook in front of you, then working on a pillow.

Using outside strand on right as knot bearer, work a diagonal bar down to center with 11 strands (Fig. 4). Work a diagonal bar from left down to center with remaining strands. Make three more diagonal bars to center directly under first bars, using outside strand as knot bearer for each. Using four knot bearer strands at center from each group of diagonal bars, tie a square knot (Figs. 10A, 10B, 10C, 10D) with four strands at center and using two strands on each side to tie knot. Tie a square knot with four strands at each side ½" below diagonal bars. Make an alternate square knot (see Fig. 11) ¼" below first on each side, using two more strands from diagonal bars and two strands from previous square knot; two outside strands are free. Make third alternate row of two square knots ¼" below last, using all eight strands on each side.

Make four horizontal bars across (see Fig. 3).

Using four outside strands on each side, make a sinnet 2¾" long. To make sinnet, tie first half of square knot, Figs. 10A and 10B. Repeat this half only. As half of the square knot is repeated, the knots will twist, making a spiral.

With remaining strands, make four vertical half hitch sinnets (Fig. 6), using four strands each. Make two double half hitches in each group of four. For second row, leave the two outside strands on each side free and make three groups of vertical half hitch sinnets (two double half hitches on each). Twist the two outside strands together; then repeat the two rows. Make four horizontal bars across.

Work the first diagonal bar pattern in reverse, tying the center square knot (eight strands) first, then the four square knots (four strands each) at each side, and last the four diagonal bars from center to each side.

To attach next wooden ring, place it on top of strands with top edge of ring 1¾" below center of diagonal bars. Tie a double half hitch with each strand around wooden ring, starting at center and working to each side; with outer four strands on each side, tie single half hitches in order to cover top half of ring, but without crowding. Bring the strands down in back of ring to bottom and tie double and single half hitches over bottom half of ring as before.

Repeat first pattern below ring. Make four horizontal bars.

continued on page 84

A long, green-beaded fringe cascading from gold bib gives a dramatic finish to a simple outfit. The bib is worked in diagonal and horizontal bars, plus alternate half-hitch sinnets and a few square knots. When bib is finished, the mounting cords become ties. Make with rug yarn or doubled knitting worsted, with the tile beads knotted in. Tile-Bead Bib, page 84.

THREE-RING BELT

continued from page 82

To end, make six sinnets of vertical half hitches (two double half hitches on each). For next row, leave two outer strands on each side free and tie five groups of vertical half hitch sinnets (two double half hitches each).

To make ties, gather strands into six groups of four each. Twist each of two adjacent groups separately, counter clockwise very tightly; then bring the two twisted groups together and let them twist together to form a heavy cord. Repeat with remaining groups in pairs, to make three cords.

On each cord, tie a knot 7″ below macrame. Cut off excess ends 5″ beyond knots. Unravel ends to make tassels.

Make second half of belt the same, starting with 12 pieces of rug yarn mounted on other half of center ring.

EVENING BAG

EQUIPMENT: See page 74.

MATERIALS: Light brown fine macrame cord, 182 ft. Matching thread. Glass beads, approximately 5/16″ diameter, with hole large enough to accommodate two strands: 28 clear; 26 amber. Dark brown velvet, approximately 20″ x 7″.

DIRECTIONS: Refer to Macrame Instructions on pages 74-77. Cut one 6-ft. long cord; fold in half and pin to working surface. Make sure this mounting cord is centered, as it will be the strap of the bag. Cut 24 7-ft. long strands; fold in half and mount on double mounting cord (Fig. 1). Separate strands into twelve groups of four. Using first group of strands at left of work, make a twisted sinnet by repeating first half of square knot (Figs. 10A and 10B) fifteen times. Sinnet will be approximately 1¼″ long. Make 11 more sinnets across work.

Using two center strands as knot bearers, make a diagonal bar of double half hitches (Fig. 4) on each half of work. Begin at center, directly below last knot of sinnet, and work out and down toward sides. Last knot of bar should measure 2½″ from bottom of outside sinnet. Be sure to leave strands between sinnets and bars loose enough to keep work flat. Make two more diagonal bars on each side directly below first, using center strands each time as knot bearers.

Anchor last knot bearer at end of left diagonal bar; slip this strand under remaining strands on left side diagonally downward; pull taut and pin again at center of work 4½″ below last diagonal bar. This strand will act as a guide in the working of the next section. Separate strands on left side of work into one group of seven strands (first

seven strands from left) and four groups of four strands. Working from center of work toward left side, make a twisted sinnet with first group of four strands, beginning directly below last diagonal bar and ending when guide strand is reached. Using next group of strands, make a flat sinnet of square knots (Figs. 10A, 10B, 10C, 10D) reaching from last diagonal bar to guide strand. Using next group, make a twisted sinnet; with next group, make a flat sinnet as before. Leave last seven strands free. Repeat on right side of work, in reverse.

Slip all strands under guide strands. Using guide strands as knot bearers, make a diagonal bar of double half hitches on each side, beginning at outside of work and working toward center. Repeat diagonal bar eight times on each side, always using outermost strand as knot bearer. Join the two center cords with two overhand knots (Fig. 12).

Thread each pair of strands with first an amber bead and then a clear bead; push beads up. Tie an overhand knot 10″ below last diagonal bar. Push beads down to knots. Trim all strands ½″ from knots. Thread each end of strap with first a clear bead, then an amber bead, then clear again. Push beads all the way to sides of work; tie overhand knots close to beads. Join all four strands with an overhand knot 7″ from first two; tie another overhand knot 2″ from last, another 4″ from last. Tie an overhand knot ½″ from end of two cut strands.

To Make Bag: Measure macrame piece, excluding fringe. Double the length and add two more inches; add one inch to the width. Cut the velvet to this size. Fold in half with right sides together. Stitch ½″ seam at each side. Turn in 1″ around top edge and slip-stitch. Turn right side out. Place macrame on top of bag with fringe extending below. Whipstitch to bag along edge, along sides at diagonal bars, and at bottom where two center strands were joined.

TILE-BEAD BIB

EQUIPMENT: See page 74.

MATERIALS: Double twist rug yarn (or doubled knitting worsted) 73 yards in color desired. Round tile beads 3/16″ diameter, about 220.

DIRECTIONS: Refer to Macrame Instructions on pages 74-77. For mounting cord, cut four pieces of rug yarn each 36″ long; tie together a few inches from each end with overhand knots (Fig. 12). Cut 22 working strands 112″ long. Double and mount each working strand over the four mounting cords as in Fig. 1. Using outside strand on each side as knot bearer, make a diagonal bar down to center (see Fig. 4). Tie knot bearers together at center by making a half hitch with one over the other. Use same knot bearers to make a horizontal bar from center out to each side.

Divide strands into groups of four and tie 11 square knots, Figs. 10A, 10B, 10C, 10D. Make a horizontal bar to left, Figs. 2A and 2B, and another to the right, Fig. 3.

Divide strands into groups of four again. Over the two center strands of each group, tie six alternate half hitches, following Fig. 8.

String a bead on the two outside strands of each group; tie strands around bead to secure bead in place, and cut off strands. Cut remaining strands in varying lengths from 6" to 9". Untwist each strand, making double the number of ends. String beads onto each end, using three or four beads on some strands and up to 10 beads on others. Knot each strand around last bead to secure them.

To finish the mounting cords for necklace, untie knots at ends and tie a square knot on each side of bib, using the four mounting cords. About 3" beyond, tie two square knots. Tie the four cords together at each end with square knot; pull ends through knot.

WISE OWL HANGING

EQUIPMENT: See page 74.

MATERIALS: Wrapping cord, about 100 ft. One straight 7"-8" long wooden stick such as a ¼" dowel. One curved twig or piece of driftwood, about 12" long and ½" diameter at center.

DIRECTIONS: Refer to Macrame Instructions on pages 74-77. Tie all knots loosely, or work will not lie flat; do not pull knot bearers too tightly when making curved and diagonal bars. Owl is symmetrical; work both halves the same, except where stated. Cut a 20" long mounting cord; fold in half and pin, centered, to working surface. Cut twelve 8 ft. long cords; fold in half and mount (Fig. 1) on double mounting cord. Divide strands into five groups of four strands with one pair of two strands at each side. Tie a square knot (Figs. 10A, 10B, 10C, 10D) with each group of four. Tie a second square knot with center group of strands. Tie a half hitch (Fig. 2A) with last two strands of second group and with first two strands of fourth group of four, directly below square knot.

Join each pair of outside strands with a pair of alternate half hitches (two center knots of Fig. 8). Using each pair of outside strands as double knot bearers, tie a curved diagonal bar (see illustration) close to last knots from sides toward center (Fig. 4).

Tie a double half hitch with left double knot bearer on right double knot bearer, pulling both ends down. Divide eight center strands into two groups of four and tie a diagonal bar toward center with each group, using outside strands as sin-

gle knot bearers. Tie a double half hitch with left single knot bearer on right single knot bearer, as before. Tie another pair of diagonal bars toward center with eight center strands, as before. This forms beak.

Divide strands into two groups of twelve strands each. With center four strands of each group, tie a loose square knot directly below diagonal bar, forming the pupils of eyes. Using third working strand in from each curved bar as knot bearers, tie a bar of five vertical half hitches (Fig. 6) on each half of work with fourth working strands. Using first working strand from curved bar as working strands, tie a bar of six vertical half hitches on each half of work with second working strands. This bar should curve slightly towards center. Using first strand on each side of beak as knot bearers, tie diagonal bars from center toward sides, with the four strands from square knot. Pull knot bearers on each half together and join with a pair of alternate half hitches, so there appears to be one uninterrupted bar. Continue tying bar knotted on first working strand, using remaining strands except double knot bearers as working strands. Work from sides toward center, and curve bar as in illustration. Join knot bearers and all others unless otherwise stated at center of work with a pair of alternate half hitches.

Using fourth strand from each side as knot bearer, tie a curved horizontal bar directly below last bar; work toward center, using four remaining working strands from last bar as working strands. On each side, bring knot bearer of this bar and of last bar together and tie a bar of half hitches toward center over double knot bearer thus formed, starting close to last half hitch so the two bars flow into one another.

Using three outside strands on each side, tie rows of alternate half hitches from sides toward center of work as follows: Starting with first outside strand, tie a half hitch (second knot of Fig. 8) on second outside strand. Using same second strand, tie a half hitch (third knot of Fig. 8) on first strand. Using second strand again, tie a half hitch (second knot of Fig. 8) on third outside strand. Using third strand, tie a half hitch (third knot of Fig. 8) on second strand. Tie a third pair of alternate half hitches in same manner, completing first row. Tie second row directly below first. Tie two rows of alternate half hitches with all strands, starting at sides and having rows meet at center, joining two knot bearers. Tie four pairs of alternate half hitches at each side, using four outside strands. Divide strands into two groups of twelve strands each. Tie a pair of alternate half hitches with two right center strands. Using second center left strand as knot bearer, tie a bar of half hitches with first center left and first center

continued on page 89

A wise owl, perched on a twig or graceful piece of driftwood, is suspended
from a dowel for an interesting wall
hanging. Owl is knotted with wrapping
cord; square knots make his eyes, while
curving diagonal bars define the con-
tours of his body (5" x 12"). Wise
Owl Hanging is on page 85.

Unusual jewelry, belt, little man are
fashioned with string and stones.
Macrame is all square-knot sinnets;
stones are glued to macrame, with coils
of string covering and reinforcing ends.
Designs are drawn with black felt-tipped
pen and made permanent with nail
polish or plastic spray. See Black &
White Jewelry, Figure on page 89.

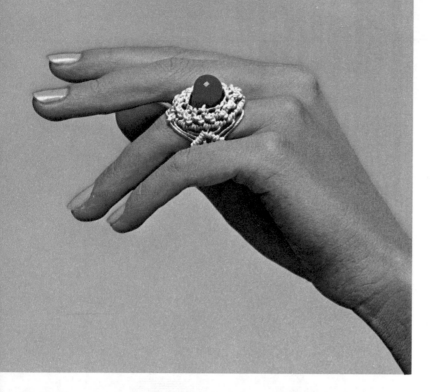

A bright-beaded macrame ring for fashion novelty! Ring is worked with half-hitch knots in fine cotton cord; diagonal bars form two diamond shapes for the shank of ring. The red oval stone is worked into the knotting. Red Bead Ring on page 91.

Keep your purse handy and secure by wearing it at your side. Pouch is worked in patterns of square-knot diamonds, twisted sinnets, and diagonal-bar panels. A felt lining and glass beads contrast with the natural linen warp. Belt Purse, page 91.

WISE OWL HANGING
continued from page 85

right strands.

Divide strands into pairs. With fifth pair from each side, tie a pair of alternate half hitches. Tie a diagonal bar towards center, using outside strand of fourth pair on each side as knot bearer. Join knot bearers at center. Divide working strands from bar into pairs and tie a pair of alternate half hitches with each two uppermost pair. Tie second diagonal bar in same manner, using outside strand of third pair as knot bearer and tying pairs of alternate half hitches with three uppermost pairs of working strands. Join knot bearers at center. Tie third diagonal bar in same manner, using outside strand of second pair as knot bearer and tying pairs of alternate half hitches with five uppermost pairs of working strands. Tie fourth diagonal bar using outside strand as knot bearer, and tying pairs of alternate half hitches with center seven pairs of working strands. Join knot bearers; tie a pair of alternate half hitches with knot bearers and adjacent strands. Tie a fifth bar by repeating fourth bar. Tie a pair of alternate half hitches with two outside strands. Tie a reversed double half hitch with second and third outside strands. Tie a curved sixth diagonal bar, using three outside strands as triple knot bearers. Work a row of alternate half hitches from sides toward center, as above, using six outside strands on each side. Work a second row, using ten outside strands. Work a third row, using all of remaining strands. Work a fourth row, using all strands. Join center strands with a pair of alternate half hitches (Fig. 7).

To form claws: Divide strands into a center pair with two pairs of strands at each side. Tie a pair of alternate half hitches with each pair. Tie an overhand knot (Fig. 12) with two center strands; pin out of the way and leave free until later. Tie another pair of very loose alternate half hitches with each of four remaining pairs of strands. Pin out of the way. There are seven outside strands on each half of work. Tie a diagonal bar toward center on each half of work, using two outside strands as double knot bearers and remaining five outside strands as working strands. Tie a second diagonal bar on each half in same manner, using knot bearers of first bar as working strands at bottom of second bar. Tie a horizontal bar on each half from sides toward center, using all strands (except center pair) as working strands, and outside strand as single knot bearer. Make sure that claws are loose enough so twig can be inserted.

Join single knot bearers at center; leave free until later. Divide remaining strands into five groups of four; work a row of square knots across work. Regroup strands and work an alternate row of four square knots, leaving two out-

side strands free at each side. Work an alternate row of three square knots, leaving two more outside strands free at each side. Work an alternate row of two square knots, leaving two more outside strands free. Work one last square knot, using four center strands. Gather four center strands by tying two overhand knots over them with adjacent strands. Trim ends of center six strands to about 1½". Weave all remaining ends into work at back; trim close to work.

Tie an overhand knot on each end of top mounting cord about 1" from edge of work; tie a second knot 1" from first. Insert straight wooden stick in loops thus formed. Insert twig or driftwood in loops formed by claws as illustrated.

BLACK & WHITE JEWELRY, FIGURE

EQUIPMENT: See page 74.
MATERIALS: White stones of various sizes. Tightly woven or twisted cord about 1/16" or 1/8" thick. Elmer's Glue-All. Black fine-pointed felt-tip marker. Clear nail polish or plastic spray. Beads, 1/8" diameter, with holes large enough to accommodate one strand of thinnest cord.

GENERAL DIRECTIONS: Refer to Macrame Instructions on pages 74-77. All cords are attached to stones by gluing on the ends; when glue is dry, coat ends and surrounding area of stone with glue and wind another cord in a flat, tight coil around glued area of stone, covering and reinforcing ends of cords. Always allow glue to dry before proceeding with next step.

To attach a loop, glue both ends of a 1" long cord to stone, forming loop. Allow to dry and cover ends of loop with coil as directed above.

For macrame strips, attach a loop as above. Calculate length of cords (see Macrame Instructions); fold cords in half and mount on loop as in Fig. 1. Macrame portions of items are flat sinnets of square knots (Figs. 10A, 10B, 10C, 10D) worked one below the other for length indicated in individual directions.

Plan designs as shown or as desired and draw on stones with felt-tip marker after the macrame portion has been completed. When designs are dry, coat stones with nail polish or plastic spray; allow to dry throughly. Assemble each as indicated individual directions.

One-Stone Black Necklace: Use fine woven cord. Glue three 3½" pieces of cord together to one end of stone for bottom. String one bead on each cord ¾" below stone and tie an overhand knot (Fig. 12) below beads to keep in place. String two more beads on each cord in same manner; trim ends to ¼". Glue two small loops about ¾" apart to top end of stone; let dry.

Mount four cords of required length on each
continued on page 90

top loop. Work flat sinnets of square knots to 6″ or desired length; tie an overhand knot with all four strands close to last knot at end of sinnet. Tie another overhand knot 3½″ below first; trim one end to 1″ and one end to 3″.

Man: Use fine woven cord. Cut four pieces required length for each macrame sinnet. Legs are made of 4″ long sinnets. Glue each group of four cords to a small round stone for foot. When dry, tie an overhand knot (Fig. 12) with each group close to stone. Work flat sinnets of square knots (Figs. 10A, 10B, 10C, 10D); glue last knot to large oval stone for torso in desired position. When dry, trim ends close to stone; cover and reinforce ends with a coil. Glue small cord bow to each foot. Neck is a 1″ long sinnet. Glue four cords of required length to medium round flat stone for head; work sinnet and glue to torso stone as for legs, using a longer cord for coil; do not trim cord used for coil. Arms are 3″ long sinnets. Glue a loop to two small stones for hands and mount cords of required length for sinnets. Work sinnets and glue to torso in desired position, using same cord as for neck to form coil to cover and reinforce ends. Work a 3″ long sinnet and glue ends to top back of head in a loop; cover and reinforce with a coil.

Black Pendant Necklace: Use fine woven cord. Join small stone to second larger stone with two very short pieces of cord as directed in General Directions. To join second stone to largest third stone, glue a loop to second stone; when dry, thread a 1″ long piece of cord through loop and glue ends of cord to third stone, forming interlocking loops. Glue loop to other end of third stone. Join two other smaller stones to each other with two 1″ long pieces of cord, stringing third stone between them. Glue loops to other ends of last two stones. Let dry.

Mount four cords of required length on each loop for sinnets. Work flat sinnets of square knots (Figs. 10A, 10B, 10C, 10D) to desired length; tie an overhand knot (Fig. 12) with all four strands close to last knot at end of each sinnet. Tie another overhand knot 1½″ below first; trim ends to 1½″.

Black Necklace with Beads and Five Stones: Use fine woven cord. Glue four 3″ long pieces of cord 3/8″ apart along wide end of a large flat pear-shaped stone. String four beads on each of two center strands and three beads on each center strand, keeping beads in place with overhand knots (Fig. 12). Trim ends close to last knot. Glue a double loop of two 1″ long pieces of cord at top, narrow end of stone. Let dry.

Calculate length of cords required to work one long sinnet (about 24″) for both halves of necklace; cut four cords. Thread cords through loop of stone; fold cords over at center to form eight strands. Tie a large overhand knot with all eight strands close to loop. Divide eight strands into two groups of four strands each. Work a flat sinnet of square knots (Figs. 10A, 10B, 10C, 10D) with each group to desired length. Divide each group of four strands into pairs; tie an overhand knot with each pair close to last knot of sinnet. Tie an overhand knot with all four strands 1″ below last knots; trim ends to 1½″. String two smaller stones on each side of first stone as in illustration, by threading a 1″ long piece of cord through edge of sinnet and gluing ends of cord to stone, forming loop.

White Necklace with Beads and Stone: Use fine twisted cord. Cut four strands of required length to make flat sinnet of square knots (Fig. 10A, 10B, 10C, 10D) of desired length. Fold in half, and, being careful not to twist sinnet, join ends by bringing four inner strands together and tying two large square knots, using remaining four strands as working strands. Trim ends to 2″ and coat with glue. While glue is still moist, form a ¾″ long post by winding a piece of cord around ends, starting close to last knot. When dry, trim ends of sinnet close to bottom of post; coat top of large flat stone with glue and attach sinnet to stone at bottom of post by winding remaining cord around top of stone in a coil. Glue five 1″ long pieces of cord to bottom of stone. String four beads on each cord; push up close to stone and keep in place with an overhand knot close to last bead; trim ends close to knot.

White Belt: Cut four pieces of thick woven rayon cord of required length. Work a flat sinnet of desired length by tying square knots (Fig. 10A, 10B, 10C, 10D) one below the other. Using all strands, tie an overhand knot (Fig. 12) close to last knot at each end of sinnet. Trim ends to about 8″ or 9″; divide strands into pairs. Glue ends of each pair to a stone. Attach a second stone to each original stone by gluing ends of two 1″ long pieces of cord to each stone; when dry, glue other ends of cords to second stone.

White Choker with Stone: Use fine twisted cord. Cut eight cords required length to work choker band. Tie all eight strands together with an overhand knot (Fig. 12) 2″ from one end. Work choker band in alternating sinnets of three square knots (Figs. 10A, 10B, 10C, 10D) as follows: * Divide strands into two groups of four strands each. Tie three square knots one below the other with each group. Regroup strands so that there is a group of four strands at center. Tie three square knots with center group. Repeat from * until choker band is of desired length. Tie an overhand knot using all strands close to last knots of sinnet; trim ends to 2″. Cut one 1 ft. long cord; tie an overhand knot at center. Tie about five more overhand knots (depending on size of stone to be used) at each side of first knot, about ¼″ apart. Glue knotted portion of cord around edge of a round, flat stone. When dry, join two ends at top of stone with an overhand knot. Weave ends into back of choker band at center sinnet; trim ends close to work and reinforce with glue.

RED BEAD RING

EQUIPMENT: See page 74.
MATERIALS: Fine, tightly twisted cotton cord, 14 ft. One bead with hole large enough to accommodate single cord; stone in illustration is oval, 5/8″ diameter at widest point.
DIRECTIONS: Refer to Macrame Instructions on pages 74-77. Cut eight 20″ long strands. String the bead at center of one strand. Pin strand to working surface for mounting cord. Fold six of the remaining strands in half and mount three on each end of mounting cord at each side of bead (Fig. 1). Pin work to working surface close to bead; wrap each end of mounting cord halfway around bead in opposite directions to meet other end where it emerges from bead; join with reversed double half hitch (Fig. 9) to make a ring around bead. Pin remaining unmounted strand in a circle around bead, close to mounting cord. Using this as knot bearer, make a horizontal bar of double half hitches (Figs. 2A and 2B) around entire stone, making two double half hitches with each of the fourteen strands. Join ends of knot bearers with a reversed double half hitch, pulling taut to begin forming the shape of a dome. Turn work over and repeat circle of double half hitches. Join ends of knot bearers with a reversed double half hitch, pulling taut as before.

Separate strands into two groups of eight strands. (Ends of added knot bearer will be used as working strands.) If stone is oval, make sure strands are divided as symmetrically as possible. Work one side of ring at a time. Join two center-strands of group with a reversed double half hitch and use as knot bearers to make diagonal bars from center down to right and to left. Make a second diagonal bar directly below first, using first working strand from first bar as knot bearer and omitting first knot bearer at bottom of bar. Tie center strands together again. Make a third diagonal bar with remaining two strands. Using original knot bearers (or first diagonal bars) as knot bearers and, using all three strands on each side, tie a diagonal bar from each side of work toward center, completing diamond shape. Repeat entire pattern on other side of ring. Holding two ends of ring shank together, join each corresponding pair of strands with a reversed double half hitch. Tie an overhand knot (Fig. 12) on each strand as close to work as possible; trim ends close to knot,

or, if desired, weave ends back into work.

BELT PURSE

EQUIPMENT: See page 74.
MATERIALS: Lily All Linen Rug Warp, natural, 235 yards. Large glass beads (about 3/8″ diameter) 33, light turquoise. Turquoise felt 5″ x 12″. Matching sewing thread.
DIRECTIONS: Refer to Macrame Instructions on pages 74-77. Cut 56 pieces of rug warp each 4 yards long. Cut two pieces rug warp each 36″ long for mounting cords. Tie mounting cords together a few inches from ends and use together (they will be used after pouch purse is finished to tie pouch to belt if desired). Mount all pieces doubled on mounting cord, following Fig. 1. Divide all strands into groups of four and tie a square knot, following Figs. 10A, 10B, 10C, 10D, with each group.

Remove work from working surface and tie mounting cords together, joining ends of macrame into a ring. Remainder of purse will be worked in a circular fashion. Knot mounting cord into a loop and pin loop to working surface, so macrame can be turned as you work around piece.

Separate two strands from each square knot and join with two strands of adjacent square knot. Tie four square knots close together with each group. Separate two strands from each square knot again and join with two strands from adjacent square knot. Tie two square knots with each group. Separate strands again in same manner and tie two square knots with each group.

Divide all strands into groups of 16 strands. Working with one 16-strand group at a time, separate two strands from each square knot, and join with two strands of adjacent knot, leaving two strands free at each side. Tie two square knots on each group. Separate strands again in same manner, leaving four strands free at each side and tie two square knots on each group. Tie two square knots with center four.

Using outside left strand (at top of third row up), make a diagonal bar down to center, using all strands from square knots. Make a diagonal bar in same manner from right side of group to center. Make seven more diagonal bars from each side to center, close together. Repeat these eight rows of diagonal bars with each group of 16 around.

Between each group, using two strands from top end of adjacent bars, tie two square knots. Separate two strands from square knot and, using two more strands on each side, tie two square knots on the two groups of four. Separate two strands from each square knot again and, using two more strands on each side, make two square knots on the three groups of four strands. Sepa-
continued on page 92

rate the strands again, and, using all 16 strands, make two square knots on the four groups of four strands. Repeat square knot pattern between all groups of diagonal bars around.

Separate two strands from each square knot at sides of each group of 16 and tie two square knots with these four strands; tie two square knots on a group of four strands at each side, leaving four strands free between each group. Repeat this all around groups of 16. Separate two strands from each square knot, and join into two groups of four strands, leaving eight strands free between each. Tie two square knots on each two groups. On next row tie two square knots with center four strands of each group.

Between the square knot groups, gather the center eight strands and tie a large square knot, using four strands as center and tying with two strands on each side. Divide four strands from this knot and, using four free strands from each side, make two groups of four and tie a square knot as before with each. Separate strands again and tie a square knot below with center eight strands. At sides of large square knots (diamond pattern), tie two square knots on groups of four, from each side down to center, separating strands for each of four rows to form bottom of diamond.

Starting at center bottom of diamond shape, separate strands into groups of four all around. Make a sinnet of each group of four by repeating the first half of a square knot, Figs. 10A and 10B, for 2″; as you work the strands will twist around.

Cut strands off 2″ below. String a bead on each group of four. With needle, bring each strand around bead and down through hole separately to secure bead. Trim all ends evenly. To close bottom of bag somewhat, bring every fourth sinnet to center. Sew them together with linen warp to form a loose ring. Remaining sinnets form an outer ring; sew edges of every other pair of sinnets together.

For tie string, cut two pieces of linen warp 4½ yards long. String a bead on the two strands to middle of strands; cross one strand on each side to opposite side. String a bead on each of the two strands; push beads close to first bead. Bring the four strands together and string another bead on all four strands; push beads close to others.

Work macrame at edge of last bead. Work square knots close together with the four strands. Continue until tie is 17″ long. Cut off strands 3″ beyond. String a bead on all four strands; push close to knots. With needle bring one end on each side around bead and down through hole of bead; pull ends out and trim all off to 1″ length.

continued on page 94

Transform old wine bottles into attractive vases by giving them macrame "slips" made of household twine. The "slips" are knotted right onto bottles, starting at the neck and working down. One bottle has an attached cover for cork cap. Directions for Pomegranate Bottle (left in picture) are on page 94; Diamond Bottle (center) and Capped Bottle (right), page 95.

BELT PURSE
continued from page 92

Run macrame tie through slits around top of purse, in and out of every fourth slit for drawstring.

For lining, sew ends of felt strip together. Cut slashes 2″ long into one long edge (bottom); overlap slashed edges to curve bottom part so it will fit in bag. Cut off overlapped edges and sew edges of slashes together; sew bottom edges together to close. Insert felt lining in purse. Cut off top edge of felt so it is ¾″ below top edge of purse. Tack lining to inside of purse around top edge with matching thread.

POMEGRANATE BOTTLE

EQUIPMENT: See page 74.

MATERIALS: Twine, 80 yards (about 1/16″ diameter). Green ½-gallon wine bottle.

DIRECTIONS: Refer to Macrame Instructions on pages 74-77. Cut 20 pieces of twine each 4 yards long. Mount 19 pieces on center of the 20th piece (see Fig. 1). Tie mounting piece around neck of bottle tightly near top, leaving equal ends. Using one end of mounting piece as knot bearer, * make a horizontal bar (Figs. 2A and 2B) around neck of bottle, tying with all strands. Tie ends of knot bearer together with a vertical double half hitch (Fig. 6).

Divide all strands (including both ends of mounting piece) into 20 pairs. With each pair of strands around bottle, tie two alternate half hitches (see Fig. 7). * Separate strands and divide again into alternate pairs. Tie two alternate half hitches with each pair around. Redivide and repeat. Repeat from * to *.

Separate strands into four groups of 10 strands each. Tie three groups loosely together, out of the way. Leaving one strand on each side of group of 10 free, separate remaining eight strands into pairs. Tie two alternate half hitches with each pair. Leaving one more strand on each side free, regroup remaining six strands in pairs and tie two alternate half hitches with each pair. Continue in this way two more rows (one pair at center).

Untie the other three groups of 10 and repeat this pointed pattern on each group around bottle.

Using 10 strands between each point, make pomegranate design as follows: Tie two center strands together ¼″ below top of point. Separate strands into two groups of five. Using right-hand group, make a diagonal bar (Fig. 4) from center down to right side, but tie two double half hitches with each of the four strands. Using next center strand as knot bearer, make another diagonal bar in same manner, tying with next three strands. Make another diagonal bar in same manner, tying

with two strands. Then make another diagonal bar, tying two double half hitches with only one strand. Using outside right-hand strand as knot bearer, make a diagonal bar down to left at ends of previous bars, tying one double half hitch with each strand. With left five strands, work same diagonal bars from center down to left, and bottom diagonal bar from left to right. Tie last knot bearers from each group together at center. Repeat this pattern around bottle with the three remaining groups of 10 strands.

Separate strands into alternate groups of 10, using five strands each from adjacent groups. Work same pomegranate design, leaving space of about 1″ to start and spacing to fit bottle shape.

Separate strands again into alternate groups of 10 and work pomegranate design, leaving space this time to fit wide part of bottle.

With two top strands on each side of each bottom pomegranate, make two sinnets of eight alternate half hitches (Fig. 7). Join sinnets by tying together one strand of each adjoining sinnet with a half hitch. Make another sinnet of four alternate half hitches with each of these pairs of strands.

With remaining six strands of each group around, make a small pomegranate design (two diagonal bars each side) and join knot bearers at center bottom of each. Make a sinnet of three alternate half hitches, using two strands each, at center and each side of pomegranates.

Group a sinnet on each side with the last three sinnets made; separate sinnets all around bottle this way into four groups; work with one group at a time to bottom of bottle. Join each side sinnet with next shorter sinnet in same manner as before (tie one strand of each together with half hitch). Make a sinnet of two half hitches with each of these four pairs. Join the two inner sinnets to center sinnet as before. Make three more sinnets at center of two alternate half hitches. Join the two sinnets at each side of center with outer sinnets. Make four more sinnets the same; join at center as before. Make three sinnets in middle and join sinnets at each side of center with outside sinnets. Make a sinnet of two reversed double half hitches (Fig. 9) with each pair on outside. Repeat this pattern with remaining three groups.

At bottom rim of bottle, using one strand as knot bearer, make a horizontal bar (Fig. 3) around bottle, tying two double half hitches with each strand to fit bottle snugly.

On bottom of bottle, using two strands each, make two alternate half hitches; divide into alternate pairs and tie one half hitch with each pair. Separate into alternate pairs again and tie one half hitch with each. Using one strand as knot bearer, make a horizontal bar in a circle, tying one or two double half hitches with each strand to keep work snug and flat on bottom. Tie knot bearer to first strand securely. Cut off all ends to 1″; tuck in.

DIAMOND BOTTLE

EQUIPMENT: See page 74.
MATERIALS: Wrapping twine (about 1/16″ diameter) 64 yards. Pale green wine bottle about 12″ tall.

DIRECTIONS: Refer to Macrame Instructions on pages 74- 77. Cut 16 pieces of twine each 4 yards long. Fold 15 pieces in half and mount along center of last piece (see Fig. 1). Tie the mounting strand tightly around neck of bottle at top. Space mounted strands evenly around neck.

Alternate Half Hitch Pattern: Separate all strands, including both ends of mounting strands, into pairs (16 pairs). With each pair, tie two alternate half hitches (Fig. 7). Separate strands and regroup into pairs using strands from adjacent knots. Tie two more alternate half hitches with each new pair. Regroup again into pairs, and tie two alternate half hitches with each pair.

Divide strands, half for front and half for back; tie back strands loosely together out of the way and work with front strands. Continue in same manner as before, regrouping pairs and leaving one strand on each side free. Tie seven rows of alternate half hitches in this manner, leaving one more strand on each side free and working down to a point.

Using outside strand on each side as knot bearer, make diagonal bars from outsides down to center (Fig. 4), but tie two double half hitches with each strand in order to widen work so it will fit bottle. Using outside strands again as knot bearers, make another diagonal bar in same manner below first. Tie knot bearers of the last bars together with a double half hitch.

Repeat to this point, using back strands. To join front and back, bring one outside strand from each side of back over to front and use as knot bearers to make another diagonal bar below. Do the same on back using two strands from sides of front as knot bearers. Make another short diagonal bar from each side on both front and back below last, tying with only two strands each.

At each side of bottle, between front and back patterns, make diamond pattern as follows: Using outside strand from front and back as center of side section, tie a double half hitch. Separate strands and, using one more strand from outside of front and back to make two pairs, tie a double half hitch with each pair. Continue separating strands and using one more strand on each side to widen pattern. Work in this manner for eight rows in all. Then make seven more rows, leaving one more strand free on each side for each row, to work down to a point.

Separate front and back halves again. Bring two center strands of front together at middle and tie a double half hitch; separate these strands. Bring next strand on each side to center, join with

strand from center and tie vertical double half hitches with each pair (Fig. 6), keeping strands taut to fit bottle shape smoothly. Continue bringing one more strand from each side to center and tying a vertical double half hitch at each side with outer strands to form an inverted V; use all strands from sides. With center strands (inside "V"), make pattern of alternate half hitches, forming a long inverted V shape within outer V, working down to bottom of bottle. Repeat inverted V pattern with back strands.

Lay bottle down and make a diagonal bar from each side of front section down over bottom of bottle to center. Tie a few alternate double half hitches on bottom of bottle to hold strands in place. Repeat with back half, bringing strands over bottom of bottle. Tie strands from front and back together across bottom of bottle, making them taut to hold macrame in place.

CAPPED BOTTLE

EQUIPMENT: See Page 74.
MATERIALS: Butcher's twine, 52 yards. Dark green wine bottle 10″ tall, with capped cork. Household cement.

DIRECTIONS: Refer to Macrame Instructions on pages 74-77. For mounting cords, cut one piece of twine 96″ long and one 10″ long. Use both together for mounting cord, laying 10″ piece along center of longer piece. Cut 14 working strands each 80″ long. Fold each in half and mount on double cord (as shown in Figure 1). Tie the double mounting cord around neck of bottle tightly. Using one end of long mounting cord as knot bearer, make a horizontal bar around bottle (Figs. 2A and 2B), using all strands to tie double half hitches. Tie the two ends of long mounting cord tightly around bottle, roll up and put out of the way to use later for cap. Tie the two ends of short mounting strand together; cut off 1″ beyond, and tuck under macrame as work proceeds.

Separate remaining 28 strands into pairs. With each pair, tie alternate half hitches (Fig. 7) for 1″. Using one strand as knot bearer, make another horizontal bar around neck of bottle and tie ends together.

Separate strands into groups of four. With each group, make a double diagonal bar to right as shown in Fig. 5. Make another horizontal bar around neck of the bottle.

To work over wider part of bottle separate strands into alternate groups of six and eight. With each of the two eight-strand groups, separate strands into pairs and tie each pair with a vertical double half hitch (Fig. 6). Separate strands and regroup into pairs, leaving one strand at each side free. Tie a vertical double half hitch *continued on page 96* with each pair. Regroup again into pairs, leaving two strands on each side free and tie pairs with a vertical double half hitch. Then tie a vertical double half hitch with two center strands.

Using outer strands on each side as knot bearer, make a diagonal bar with each, down to center (Fig. 4). Using the four strands from each diagonal bar separately, work as follows from outside to inside of each group: Tie a vertical double half hitch with two outer strands. Using one strand from this knot and next strand, tie another vertical double half hitch. Repeat, adding last strand. Work in this manner again, using three outer strands, then only two outer strands. Using inner strand of each group as knot bearer, make three diagonal bars from center outward.

With the two six-strand groups, make first and second rows in same manner as for eight-strand groups. Then tie the two outside strands on each side with a vertical half hitch. Divide into two groups of three, and tie a vertical half hitch with each of the two inner strands. Cross the two center strands to rejoin groups and tie a half hitch with them. Using outer strands as knot bearers, make a diagonal bar from each side to center. Repeat the center half hitch and diagonal bars two more times. Tie last knot bearers together at center.

Cut eight more pieces of twine each one yard long. Make a horizontal bar around bottle, using a center strand from eight-strand group as knot bearer and tying two double half hitches with each working strand; mount two extra strands on knot bearer between each six and eight-strand group as you work around.

Work with strands below each six-strand group, plus two new strands on each side first. Divide these ten strands into two groups of five, and tie a square knot with each (Fig. 10A, 10B, 10C, 10D), using three strands at center of each. Then tie a square knot below with center six strands. On each side of square knot, tie two vertical half hitches with two outside strands. Repeat first two square knots.

Leave these strands and work with four strands from each side of adjacent eight-strand group, plus two other added strands.

Using two strands (below center of eight-strand group), tie a vertical half hitch. Using next (third) strand in as knot bearer, make a bar vertically, using first two strands to tie half hitches. Tie fourth strand and top strand from vertical bar with a half hitch; tie two end strands from vertical bar with a half hitch. Make a vertical bar, using fourth strand as knot bearer. Make two half hitches again. Tie the added strands with a double vertical half hitch, then use one as knot bearer and make a vertical bar. Make four more vertical

bars next to last, using top strand each time as knot bearer; tie knots with one less strand each time, leaving last strands free. Join ten-strand group to this group by crossing adjacent strands. Use strand from ten-strand group as knot bearer to make a horizontal bar below the vertical bars. Make four more horizontal bars below, using one less strand for tying each time. At ends of bars, tie two strands together with alternate half hitches for about 1". After completing this much with each group around bottle, tie ends of half hitches from the horizontal bars together, at center of space, adjusting length if necessary; they should reach the bottom of the bottle.

To finish the ten-strand square knot groups, repeat top half in reverse. Then cross two center strands loosely. For center tassel, cut four pieces of twine 5" long and mount all together on the crossed strands. Tie the five strands on each side of tassel with a square knot. Trim ends of all strands even with bottom of bottle and cement macrame securely around the entire bottle.

To make cap cover and attached cord, use the two strands set aside at top of bottle. Tie them together with alternate half hitches for about 10". Leave 1" and cut off ends. Fold this knotted cord in half and attach 1" ends inside second horizontal bar around neck of bottle. Cut eight pieces of twine each one yard long. Use one as mounting cord and mount remaining seven onto this one. Tie ends of mounting cord together tightly around folded end of double knotted cord. Glue folded end of cord to top of cord cap and let dry thoroughly.

Divide all strands, including ends of mounting cord, in pairs and tie with half hitches as at beginning of bottle, making them loose enough to fit over cork cap. At bottom of cap, tie each cord separately with three overhand knots and cut off excess twine.

A versatile window shade is worked in an all square-knot pattern with cable cord. Wooden drapery rod is used in place of the mounting cord. The end strands forming the full fringe can be cut the same length or trimmed unevenly as shown opposite. The shade also makes an attractive wall hanging or a room divider. See directions for Window Shade on page 100.

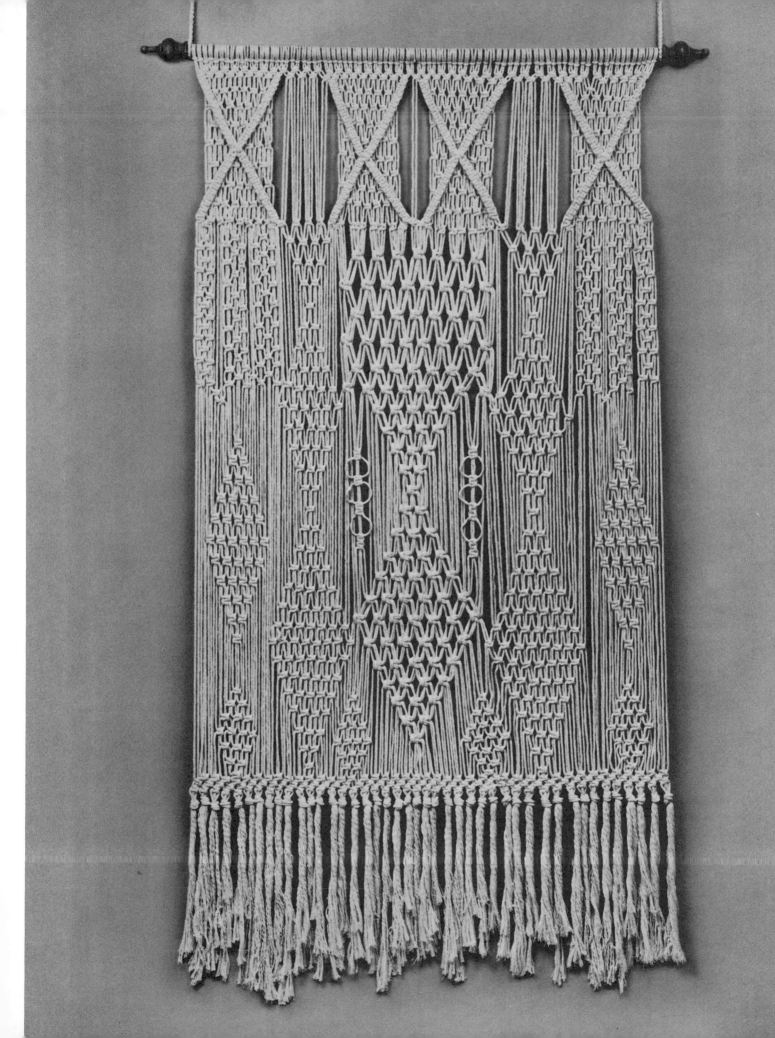

This decorative red pillow is knotted in a very simple allover pattern of alternating square knots. The pillow, 13″ square, is worked in heavy rug yarn and has a lining in contrasting color showing through. If you are covering a foam rubber pillow, the pillow itself can be used for the working surface. Directions for the Square Knot Pillow given on page 100.

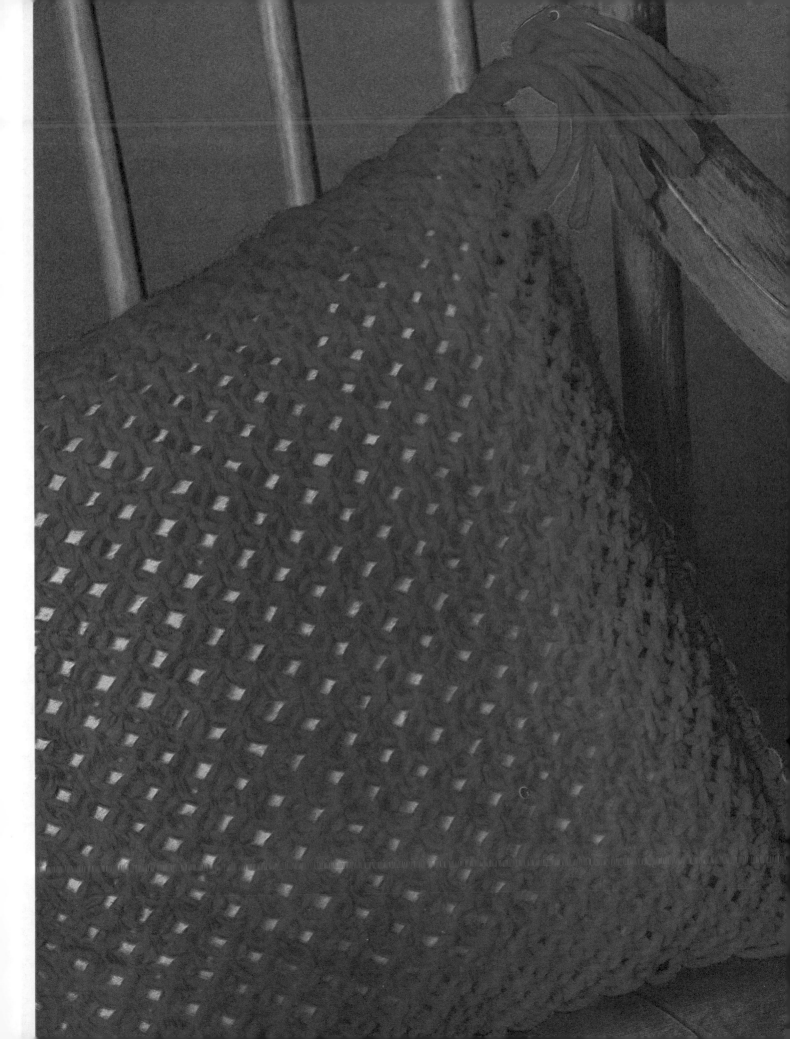

WINDOW SHADE

SIZE: 40″ x 78″.

EQUIPMENT: See page 74.

MATERIALS: Conso cable cord, style 60088 #80 natural, 1275 yards. Wooden drapery rod 40″ long, with finials. Rod hangers.

DIRECTIONS: Refer to Macrame Instructions on pages 74-77. Cut 85 pieces of cable cord each 15 yards long. Fold each in half and mount on drapery rod following Fig. 1. Attach rod hangers to wall and suspend rod from hangers at convenient working height. As work progresses, pull rod up until it can be put on hangers. Roll up each of 170 strands and hold with rubber bands.

Divide strands into groups of four and, 1″ below mounting, tie a square knot (Fig. 10A, 10B, 10C, 10D) with each group across. Separate two strands from each knot and join with two strands from adjacent knot, and tie a square knot with each group directly below first row.

Leave two center strands hanging free. Make a sinnet on each side by tying square knots with each group of four strands on each side of center. Tie knots closely, one under the other, to make sinnets 7″ long.

For next pattern on each side of center sinnets, use a group of 26 strands on each side separately. Tie two alternate rows of square knots (Fig. 11), each 1″ below last row. Repeat alternate square knot pattern for six more rows, making space between rows a little wider.

Leave next 14 strands on each side free. With next four strands on each side, make a square knot sinnet. With next 28 strands on each side, make alternate square-knot rows as at center.

With each outside group of four, make a square knot sinnet. Bring two sinnets together at each side and tie the eight strands of each together with a large square knot, using four strands at center and two on each side for tying. Repeat the square knot with middle four sinnets, joining two each. Separate each pair of sinnets and continue square knot sinnets on each four strands for 7″ more. Bring sinnets of each pair out to sides. Make a row of square knots across all strands.

Next center pattern is worked using eight strands for each square knot; with four strands at center, tie knot with two strands on each side. Make first row of knots about 1½″ below last row. Following illustration, divide four strands from each knot to make the alternate rows of knots. Work down to center point of this pattern, making one square knot. Leave two strands free at sides of center pattern.

Next pattern at each side is made with four strands for each square knot; follow illustration for number of rows and knots, working down to same length as center pattern.

The panels at outsides are worked in three separate sections of 10, two free strands, 10 and eight at outer edge. Tie square knots with four strands each as shown, using one strand from each side of center knot and outer three strands for second row of the 10-strand groups.

The loop patterns at each side of center are made with four strands each. Tie three square knots with each group. Then, 2″ below, tie three more square knots; push them up to within 1″ of last three, forming the loops at sides. Then make four rore square knots and repeat the loops.

Continue making square-knot patterns, following illustration, down to bottom. Then make three rows of alternate square knots, using four strands for each. For bottom edge, tie each group of four strands together with an overhand knot (Fig. 12).

Trim off ends of strands unevenly as shown, or cut them all the same length if desired. Unravel each strand to make a full fringe.

To use macrame as a wall hanging, make two sinnets, using two strands each and tying vertical half hitches, Fig. 6. Make each sinnet twice the length desired. Fold each around end of pole and tie ends together. Hang from molding or hooks.

SQUARE KNOT PILLOW

SIZE: 13″ square.

EQUIPMENT: See page 74.

MATERIALS: Rug yarn, about 90 yards of one color.

DIRECTIONS: Refer to Macrame Instructions on pages 74-77 and "How To Make a Pillow" below. Cut a 20″ long mounting cord; pin to top edge of pillow. Cut 36 80″ long strands; fold in half and mount, using picot mounting (Fig. 13). Separate strands into groups of four strands each. Starting with first group of strands on left, work a row of 18 square knots (Fig. 10A, 10B, 10C, 10D) across entire work. Work an alternate row of square knots (Fig. 11) below first, leaving even space between rows. Continue working alternate rows of square knots until work measures 13″ in length. To finish, cut a 15″ long knot bearer. Starting at left of work, work a horizontal bar of double half hitches (Fig. 3) across entire work, close to last row of alternate square knots. Using last two strands, work a square knot at end of bar to close it. Turn work over to wrong side. Starting from left, draw first strand through back of second double half hitch. Draw second strand through back of first double half hitch. Picots are thus made, similar to mounting at top. Repeat across entire work until all strands are used. Trim ends of strands to 1″; sew work onto fabric cover, each stitch going through double half-hitch bar, allowing picots to remain free.

Tassels: For each tassel, cut nine 8″ long strands and one 10″ long strand. Thread strands through corner loop of work; fold strands over at center; using 10″ long strand, tie two overhand knots (Fig. 12) around remaining strands close to work.

HOW TO MAKE A PILLOW

EQUIPMENT: Scissors. Sewing needle.

MATERIALS: Aunt Lydia's Heavy Rug Yarn (or other heavy yarn). Cotton fabric in matching or contrasting color. Matching sewing thread. Knife-edged foam-rubber pillow form, 13″ square.

DIRECTIONS: Cut two 14″ square pieces of fabric. With right sides facing, place two fabric pieces together and stitch, making a ½″ seam and leaving an 8″ opening for turning. Turn pillow cover to right side. Insert pillow form and sew opening closed. Since macrame piece is made the size of pillow top, covered pillow may be used as working surface. Sew finished macrame to pillow along edges on all four sides, using thread to match yarn.

SHADOW BOX FIGURES

EQUIPMENT: See page 74.

MATERIALS: For each doll: Cable cord #15 (chalk line), four 150-yard balls. Wooden finial ball 3″ in diameter with wide hole. Wooden beads: one 5/8″ in diameter; two 7/8″ diameter; five 1″ diameter; 12 3/8″ diameter. Wooden dowels: 1/8″ diameter, 25″ long; ¼″ diameter, 8″ long. **For Frame:** Clear pine 3/8″ thick, 3 3/8″ wide, 10 feet. Heavy mounting board, 1 sheet 28″ x 44″. Turquoise felt 36″ wide, 1 yard. All purpose glue. Small finishing nails. Large straight pins.

DIRECTIONS: See "How to Macrame" on pages 74-77.

Boy: It will be easier to make the dolls if they are suspended from a hook. To do this, cut four strands of cord each 312″ long. Mount the four strands on mounting cord, Fig. 1, making 8 strands. If you wish to display the dolls hanging free, make a twisted sinnet 12″ long by using two outside strands at outside of the eight strands to tie half of a square knot, Figs. 10A, 10B; work over four center strands.

To display dolls in shadow box, do not make sinnet, but knot all strands together and catch on a hook.

Thread the eight working strands through 3″ finial ball for head, then through a 1″ and a 5/8″ bead for neck. Mount these strands on center of a ¼″ dowel 8″ long, using double half hitches (Figs. 2A and 2B). Cut 16 more pieces of cord each 184″ long. Mount these on dowel (half each side of center strands) with double half hitches, making

32 more working strands for a total of 40 strands. Push a 7/8″ bead onto each end of dowel. As work progresses, push a 3/8″ bead onto each end of each 1/8″ dowel.

Work a row of square knots across these 40 strands (Figs. 10A, 10B, 10C, 10D). Decrease next row by discontinuing the two outer strands on each side; work square knots across 36 strands, using two strands from adjoining knots. Cut off the two outer strands and weave ends through knots on back. Make two more rows of square knots in same manner. * Decrease on next row and work three rows of square knots; repeat from * three times (24 strands remaining). Divide strands into five groups of 5, 5, 4, 5, 5. With each group, work a sinnet of alternate half hitches, Fig. 8, for 1½″ (use three strands in center on groups of 5 and two strands in center on groups of 4). Cut off one strand on two outer sinnets on each side and run ends up back of work (20 strands). Mount the 20 strands on a 1/8″ dowel 3¼″ long, using double half hitches. Work three rows of square knots as before.

Mount the strands on another 1/8″ dowel 3¼″ long. Make five vertical sinnets of alternate half hitches as before in groups of four. Mount strands on another 1/8″ dowel 4¼″ long, adding four double strands evenly spaced, to make 28 working strands. Divide strands into three groups of 9, 10, 9. Work double diagonal bars with each group, leaving center strand of the 9 groups hanging down in back. Tie center four strands of each group with a square knot (tie over center strand of 9 groups). Make double diagonal bars down in opposite direction, still leaving center strand of 9 groups free.

Mount all strands on a 1/8″ dowel 4½″ long with double half hitches, adding two double strands at center (32 working strands).

For legs, use 16 strands each. Divide each leg into three groups of 5, 6, 5, and work three vertical sinnets for each leg (Fig. 8) for 5¼″. Mount strands from both legs on a 1/8″ dowel 4″ long (pass several strands of each leg down in back of dowel to keep width even); leave a ¼″ separation between legs. Continue making rest of leg the same for 5¼″. Mount strands again on a 1/8″ dowel 5¼″ wide; spread bottom of each leg across dowel. Lace the three sinnets of each leg together with separate cords through loops at edges of posts. Cut off one strand at each side of each leg and weave ends into back of knots. Pull the 14 remaining strands of each leg through 1″ beads for feet. Push beads up against dowel and knot each strand below bead. Knot each strand again 1½″ below bead and cut off excess cord.

For arms, mount 7 strands 100″ long on each end of shoulder dowel (14 strands each). Divide each arm into two groups of 7 and work two ver-
continued on page 104

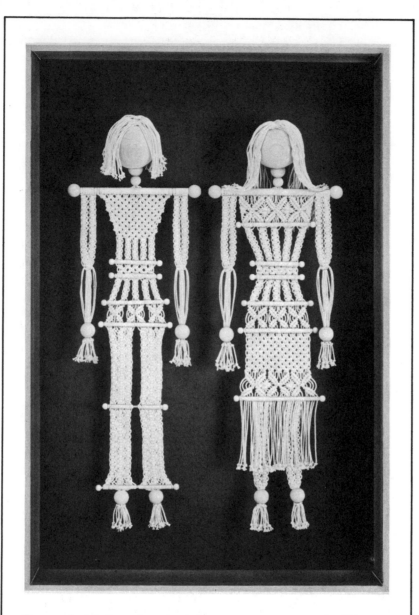

Boy and girl figures are a very contemporary couple. Figures, knotted in chalk line, have ball finial heads, with wood beads and dowels holding the shapes of the bodies. Mount them in a felt-lined shadow box, as shown above, or suspend them with a cord. See the directions for Shadow Box Figures on page 101.

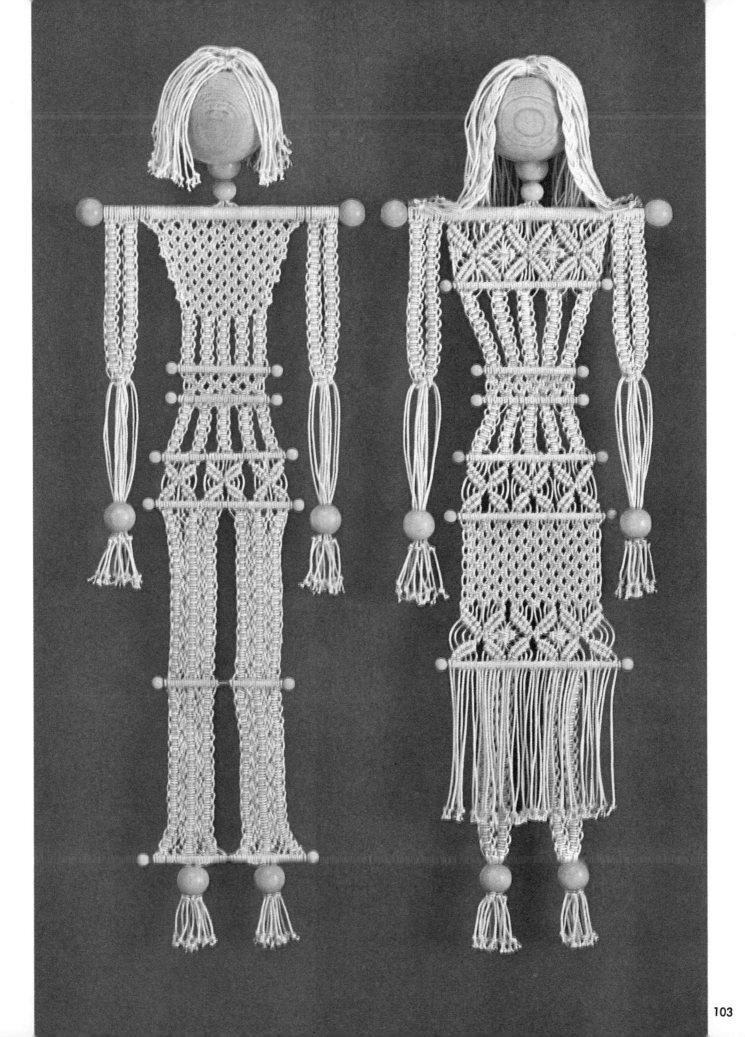

SHADOW BOX FIGURES
continued from page 101

tical sinnets (Fig. 8) for 4¾". Bring the 14 strands all together and tie with a square knot, using two outside strands on each side for tying. Thread strands through beads and knot as for feet.

For hair of hanging dolls, use a circular mounting cord at top of ball head tied loosely around twisted sinnet. Mount 44 strands 10" long (Fig. 1). Knot the end of each strand and arrange around head.

For hair of framed dolls, cut 44 pieces of cord 10" long. Tie all together at midpoint with one of the beginning strands. Knot ends and arrange down sides of head.

Girl: Start same as for Boy, adding one extra strand with double half hitch on shoulder dowel (42 strands). Divide strands into three groups of 14 strands each. With each group, work double diagonal bars. Tie center four strands of bars together with a square knot. Tie a square knot around center six strands between bars with two strands at each side. At outer edges, tie a double half hitch with the five strands. Make double diagonal bars down in opposite directions. Mount all strands on a 1/8" dowel 5" long, weaving 12 strands (evenly spaced across) into back of knots and cutting off these 12 ends (30 strands).

Divide strands into five groups of 6 strands each and make five vertical sinnets (Fig. 8) 2½" long. Mount strands on another 1/8" dowel 3¼" long, passing eight strands (evenly spaced across) in back of dowel; cut off and weave in two strands on back (28 strands).

Work three rows of square knots, alternating rows of knots by using two strands from adjacent knots of previous row.

Mount 20 strands on 1/8" dowel 3¼" long, passing eight strands in back of dowel. Divide strands into five groups of 6, 5, 6, 5, 6. Work five vertical sinnets (Fig. 8) 1½" long. Mount all strands on a 1/8" dowel 4½" long; add one double strand, making 30 strands.

Divide into three groups and work double diagonal bars. Tie with a square knot where bars meet and make double diagonal bars down in opposite direction. Mount all strands on a 1/8" dowel 5" long, adding three double strands (36 strands). Work in rows of square knots, alternating knots in each row for 2¾". Divide strands into three groups of 12 and work double diagonal bars, tying strands between bars with square knots as for first pattern.

Mount all strands on 1/8" dowel 5¾" long, adding three double strands evenly spaced across. Cut off strands, leaving 4¾" ends; knot each end for skirt fringe.

For legs, cut 14 strands of cord each 50" long. Mount 7 strands of cord each an equal distance from center of dowel by pulling each halfway through knots on back of dowel (14 strands for each leg). Make legs in same manner as Boy's arms, 6" long. Pull ends through beads and knot. Make arms same as Boy.

Make hair same as Boy, cutting strands 15" long. Arrange hair around head; braid 9 strands together on each side of front.

Shadow Box: Cut mounting board 23" x 35" for background. Cut two sides 3" x 35"; cut two ends 3" x 22¾". Glue felt to one side of background piece. Glue felt to one side of each side and end, extending felt over one long edge for front.

Cut pine strips 36" long for sides and 23" long for top and bottom. Glue and nail strips together with butt joints for shadow box frame. Attach background in frame with glue and large straight pins toenailed through back of mounting board into sides of frame. Glue felt-covered sides, top and bottom strips inside frame.

To attach dolls, make two holes through background about 5½" from top and 6½" from sides. Start a nail hole in center back of each doll head with a common nail; remove nail. Holding doll head in position in shadow box, hammer nail through hole in background, into hole in head.

Metal Foil Tooling

The repoussé technique of raising metal from
the reverse side by hammering or pressing to form a
design on the front has been popular for centuries.
Thick pieces of metal had to be heated before
shaping, and craftsmen needed not only a forge, but
strong tools. In contrast, the tooling presented
here is done on thin aluminum foil, and the fine
portions of the design can be incised with boxwood
modeling tools or similar objects, such as a blunt
needle or discarded ball-point pen; larger design
areas may be shaped with the bowl of a spoon!
The work is usually done on a pile of newspapers
or a hard rubber mat so that the foil can be kept
flat when the design is recessed. For the more
detailed pieces, the design is worked from the
front as well as the back to give greater variety.
Large raised areas, which might become crushed
with use, may be reinforced with wads of absorbent
cotton soaked in glue; these wads are used to fill
the depressions on the back side of the work before
the tooled pieces are mounted onto a firm surface.
Tooling is a fun craft for all the family to enjoy!

COLUMN CANDLE BASES

EQUIPMENT: Tracing paper. Pencil. Ruler. Scissors. Wooden modeling tools with a pointed end, flat end, and round end (an orangewood stick or a sharp pencil with eraser and a pencil with eraser removed can be used in place of modeling tools). Old newspapers for padding. Cellophane or masking tape. Drill with 3/32" bit. Brush for stain. Compass.

MATERIALS: Maid-O'-Metal coppertone tooling foil, 38 gauge, small roll (one side copper color, other side aluminum). Clear pine blocks, 2¾" x 2¾" by 4", 7", or 11" long (you can use any length desired). Walnut stain. Contact cement.

DIRECTIONS: Use actual-size illustration on left for middle-sized pattern; to make smaller or larger patterns, mark rectangles on tracing paper the same width, 3½" long (smaller) and 10 5/8" long (larger). Mark 1/8" border on all edges. Center and trace large flower motif in each rectangle, then continue diagonal lines to fill in rectangles; continue small flowers of dots.

For tooling, be careful to keep foil smooth and flat; if any portion has a definite crease, discard it. Tape pattern on foil with a padding of newspapers underneath. For each base, make two sections of copper color and two sections of aluminum color. With pointed modeling tool or orangewood stick, trace over outline of section and inner border line. Turn foil to other side and trace over center flower and go over all diagonal lines (use ruler to make them even). With pointed tool or sharp pencil, make dots along border. With round tool or eraser, press in center of flower. Turn foil back again to other side; make dot designs within diamond areas with pointed tool, stick, or pencil point. It is easier to make this design by first lightly pressing end of pencil with eraser removed to form circle on foil and then pressing dots around circle line. On same side, make line around flower center, then with round tool or pencil eraser, press in area of flower
continued on page 108

A completely new and stunning effect is created by covering wood blocks with gleaming foil. The candle base, at the left, is actual-size, and the illustration may be used as pattern. The tooling foil is reversible — aluminum on one side, and a copper tone on the other. Sides of the foil are alternated around each wood block. For Column Candle Bases, see above.

COLUMN CANDLE BASES
continued from page 106

petals, smooth area directly outside of flower, and then smooth all other flat areas. For top piece, mark 2 3/8″ square on foil with pointed tool, mark 1/8″ border as for sides, turn to other side and dot along border; mark and cut ¼″ diameter hole out of center. Cut all foil pieces.

Drill 2″ deep hole in one end of wood. Stain wood; let dry. Cement foil on sides of wood, alternating copper and aluminum colors. Center and cement top piece over end with hole.

MAILBOX POST AND PLANTER

Note: Directions are for 6-ft. tall post; it can be topped with a lamp if desired. Directions for a 40″ post ending at top of mailbox are in parentheses.

EQUIPMENT: Regular workshop tools.

MATERIALS: Redwood lumber: **For Post:** 2 pieces 8 ft. long (64″ for shorter post), 1″ x 4″ (A); 2 pieces 8 ft. long (64″ for shorter post), 1″ x 2″ (B); 2 pieces 18″ long, 2″ x 4″ (C); 2 pieces 8″ square, 2″ thick (D); 1 piece 2″ square, 1″ thick (E). **For Planter:** 2 pieces 24″ long, 1″ x 8″ (F); 2 pieces 1″x 8″ x 6″ (G); one piece 21 ¾″ long, 1″ x 6″ (H). Aluminum flathead wood screws 3″ long. Finishing nails. Cement. Mailbox, 21″ long, 8½″ wide, 11″ high.

DIRECTIONS: Dig a 2 ft.-square hole 2 ft. deep (or below frost level).

Post: Assemble hollow post, following Fig. 1 on page 111; wood pieces corresponding to letters in diagram are given in Materials; leave back off until arm supports are attached. Use finishing nails or screws as desired. Mark a line around post 2 ft. from one end to show ground level. Enlarge pattern for arm supports on page 111 by copying on paper ruled in 1″ squares. Cut two from 8″-square pieces of wood. Mark position of the two arms C, one 40″ up from ground level and one 30″ from ground level (for shorter post, top arm will be at top of post). Attach a support for underneath each arm with screws from inside post. Attach arms with countersunk screws from top of arm into support. Glue and nail 2″ wood square in top of post; a hole for threaded pipe can be drilled in center if desired. Set post in hole; imbed in cement up to within 6″ of ground level. When cement has hardened, fill remaining 6″ with topsoil. To decorate supports, see Tooled Mailbox on this page.

Planter: Drill six holes evenly spaced around bottom piece H, Fig. 2, near edges for water drainage. Assemble sides and ends of redwood pieces, following Fig. 2 and using finishing nails. Fit bottom in and nail. To decorate, see Tooled Mailbox at right. Screw planter to lower arm.

TOOLED MAILBOX

EQUIPMENT: Kitchen shears. Wooden modeling tools with pointed, flat and round ends (or an orangewood manicuring stick may be used). Tracing paper. Pencil. Newspapers for padding. Soft rags. Drill with metal bit. Masking tape.

MATERIALS: Aluminum tooling foil 36 gauge, 12″ wide: for large galvanized mailbox about 21″ long, planter, and arm support decorations, 7 feet. Wooden knob with screw (to replace mailbox catch) and magnetic catch. Miracle Black Magic adhesive, Dark brown flat oil paint for antiquing. Small amount of pale gray paint.

DIRECTIONS: Trace actual-size patterns on page 111; complete quarter-pattern for the center. Be careful to keep aluminum smooth and flat; if any portion has a definite crease, discard it. Tape pattern on aluminum. With pointed modeling tool go over outline on pattern and all design lines. Border patterns A and B are to be repeated to a length of 27″. To repeat border B, trace complete design once, lift pattern and replace, matching small half-circles and with straight double lines at sides. To repeat border A, trace complete design (including plain circle), lift pattern and replace with straight double lines at sides and design circle on top of marked plain circle. Place center design on a 27″ length of aluminum; mark complete design only twice, placing pattern 1″ from each end of aluminum. Cut aluminum away outside of straight lines on each side of design. After borders A and B have been repeated for 27″, cut away aluminum outside double lines at each side.

For tooling, lay cut piece of aluminum on newspaper padding with marked side up (this is right side). Mark lines of design on right and wrong sides, following individual directions below. Areas indicated by X's are pressed down on right side with a flat tool. To do this, press and rub from center of areas towards marked lines; this will raise the lines on right side. Areas indicated by Z's are to be stippled on right side
continued on page 110

Multipurpose mailbox post, opposite, supports an ornately decorated planter and mailbox. Post is made of durable redwood. The mailbox and planter designs are worked on aluminum tooling foil, which is then antiqued to highlight pattern. Post can be cut at mailbox height or topped with lamp. Directions for Tooled Mailbox, Mailbox Post and Planter are here.

TOOLED MAILBOX
continued from page 108

with pointed tool.

Border A: Using pointed tool, go over lines of petals and center circles on right side, and lines of petals and stems. Turn aluminum over and, with round or pointed tool, press areas between double petal lines and in small circles; press between lines of leaves and stems. Turn aluminum to right side. Rub and press areas indicated by X; stipple areas indicated by Z. Stipple a line outside leaves and stems.

Border B: Go over double lines of design and around circles with pointed tool on right side. Turn aluminum over to wrong side, and, with round or pointed tool, press down between double lines in center of petals and in circles. Turn right side up and stipple areas indicated by Z.

Center Panel: Go over all lines of large flower circle on right side, around tiny petals in small circles, around circles between scrolls with pointed tool. Turn aluminum over, and, with round or pointed tool, press down between double lines of large flower circle, inside tiny petals and center, inside circles between scrolls, on all lines of large scrolls, and inside small scrolls. Turn to right side. Press and rub area indicated by X; stipple areas Z.

Front Panel (door of mailbox): Trace panel shape from mailbox inside rim and cut shape from aluminum. For tooling, use the double flower design of border B, placing it horizontally just above center of panel. Across bottom of panel, use three circles 3, separated by scrolls 2 from center design pattern. At top of panel, use two scrolls 2 about 1½" apart.

Remove latch from mailbox. Using Miracle adhesive liberally, apply with a putty knife on back of tooled aluminum, so it will fill indentations; press front panel on mailbox door. Paint wooden knob pale gray. Drill a hole between scrolls at top of door and attach wooden knob. Place borders and center panel around mailbox with borders A at ends and borders B between center panel and A. On one border A, cut a notch out of aluminum to accommodate mailbox flag. Attach tooled pieces with adhesive; trim off any excess at bottom edges of each piece. Adhere magnetic catch with adhesive inside top front.

Note: If there is a mail slot in door, cut aluminum away around slot before adhering; tool a stippled line around slot.

To antique, rub brown paint over all tooled aluminum and knob with soft rag. With clean rag, wipe off excess paint; rub softly to remove paint from raised areas, leaving indentations darkened. Let dry.

Post Decorations: For supports under mailbox and planter arms of post, cut four triangles of aluminum, cutting on inner curved line of support pattern. Trace designs marked 1, 2, 3 from tooling designs for center piece of mailbox. Mark designs on aluminum pieces as indicated on support pattern. Tool designs as directed for center piece of mailbox; press and rub background on right sides of pieces. Adhere a tooled piece to sides of each triangular support. Antique.

Planter: Using border A, cut aluminum strips to fit sides and one end of box. Tool as directed for border A. Adhere to center of sides and end of planter. Antique.

LAMPSHADE TRIMS

EQUIPMENT: Tracing paper. Pencil. Ruler. Compass. Scissors. Orangewood manicure stick (or wooden modeling tool with pointed end and flat end). Newspapers for padding. Hole punch. Masking tape. Soft cloth.

MATERIALS: Plain, inexpensive lampshades. Copper tooling foil. Copper polish. Colorless nail polish. All-purpose glue.

DIRECTIONS: Trace patterns for fish, fish scales, snail, flowers, and leaves on page 114; complete half and quarter-patterns indicated by dash lines. Place piece of foil right side up on padding of newspapers. Tape pattern on foil. With pointed end of stick, trace over outline and all design lines. Remove pattern and go over lines again to make them sharper. To form raised areas, press on wrong side of foil with flat end of stick or pencil eraser. To form indented areas, press on right side of foil. To stipple, make dots with pointed end of stick or sharp pencil. When design is finished, shine right sides with polish and cloth. Coat with nail polish; let dry. Arrange pieces around lampshade; glue in place.

For fish shade, cut simple long and short grasslike pieces and circles of foil. For flower shade, vary treatment of flower centers; make them raised, indented, stippled, perforated, or cut out. For simple geometric designs, cut diamonds, circles, squares, and rectangles. Tool simple lines on pieces as shown in illustrations on pages 112 and 113, or ad-lib your own designs. For fish-scale shade, place larger pieces around bottom border. Overlap each row as you work up. Fill in areas at bottom row with small foil triangles.

"STUDDED" MIRROR FRAME

SIZE: 16" x 20".

EQUIPMENT: Tracing paper. Pencil. Ruler. Scissors. Wooden modeling tools with pointed, flat, and
continued on page 116

BORDER A

CENTER

BORDER B

FIG.1

FIG. 2

Actual-size tooling designs for mailbox and planter are given above (Borders A and B, Center); enlarge arm-support pattern, which also has tooling design.

Follow Figures 1 and 2 for assembling the post and planter. Dotted line at C of Figure 1 shows where to cut post if a lamp (optional) is not used at top.

Six shiny and bright lamp-shades glimmer with tooled copper cutouts in easy geometrics or sprightly nature motifs. Tooling foil is cut in desired shapes, embossed or impressed with the point of a pencil, and glued to a ready-made lampshade. See the directions on page 110.

Actual-size quarter-pattern at left is for corner of
"Studded" Mirror Frame, shown on opposite page.

FISH
SCALES

Trace patterns for Lampshade Trims (above); half
and quarter-patterns are indicated by dash lines.

A regal silvery mirror frame is made with aluminum tooling foil over plywood. The "studs" are formed with the help of a partial pattern you make yourself, showing rows of circles; a pattern for the corners is on opposite page. For "Studded" Mirror Frame, see page 110.

"STUDDED" MIRROR FRAME

continued from page 110

round ends (or an orangewood manicure stick may be used). Newspapers for padding. Masking tape. Putty knife.

MATERIALS: Aluminum tooling foil 36 gauge, 12″ wide, about 3 feet. Heavy cardboard: four 4″ square pieces; two 4″ x 12″ pieces; and two 4″ x 8″ pieces. Miracle Black Magic Adhesive. Plywood, ½″ thick, one piece 16″ x 20″. Mirror 8″ x 12″. For hanging, one picture hanger loop.

DIRECTIONS: Trace actual-size pattern; complete quarter-pattern indicated by dash lines. Make four corner pieces as follows: Cut a 5¼″ square of tooling foil. Place 4″ cardboard square on duller side (wrong side) of aluminum, leaving two adjacent ½″ margins (inside) and two adjacent ¾″ margins (outside). With pointed tool, trace around cardboard on foil. Remove cardboard. Tape centered pattern to right side of aluminum, and go over the outlines of pattern with pointed tool. For tooling, lay piece of aluminum, wrong side up, on newspaper. With pointed tool, press areas between double circle lines and double geometric border lines. Turn work to right side and press area A between circle and border with flat tool. To do this, press and rub from center of area towards marked lines. Turn work to wrong side and, with round tool, press and rub area of each circle with a circular motion, beginning at center and working outward toward marked line. Turn work to right side and, with pointed tool, stiple background to marked lines of square and area B inside large circle.

Make two side panels as follows: Cut a 13″ x 5¼″ piece of aluminum. Place 4″ x 12″ piece of cardboard on wrong side of foil, leaving ¾″ margin on one long side (outside) and ½″ margins on remaining sides. With pointed tool, trace around cardboard on foil. Remove cardboard and lay foil, right side up, on newspaper padding. Make a partial paper pattern of two or three horizontal rows of five evenly spaced ½″ circles; begin first row ¼″ from marked line on short side, and leave ¼″ between rows. Place pattern on right side of foil and, with pointed tool, trace outline of circles. Repeat, using pattern, until there are 16 horizontal rows of circles. Turn to wrong side and press and rub area inside circles as for corner pieces. Turn work to right side and stiple background up to marked outline of cardboard rectangle.

Make a top and bottom panel as follows: Cut a 5″ x 9¼″ piece of aluminum. Place a 4″ x 8″ piece of cardboard on wrong side of aluminum and mark outline, leaving same margins as for side pieces. Press and rub 11 horizontal rows of five evenly spaced ½″ circles, using partial pattern to mark them on right side of aluminum first. Stiple background.

Finishing: Apply Miracle Adhesive to back of mirror with putty knife; press to center of plywood piece. Apply adhesive liberally with putty knife to back of

tooled aluminum, so it fills indentations; gently press corresponding cardboard pieces to back of foil, within marked outlines. Fold ½″ margins to back of cardboard, cutting away excess foil at corners. Apply adhesive to cardboard backs and foil margins; place on plywood around mirror (see illustration), folding ¾″ margins over sides of plywood and around to back. Cover edges of aluminum on back with tape. Attach picture-hanger loop to center back, near top.

"MEXICAN" MIRRORS

EQUIPMENT: Kitchen shears. Wooden modeling tools with a pointed end, flat end, and round end (or an orange stick may be used). Tracing paper. Pencil. Coping saw. Small paintbrush. Masking tape. Newspapers for padding. Carbon paper. Sandpaper. Tweezers (optional).

MATERIALS: Aluminum tooling foil, 36-gauge, 12″ wide: 6″ x 12″ for Round Mirror; 15″ x 12″ for Oval Mirror; 22″ x 12″ for Oblong Mirror; 24″ x 12″ for Diamond Mirror. Unframed mirrors: One 2½″ diameter for Round Mirror; one 3½″ x 5¼″ for Oval Mirror; one 5″ x 7″, six 1¼″ diameter, and six 1″ square for Oblong Mirror; one 6″ diameter, four 2″ diameter for Diamond Mirror. Silver beads 1/8″ diameter and 1/16″ diameter. Clear pine 3/8″ thick: 7″ square for Round Mirror; 9″ x 13″ for Oval Mirror; 11″ x 14″ for Oblong Mirror; 13″ x 13″ for Diamond Mirror. Flat black paint. Elmer's Glue-All. Metal picture hanger loops.

DIRECTIONS: Trace actual-size quarter-patterns on pages 118-120 for mirror frames; complete patterns. Make a separate pattern for each numbered piece; each No. 1 is the complete background piece; the other numbers are separate pieces to be tooled and placed as shown on background piece. On Oval Mirror, piece 4 is placed on the X on background. The mirrors are centered and either overlap separate pieces or are in the middle of separate pieces.

Be careful to keep aluminum smooth and flat; if any portion has a definite crease, discard it. Use brighter side for front. Tape background pattern on aluminum. With pointed modeling tool, trace over outline of each pattern and all design lines of each background pattern—both red and black. Transfer the other numbered patterns onto aluminum in same manner. Remove patterns and go over lines again to make them clear. Cut out each piece carefully.

For tooling, lay cut piece of aluminum, brighter side up, on a padding of newspaper. The black lines and black areas are tooled on the front; red lines and red areas are tooled on back. With pointed tool, work over all black lines of design. Use round or flat-end tool to press down
continued on page 118

These eye-catching mirrors in four shapes and sizes have the quality of folk art. Designs are tooled on aluminum tooling foil (the quarter-patterns are shown actual-size, pages 118-120). Foil is glued to wooden backings; small unframed mirrors decorate the two largest frames. Silver plastic beads make an attractive border for "Mexican" mirrors opposite.

"MEXICAN" MIRRORS
continued from page 116

solid black areas. Work slowly and go over lines and areas as necessary to make design well defined. Turn aluminum piece over and tool all red lines and areas of pattern in same manner. Repeat tooling on both sides to make designs clear and dimensional. Plain background areas around designs are tooled by pressing with pointed tool on aluminum from front at random (except where mirrors and other pieces are placed).

For wood backing, add 1/8″ all around each background pattern. Trace outline onto 3/8″ pine with carbon paper and cut out with coping saw.

Sand edges smooth. Paint sides and front of each piece black. When completely dry, glue background aluminum on wood with even margin of wood all around. Then glue each numbered piece in place as shown on pattern. Glue mirrors on, centered over numbered pieces as indicated by short dash lines on patterns for Round, Oblong, and Diamond Mirrors; on Oval design, place mirror overlapping edges of pieces. Around the edge of each mirror, glue silver beads, using the larger beads around the larger mirrors and for the small Round Mirror, and smaller beads around the smaller mirrors. You may find tweezers helpful.

Attach a picture hanger loop to center back of each mirror, near top edge.

OVAL MIRROR

ROUND
MIRROR

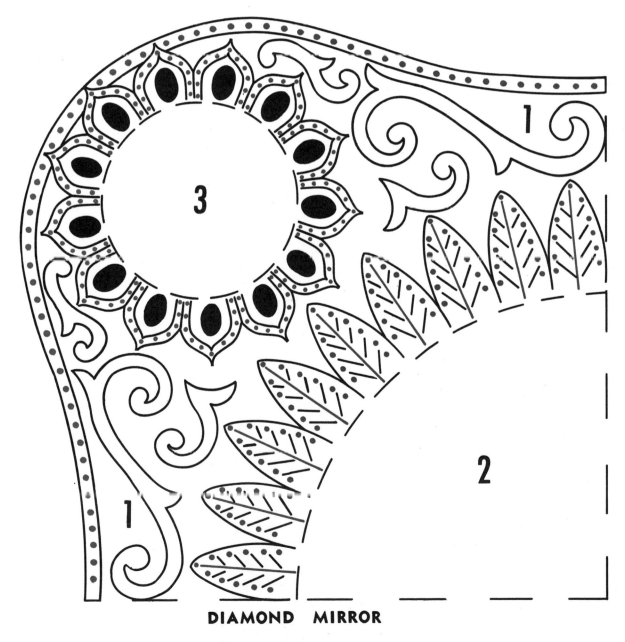

DIAMOND MIRROR

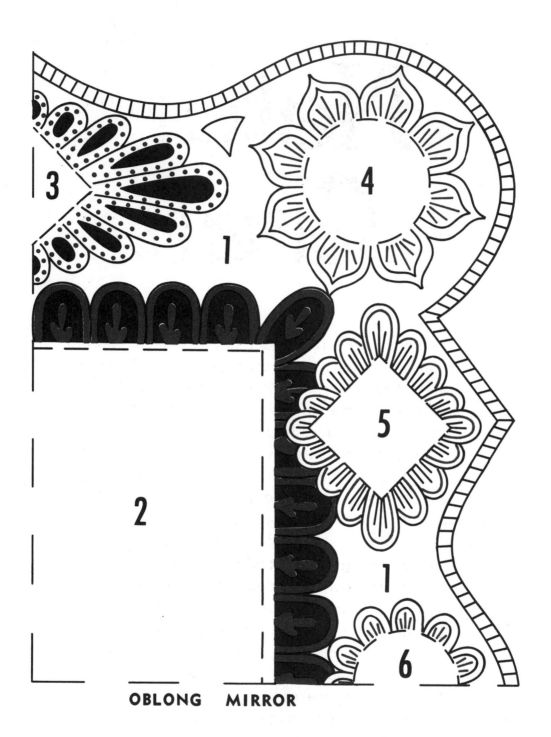

OBLONG MIRROR

Nature Crafts

The current interest in ecology has made nature's products into popular craft materials. Furthermore, each flower, leaf, or shell is so beautifully formed that whether one studies a blade of grass or a pine cone he is taught a lesson in design—this way he learns the perfect ratio of each part to the whole. With a little imagination, beautiful arrangements can be made from dried flowers and grasses; whimsical animal shapes may result from combining a few leaves; rich looking costume jewelry is created from small shells sprayed with gold paint; while a number of various sizes of pine cones produce astonishing creatures. Everyone in the family can turn a walk in the country or a stroll on the beach into a hunt for exciting "art materials"; but *please,* be very sure that no rare wild flowers or plants are collected! Also, before picking leaves at random, be sure that you know poison ivy, oak, and sumac or any other plants to which you may be allergic—in the fall these plants have very tempting colors! But most important of all is to learn good design and color harmony from the best teacher of all—Nature herself.

DRIED FLOWER PICTURE

SIZE: 22¾" x 27", framed.

EQUIPMENT: For Pressing Method: Large quantity of newspapers. Suit boxes, or similar objects for light weight. **For Borax Method:** Cardboard boxes at least 3" deep. Powdered borax. Small watercolor brush. Spatula. Plant markers. **For Framing:** Backsaw and miter box. Small flat paintbrush. Hammer. Nail set. Clean rags. Straight pins.

MATERIALS: Delicate wild flowers and garden flowers, such as Queen Anne's lace, black-eyed Susans, poppies, bachelor buttons, petunias; wild grasses, ferns, and other foliage; small pieces of flat bark. White fabric such as monk's cloth, 24" x 28". Cotton batting, 20" x 24". Plywood, ¼" thick, 20" x 24". Pine stripping, ¼" thick, 1½" wide, 8 feet. Flat picture molding, ¾" thick, 1½" wide, 9 feet. Simulated bamboo molding, 5/8" wide, 9 feet. Wood putty. Flat white paint. Flat cream-color paint. Brown oil stain. Finishing nails. Carpet tacks. Elmer's Glue-All.

GENERAL DIRECTIONS: Note: When picking wild flowers, be sure of what you are handling. The results of carrying home the attractive foliage of poison ivy or poison sumac can be disastrous. It is also wise to check your state conservation list of plants that cannot be picked if growing wild (for example, use cultivated ferns, not wild ferns).

Pick floral material in perfect conditon; a small hole in a petal will be a large hole when dried. Pick flowers at their peak of bloom; if too mature, they will shatter in drying. Pick flowers on a dry day. Be sure there is no moisture in the flower heads; if there should be any, allow stems to stand in 2" or 3" of warm water until flower heads are completely free of moisture. Cut off or wipe wet part of stems before processing. Strip all leaves from flower stems. Be sure there are no insects in the flower heads. Flowers shrink in drying, and you need a good selection when making arrangements, so dry at least twice as many as needed.

If you wish to develop special lines or curves, with either pressing or borax method, gently shape curves by hand before drying.

Humidity is the enemy of dried flowers. Most dried material will keep indefinitely provided it remains dry. There is no need to worry during the season when the house is artificially heated and humidity is low, but during humid weather your preserved flowers should be kept in a dry place. Store them in suit boxes to protect from humidity and dust. Protect your flowers from continuous exposure to strong daylight; some may fade. Handle them carefully, for most dried flowers are brittle and will break easily.

Pressing Method: Place plant material between several thicknesses of newspaper. Be careful to spread out flat; see that pieces do not touch or overlap. Put under a rug that is not walked on frequently or under light weights such as suit boxes for a more dimensional, less flat appearance. Press under heavy weight for a very flat appearance. Allow to remain undisturbed for a minimum of three weeks, until thoroughly dry; however, if material was very moist, change newspapers every three or four days to avoid mildew.

Borax Method: For best results, choose fluffy light-textured flowers with round heads, such as black-eyed Susans. Heavy-textured flowers such as lilies, succulents, and large marigolds are difficult to dry in borax. Pour borax, free from lumps, into box to depth of 2" or 3". Whenever possible, remove stem from the flower head; dry stem separately. Place flowers face down in the borax. Put flowering sprays directly on borax; pour more borax carefully around and over flowers until completely covered. Allow some borax to lie between the petals as support to retain natural form of flowers. Place markers in box with names of flowers and the dates. Length of drying time depends upon the texture of the flowers. With this method, it is very important not to overdry the flowers. Place an extra flower in the box for testing; it is dry when the texture resembles that of taffeta.

In removing flowers from borax, work carefully. Place spatula under flower head and lift gently. Any borax left clinging to flowers may be removed with watercolor brush. If petals fall from flowers, replace with a bit of glue.

Making Arrangement: Place one layer of cotton batting over plywood background; tack in place and cover tacks with batting. Stretch monk's cloth over padding, using pins to hold fabric on edges while stretching and straightening; be sure threads of fabric are straight. Turn excess fabric to back of board and glue; pin until dry.
continued on page 126

Delicate blooms, ferns, and grasses from the garden or meadow are "planted" in bark for a composition of lasting beauty. First, the foliage is dried — either in borax (for round, fluffy flowers) or between layers of weighted-down newspapers. The arrangement is glued to a padded backing covered with monk's cloth and framed with "bamboo" molding. Directions above.

Whimsical pictures are created from dried plant material. Each is truly one of a kind. The method is easy: leaves, ferns, grasses, and seaweeds are pressed between newspapers, dried for several weeks, and then are glued to a gessoed backing. Forms of the plant material, with various shapes and subtle coloring, suggest the subject. Follow our ideas above and opposite — the owl, turtle, rooster and hen — or make portraits-from-plants of your own design. See directions for the Dried Leaf Pictures on page 126.

DRIED FLOWER PICTURE
continued from page 122

Arrange flowers, stems, and foliage on fabric background, keeping it light and airy. Use small ferns at bottom of arrangement. Attach flowers, stems, and foliage to fabric with little dabs of glue. Glue small pieces of bark over ends of stems and ferns at bottom.

Framing: Cut pine stripping to fit around plywood picture with butt joints. Paint strips white on all sides. When dry, nail around picture with one ¼" surface even with back of plywood; stripping extends 1¼" on front for shadow-box effect. Cut picture molding with mitered corners to fit over pine stripping. Glue and nail molding together; let dry. Cut bamboo molding with mitered corners, ¼" shorter than picture molding pieces. Place on top of picture frame, matching miters and glue in place; let dry. Countersink all nails; fill holes with wood putty. Paint frame cream color. When dry, antique by brushing on stain and wiping off excess; let dry. Brush bamboo "joints" lightly with white paint. Dry. Glue frame on shadow box.

DRIED LEAF PICTURES

EQUIPMENT: Newspapers. Press consisting of two plywood boards 12" x 18" and two pieces of cardboard 12" x 18". Strong cord. Watercolor brush #3. Flat paintbrush, 1½". Cheesecloth. Clean white paper. Heavy weights such as books.

MATERIALS: Plant material such as leaves, wild grasses, ferns, and seaweeds. Masonite board, matboard, or canvasboard (sizes vary from 9" x 12" to 14" x 22"). Liquid gesso. All-purpose glue.

DIRECTIONS: Note: When picking wild flowers, be sure of what you are handling. The results of carrying home the attractive foliage of poison ivy or poison sumac can be disastrous. It is also wise to check your state conservation list of plants that cannot be picked if growing wild (for example, use cultivated ferns, not wild ferns).

To Dry Plant Material: Collect plant material desired for picture. To press, put plant material carefully between several layers of newspapers, then put between corrugated cardboard so that air may circulate, then put between plywood boards. Tie firmly together with strong cord to apply pressure on plants. Store in dry, warm place (attic is good) for four to six weeks. If material was very moist, change newspapers every three to four days to avoid mildew. When material is dry and completely flat, remove from press and store between pages of old magazines until ready to use.

To Arrange and Design: Cover board with two coats of gesso, using flat paintbrush; let dry thoroughly. Select and arrange plant material on board. Refer to illustrations for designs or work out your own, keeping in mind contrast, balance, and continuity of line. Make tiny pencil marks on background to indicate position of dried plants. Lift plants off and place wrong side up on clean sheet of paper. Gently apply glue on reverse side of plants with watercolor brush. Replace in position on board. Press down firmly, especially around edges. Make sure no air bubbles remain. Wipe off excess glue. When picture is finished, cover it with piece of cheesecloth and clean paper. Weight down heavily and evenly for several hours or overnight. Remove cheesecloth gently. Frame as desired.

CORN-COB PLAQUES

EQUIPMENT: Small handsaw. Small, flat paintbrushes. Scissors. Sharp knife.

MATERIALS: Dried corn cobs, kernels, and husks. Scrap lumber ½" thick, about 8" wide. Red food coloring. Shellac. All-purpose glue. Screw-in rings for hanging.

DIRECTIONS: With saw, cut wood for each plaque 8" x 10". Leave edges and sides rough; cut nicks into edges for more rustic look if desired. Dilute food coloring with water. With flat brush, color one side (front) and edges. When dry, coat front and edges with shellac.

With saw, cut corn cobs in slices crosswise to make circles. Cut some circles into quarter wedges. Referring to illustration, arrange design on wood plaques as shown or as desired, using cob slices and yellow, red, and black kernels to accent or as part of basic design. Cut leaf and stem shapes of husks and arrange in place. Use corn cob sliced in half lengthwise for long, thick leaves shown on one plaque. Glue all pieces on plaques. With paintbrush and diluted coloring, touch up cob edges and husks as desired. Insert hangers in top.

Cleverly arranged designs on distressed-wood plaques make attractive wall decorations. The "flowers" are corn cobs sliced into circles and quarter-circles. Leaf and stem shapes are cut from husks. Corn kernals in various colors accent the "flowers." Following illustration, opposite, designs are glued on natural or stained-wood plaques. Directions above.

WHITE STILL LIFE

EQUIPMENT: Ruler. Saw. Hammer. Sharp scissors. Plastic bowl. Waxed paper. Small, flat paintbrush.

MATERIALS: Wood: plywood ¼" thick, 12" x 18"; lattice strips 3/8" x 1 3/8", 6 feet. Small finishing nails. All-purpose glue. Dried or plastic weeds and pods. Plaster of Paris. White spray paint. Paint for frame.

DIRECTIONS: Note: When picking wild flowers, be sure of what you are handling. The results of carrying home the attractive foliage of poison ivy or poison sumac can be disastrous. It is also wise to check your state conservation list of plants that cannot be picked if growing wild (for example, use cultivated ferns, not wild ferns).

Saw wood strips for frame, two 12" long and two 19" long. Center and nail the two shorter strips at top and bottom of board, the two longer strips at sides forming butt joints; make sure that the board is centered on the frame so that there is equal amount of depth on both front and back. Spread glue around joints of frame to seal, so plaster will not leak through when it is poured into frame. Place waxed paper under frame.

Cut weeds and pods for arrangement desired or illustrated to fit inside frame. Spray weeds and pods with several coats of white paint; let dry. Prepare plaster in bowl following directions on package. Pour a thin layer of plaster into frame and immediately transfer plant arrangement into plaster-filled frame, lightly pressing weeds and pods into plaster. Spray entirely with white paint. Paint frame desired color

SHELL FLOWER PLAQUE

EQUIPMENT: Hand drill. Pliers. Wire cutters. Scissors. Ruler. Compass.

MATERIALS: Shells in various sizes and shapes. Heavy and fine florist's wire (covered with green tape) for stems. Plain fine wire. White cotton piping with cord removed. Green pipe cleaners or chenille stems for hyacinths. Thin white cardboard for mum and round petal flowers. Small amount absorbent cotton. Straight pins. Stiff, heavy cardboard 11½" x 16½". Green burlap 15" x 20". White felt 1½" x 18". All-purpose glue.

DIRECTIONS: Use heavy wire for all stems except lilies of the valley. Assemble flowers as directed below, then coat stems thinly with glue and insert into piping.

For hyacinth, use about 90 conical shells all approximately the same size. Cut a 1" length of pipe cleaner or chenille stem for each shell; glue
continued on page 130

The striking white-on-white still life consists of an imaginative composition with dried or artificial pods and weeds. The plants are arranged as desired and sprayed with white paint. After the wood frame has been assembled, plaster of Paris is poured into it. The arrangement is then set in the wet plaster. Directions for the White Still Life are at right.

end into each shell cavity; let glue dry. With plain fine wire bind pipe cleaner ends together to length of heavy wire, covering top section of stem with mass of shells.

For mum, use pointed, elongated shells in three sizes. Cut 3″ diameter circle of cardboard and of felt. Glue felt to cardboard. Make two holes in center of circle about ¼″ apart. Glue largest shells with points outward around outer edge. Continue gluing shells in circles to fill area, but leave holes uncovered. When dry, thread one end of heavy wire through center holes (in one and out the other), extending other end for stem; with pliers, twist end behind flower. Glue small white snail-like shell to center of flower covering holes and wire. Crush small shells; spread glue on back of cardboard disk and sprinkle with crushed shells.

For lily of the valley, use tiny white snail-like shells with small points. Glue small wads of cotton into shell openings. Dip fine florist's wire 6½″ long in glue and insert into cotton. When dry, group several together and twist one wire around other wires to hold all in place.

For round petal flowers, use bivalve shells in varied sizes and conical shells. Cut circles of cardboard and felt slightly smaller than group of selected shells. Glue felt to cardboard. Make two holes in center of circle about ¼″ apart. Glue shells to felt side in a variety of ways: Some of the large shells can be placed face down with areas between shells and center filled with smaller, conical shells; larger shells can be placed face up, overlapped around edges, with tiny bivalve shells overlapping and filling in center area. Before centers are filled, thread end of heavy wire through center holes (in one and out the other), extending other end for stem. With pliers, twist wire end in place behind flower. Crush some small shells; brush glue on back of disk and sprinkle with crushed shells.

For simple flower, use two bivalve shells, one larger than the other, and one dark snail-like shell. Drill two holes in base of larger shell. Thread one end of length of heavy wire through holes (in one and out the other), twist together with pliers at back of shell to hold in place. Glue smaller shell inside larger. Glue snail-like shell in place for flower center.

For background, cover one side of large cardboard with burlap; bring edges to back, making sure front is smooth; glue edges to back securely. Carefully pin and glue flowers in arrangement on burlap-covered cardboard. Tie strip of white felt into neat bow; trim ends as shown. Pin and glue bow over stems.

A myriad of seashells in assorted sizes, shapes, and colors are assembled to make a bouquet of lilies of the valley, hyacinths, and other flowers — both real and imaginary. The shell flowers are arranged on a backing of burlap-covered cardboard; a neat felt bow adds the final touch for a summery wall hanging. See the directions for Shell Flower Plaque, page 129.

GOLDEN SHELL JEWELRY

EQUIPMENT: Drill and 3/8″ bit for pendant. Old soft toothbrush.

MATERIALS: Shells. Sea creatures. Coral. Household cement. Pearl beads, various sizes. Tiny glass beads. Stones from old costume jewelry. Wood filler. Gold and silver spray paint. Beading needle and thread. Fasteners for pins, earrings, and cuff links. Gilt cord.

DIRECTIONS: If shells are picked from the beach, scrub with old toothbrush; dry. Sea creatures must be completely dried out. With wood filler, fill out cavities of shells where needed to attach fasteners. Arrange shells as desired; then cement each piece separately; let dry 48 hours. Spray gold or silver. For splattered effect, press valve very lightly so that mostly air is released. Add pearls, stones, and contrasting color shells. When dry, cement fasteners in place.

Cornucopia: Spray cone-shaped shell. Make a tassel of 20 strands of 25 small pearl beads, each on doubled thread with glass bead in place of knot. Tie strands together. Fill shell cavity with cement, poke thread ends into cavity; let dry.

Rose: Fill cavity of one round-shaped shell with wood filler; let dry. Spray this shell, five large, and four small shells, round-shaped, with gold, front and back. Use filled shell as base; cement large shells to it in flower shape. Prop each shell in place until cement sets. Cement smaller shells around center as shown. Cement large pearl bead at center.

Pendant: Mark position for holes about ½″ apart. Drill 3/8″ holes in oyster shell, dipping shell in water repeatedly while drilling to prevent cracking; dry. Spray shell silver; splatter with gold. Insert gold cord or chain through holes.

Abstract Pin: Use interesting bits of shells and coral with contrasting textures. Spray some gold, some silver. Cement in desired arrangement, using a long, whole shell, or a long piece of shell as the base.

Earrings: Spray two matching small shells gold or silver. Fill an area on inside of each, making a flat place to cement on the earring backs.

FISH PRINT

EQUIPMENT: Paintbrushes: large, flat; 1″; retouching No. 3. Waxed paper. Flat working surface. Extra-fine steel wool.

MATERIALS: One fresh fish. Rice paper larger than fish. India ink. Plywood or masonite larger than fish for backing. Clear, satin-finish varnish. All-purpose glue. White and yellow acrylic paint in tubes. Liquid gesso. Polymer medium.

DIRECTIONS: Cover working surface with
continued on page 136

Sea creatures and shells collected on the beach can be dried, then sprayed with gold or silver paint to make glamorous pins, pendants, clips, and earrings. Tiny shells or bright stones from old jewelry can be glued to large shells to make stunning cluster pins. Strands of pearl beads accent a cone-shaped shell. Broken bits form an abstract pin. Directions left.

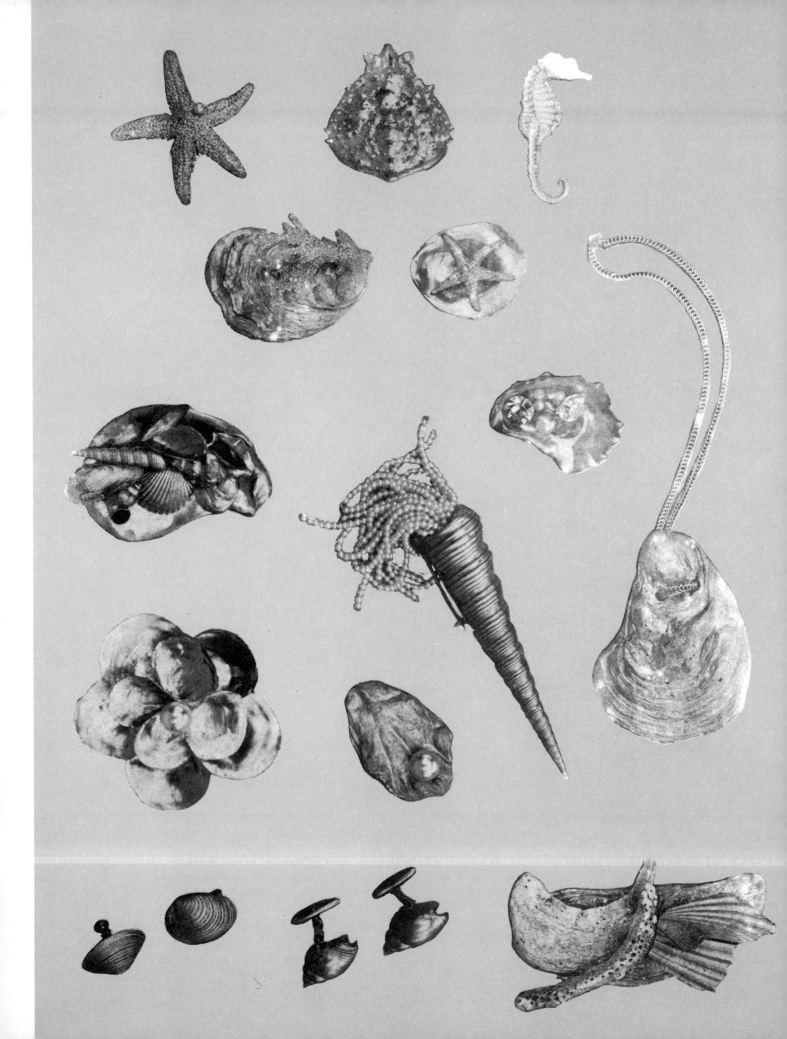

Little golden birds perch in branches, left, to group for a wall decoration. To make a bird, place a small pinecone with stem at top; add a beak by pulling a "petal" from the back of cone, then gluing to the front near top, with the pointed end of petal protruding. Paint birds gold, then glue on plastic movable eyes. Find pieces of scrap wood about 9" or 10" long and glue the birds in forked branches. Arrange several in an interesting grouping.

Pinecone animals at right are created with cones and seeds, a bit of glue. Gather cones in many shapes and sizes; let the cone itself suggest your animal: round and flat for a turtle's back, long and thin for a dachshund's torso. If you like, trim the cone with scissors for a better shape. Fit cones together, dripping glue around joining wherever possible. Give your animals eyes and mouths with acorns, corn kernels, apricot pits and seeds.

This Japanese-style print is created in an unusual manner. To transfer the shape and texture of fish, a fresh fish is painted with India ink. Rice paper is placed over it and gently patted until design is imprinted. Plywood or masonite is used as a backing. Directions for Fish Print start on page 132.

FISH PRINT
continued from page 132

waxed paper. Place fish on waxed paper. With 1″ paintbrush, quickly paint top surface of fish with ink. Carefully place rice paper over fish; gently pat until fish outline and markings are transferred to rice paper. Do not move paper while transferring or print will smudge. Lift paper carefully from fish; let dry. Fill in any missing lines with ink and retouching brush. Tear edges of print unevenly.

Coat backing with gesso. When dry, mix small amount of white with yellow paint; thin with water. Paint entire backing. When dry, adhere fish print to backing with polymer medium. Carefully press out all air bubbles; let dry. Paint over rice paper, around fish print with paint mixture. When dry, coat entire surface with polymer medium; let dry.

Paper Crafts

Most paper today is made from cotton or wood pulp, but its ancestry is traced from papyrus through parchment and vellum to paper made of linen. It was the Chinese who invented paper as we know it today.

Paper is a very important craft material and has a multitude of possibilities. It can be cut, curled, and colored; it is delicate, tough, thick or thin; it may have the texture of chiffon, linen, leather, or wood. There are all kinds of paper: construction, tissue, cellophane, crepe, cardboard. Few materials are more economical, or more available. With this versatile material, you yourself set the limitations. Some of the items in this section look like papier-mâché but are actually made from pieces of egg cartons. However, the beautiful Madonna is made in the true papier-mâché technique—layers of paper are glued, pressed together, and molded when moist to form her body and garments. When dry, papier-mâché hardens and may be painted with water colors or oils. Beauty is something one feels with the heart. With a material as flexible as paper, one's imagination is uninhibited to create many beautiful objects.

VANITY FANCIES

EQUIPMENT: Paper for patterns. Tracing paper. Pencil. Ruler. Scissors. Two small bowls. Small flat and pointed paintbrushes for gesso, paint, and lacquer. Clean, soft rag. **For Powder Box:** Drill with 1/8″ bit. **For Hand Mirror:** Coping saw. Wood file. Aluminum foil. Sandpaper.

MATERIALS: Cardboard. Masking tape. Newspaper. All-purpose glue. Split peas, rice, and barley for flower centers. Gesso. Tempera paints in desired or illustrated colors. Van Dyke brown for antiquing. Clear brushing lacquer. **For Tissue Box Cover:** Fancy braid ½″ wide, 1 yard. **For Powder Box:** Round, one-pound fruitcake tin or equivalent (approx. 6″ diam.). Small wooden knob with screw 1/8″ diameter. **For Hand Mirror:** Plywood 3/8″ thick, 10″ x 17″. Mirror glass 7¼″ diameter (have it cut by a glass cutter if not readily available). Heavy string 1⅔ yards. Ribbon ½″ wide, ½ yard.

GENERAL DIRECTIONS: Enlarge patterns on page 140 for mirror and tissue box by copying on paper ruled in 1″ squares; trace actual-size patterns for flowers; complete all half patterns indicated by long dash lines.

For each piece, prepare basic shapes as indicated in individual directions. Cover with papier-mache where indicated. To make papier-mache, tear newspaper into about 1″ strips. Fill one bowl with water and the other with glue. Dip newspaper strips in water, then in glue. Apply and smooth each piece with fingers as you apply it to shape. Cover each shape with overlapping papier-mache pieces until completely covered; let dry.

Using patterns, cut flowers and leaves of cardboard; vary shapes, curve and overlap petals; cut as many as needed to complete design area. Arrange and glue in place. For flower centers, glue on split peas, rice, barley, or other similar shapes.

When design is complete, paint entire piece with gesso, getting it into all crevices. When dry, paint as illustrated or as desired with tempera paints; let dry. Lacquer entire piece and let dry. Antique piece with Van Dyke brown mixed with a little water; brush it on and wipe off excess with clean rag. When dry, lacquer again and let dry.

Tissue Box Cover: For basic shape, cut five pieces of cardboard: two 4¼″ x 10¼″ for sides; two 4¼″ x 5½″ for ends; one 5½″ x 10¼″ for top. Using pattern cut opening out of top piece. Secure all pieces together with masking tape, leaving bottom open. Cover inside and outside with two complete layers of papier-mache. Glue braid around bottom edge as illustrated. Cut and *continued on page 142*

Spring flowers in gay profusion decorate this three-piece vanity set. The hand mirror, tissue box cover, and powder box are all covered with papier-mâché, trimmed with cardboard cutouts. Split peas, rice, and barley are used for flower centers. The painted pieces are then lacquered and antiqued. See the directions for Vanity Fancies starting at the left.

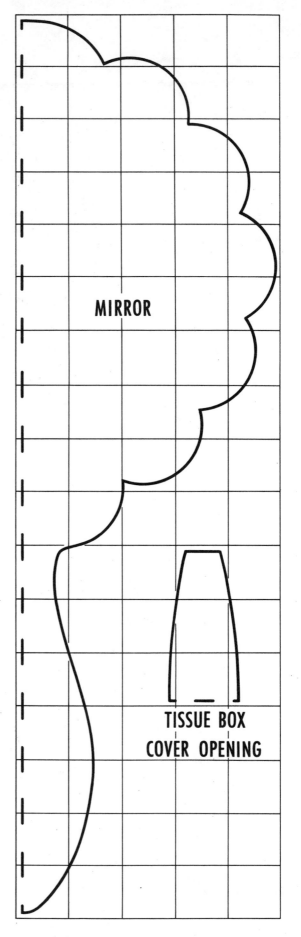

MIRROR

TISSUE BOX
COVER OPENING

*Vanity Fancies: Trace actual-size patterns,
left; enlarge patterns above on 1" squares.*

The rich-toned fruit bowl, made of a cardboard circle cut and taped to bowl shape, is decorated with cardboard fruit. Cardboard petals of poppy bowl are cut separately, then joined for bowl shape. String adds design and texture to center. Glued-on leaves of green tray are veined with a dry ball-point pen. See pages 142 to 143.

glue cardboard flowers and leaves on top. Finish, following General Directions.

Powder Box: Cover tin box and lid with one complete coat of papier-mache: For lid, cover top and sides; for box, cover bottom and sides only up to rim; let dry. Make sure lid still fits. Cut flowers and leaves of cardboard and glue on lid. Finish, following General Directions. Paint knob; let dry. Drill hole in center top of lid; attach knob to center of lid with screw.

Hand Mirror: Make tracing of mirror outline; transfer to wood by placing tracing pencil side down on wood and retracing lines on wrong side with pencil. Cut out shape with saw. With wood file, bevel all edges from top surface to bottom edge on one side. Sand smooth. Wrap mirror glass with aluminum foil; center on flat side of wooden shape. Cover both sides of shape with one complete coat of papier-mache, leaving mirror area uncovered. Glue string dipped in glue around mirror. When dry, remove mirror. Turn to other side. Cut flowers and leaves of cardboard; overlap and glue as illustrated to cover top part of shape. Press string dipped in glue along handle as shown. Tie ribbon into bow with streamers; dip in glue and put in place on handle. Coat mirror shape with gesso and finish, following General Directions. Glue glass in place.

LEAF TRAY

EQUIPMENT: Paper for pattern. Ruler. Pencil. Scissors. Small, flat paintbrush. Small bowl. Dish. Compass. Dry ball-point pen. Soft, clean rag.

MATERIALS: Lightweight cardboard 17″ square. Newspaper. All-purpose glue. Masking tape. Heavy string. Liquid gesso. Tempera paints: medium yellow-green and Van Dyke brown. Clear lacquer.

DIRECTIONS: With compass, mark 12½″ circle on cardboard and cut out. Enlarge leaf pattern on page 143 by copying on paper ruled in ½″ squares. Cut 14 leaves from cardboard.

Cut seven slashes from edge of cardboard circle toward center, 4″ long, spacing evenly around edge (about 5½″ apart). Overlap edges of slashes 1/8″ and tape together to form a slightly concave tray.

Fill bowl with water and put some glue in dish. Tear newspaper into pieces about 1″ square. Apply pieces of newspaper to both sides of tray as follows: spread glue over a small area of tray; dip finger into water, then in glue and press paper pieces onto glued area, overlapping them to cover. Dip finger in water and glue and

smooth over pieces. Continue in this manner, covering entire tray. Cover both sides of tray with at least three layers of newspaper. Glue cardboard leaves around tray on top and on bottom, with tips of leaves at edge of tray.

Dip string in water and glue, then apply string around edge of tray on bottom, forming a loop between each leaf. Let dry.

Coat tray on both sides with gesso. When dry, score veins in leaves with dry ballpoint pen. Paint entire tray green; let dry. Coat with clear lacquer; let dry. Antique tray with Van Dyke brown paint mixed with a little water; apply with brush all over tray and wipe off excess with rag. When dry, lacquer entire tray again.

POPPY BOWL

EQUIPMENT: Paper for pattern. Ruler. Pencil. Scissors. Small, flat paintbrush. Small bowl. Dish. Compass. Soft, clean rag.

MATERIALS: Lightweight cardboard 16″ square. Newspaper. Masking tape. All-purpose glue. Heavy string. Liquid gesso. Tempera paints: yellow, orange, red, light yellow-green, Van Dyke brown. Clear lacquer.

DIRECTIONS: Enlarge petal and leaf patterns on page 143 by copying on paper ruled in 1″ squares. Complete half-pattern for petal, indicated by dash line. Cut five petals of cardboard. Cut four slashes in each petal as shown on pattern and one on half-pattern line for center. With compass, mark a 2½″ diameter circle on cardboard and cut out.

Overlap the slashes in each petal slightly and tape to hold. Place each petal under the 2½″ circle, overlapping each to form bowl shape; tape securely on inside and outside to circle; glue overlapping petals together.

Following directions for the Leaf Tray at left, cover inside and outside of bowl with at least three layers of newspaper. Dip string in water and glue. Press a piece of string on outside of petals around top and about halfway down one side of each. Cut short pieces of string; dip each in glue and water and press onto inside center of poppy at various angles in a 2½″ diameter area. Let dry thoroughly.

Coat bowl on both sides with gesso. When dry, trace leaf on outside of each petal, with bottoms of leaves meeting at center. Paint inside of bowl orange, shading to yellow at center (string area). When dry, paint lightly on inside with red, leaving some orange and yellow at center; wipe off some red around center of each petal. Paint center area green. Paint outside of bowl orange, except leaves. When dry, paint over lightly with red. Paint leaves green. Lacquer and antique bowl with Van Dyke brown, following directions for the Leaf Tray.

FRUIT BOWL

EQUIPMENT: Paper for patterns. Pencil. Ruler. Scissors. Small flat and pointed paintbrushes. Small bowl. Dish. Compass. Soft, clean rag. Dry ball-point pen.

MATERIALS: Lightweight cardboard two pieces about 17″ square. Newspaper. All-purpose glue. Masking tape. Heavy string, 5 yards. Liquid gesso. Tempera paints: yellow-gold, light yellow, orange, red, purple, yellow-green, white, Van Dyke brown. Clear lacquer.

DIRECTIONS: With compass, mark a 16½″ circle on paper and cut out for pattern. Enlarge fruit patterns, below left, by copying on paper ruled in 1″ squares. Short dash lines indicate overlapping pieces. Cut each fruit piece from cardboard.

Fold paper circle pattern in half twice to divide into quarters; open pattern. Mark a 6″ square in center of circle, with corners at folds. Refold circle with marked square on outside. Cut off a wedge on each folded side from edge to corner of marked square. Open pattern; bend up each side on marked square line, matching edges of wedge cutouts. If sides do not slant up enough, refold pattern and cut wedges a little wider.

Using pattern, mark bowl on cardboard and cut out. Score cardboard along marked square lines. Fold up sides and tape, matching corners together on inside and outside.

Following directions for the Leaf Tray at left, cover inside and outside of bowl with at least three layers of newspaper. Glue a group of fruit or a grape cluster to each section of bowl on inside. Dip string in water and glue; press a piece of string around bottom inside of bowl, around top inside, and around top outside ¼″ from edge; glue two rows of string around bottom outside of bowl. Let dry thoroughly.

Coat bowl on both inside and outside with gesso. When dry, score veins in grape leaves; using ball-point pen, press dents into orange, lemon, and strawberry for rough texture. Paint bowl yellow-gold. Paint fruit and leaves in natural colors, wiping off some paint to make lighter high-lights; shade orange with a little yellow at top; shade pear with orange at wider part. Paint bottom outside string and bottom inside string red. Paint remaining string white. Let dry. Lacquer and antique bowl with Van Dyke brown, following directions for the Leaf Tray.

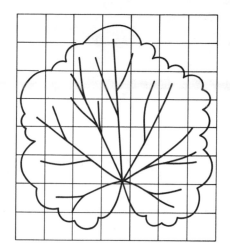

Leaf Tray: Enlarge pattern for leaf on ½″ squares.

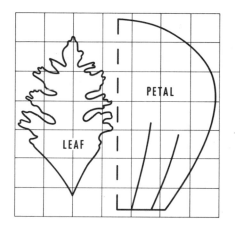

Poppy Bowl: Petal and leaf to enlarge on 1″ squares.

Fruit Bowl: Fruit patterns to enlarge on 1″ squares.

143

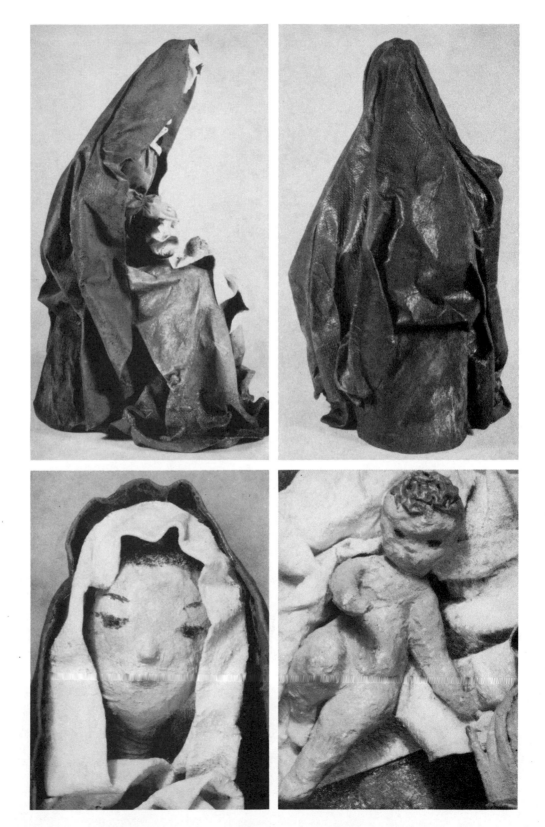

A serene madonna and child radiate loveliest of holiday themes. The sculpture is a perfect decoration for the mantelpiece or table. The photographs at right show how carefully the figure, including back, was modeled. Close-ups show texture and other details. See the directions for the Papier-Mâché Madonna, page 149.

Construction of figure for the Papier-Mâché Madonna is illustrated. Wads of newspaper are placed on a wire armature; shape is modeled with paste-dipped strips of paper toweling. In photograph, sculptured figure is in place on a seat. Long lines of figure and position of head, torso, limbs retain characteristics of an El Greco, inspiration for the Madonna.

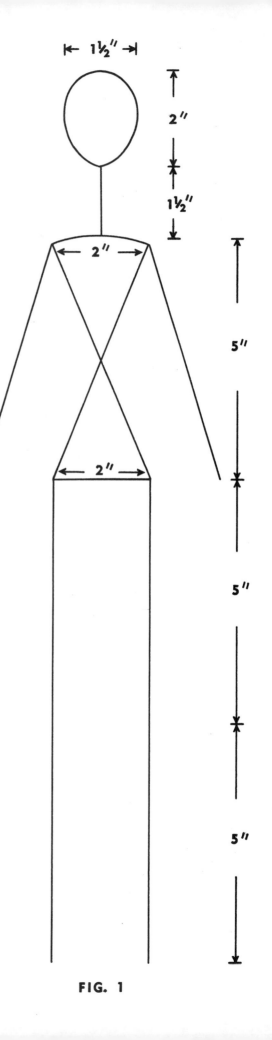

FIG. 1

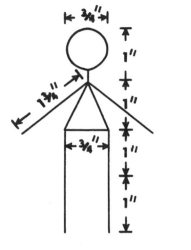

FIG. 2

FIG. 6

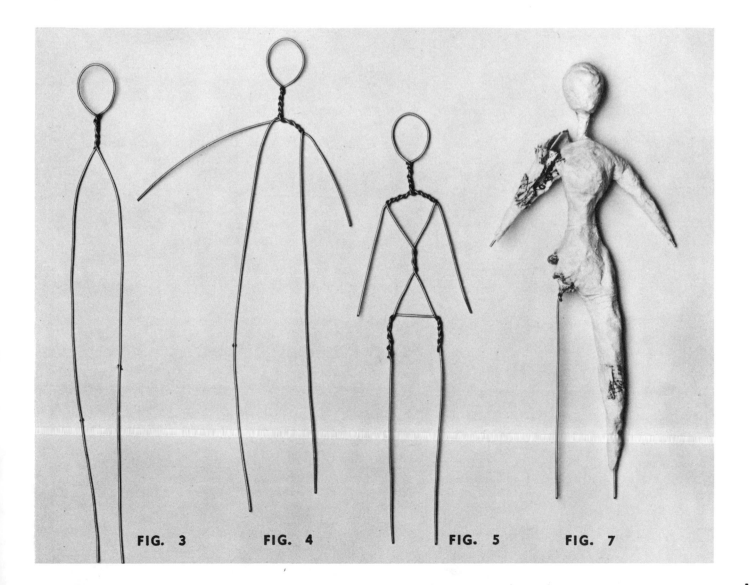

FIG. 3   FIG. 4   FIG. 5   FIG. 7

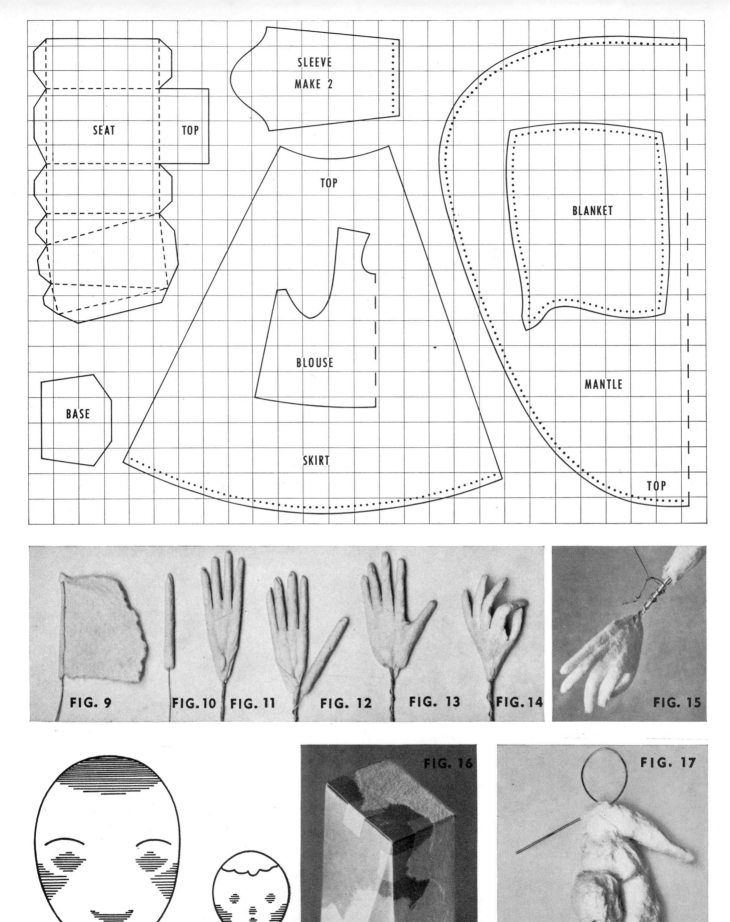

SEAT

TOP

SLEEVE
MAKE 2

TOP

BLANKET

BLOUSE

BASE

MANTLE

SKIRT

TOP

FIG. 9   FIG.10   FIG. 11   FIG. 12   FIG. 13   FIG.14   FIG. 15

FIG. 16

FIG. 17

MADONNA   BABY

FIG. 8

PAPIER-MACHE MADONNA

EQUIPMENT: Scissors. Ruler. Compass. Wire-cutting pliers. Paper for patterns. Pencil. Single-edged razor blade. Measuring cup. Mixing bowl and spoon. Paper cups for mixing paints. Camel's hair paintbrushes, one very fine, one about No. 7, one wider (optional). Damp and dry cloths.

MATERIALS: Galvanized wire; 18-gauge, 20-gauge, 26-gauge. Newspapers. Single-ply paper toweling. Flour, for paste. Paint: flat white; fire-engine red enamel; white enamel; royal blue enamel; brown spray enamel. Lightweight cardboard. All-purpose glue. Masking tape. String.

DIRECTIONS: Enlarge patterns for garments and seat, on page 148, by copying on paper ruled in 1″ squares. Complete half-patterns indicated by long dash lines. Use dimension patterns, Figs. 1 and 2 on pages 146-147, as guides for making wire armatures.

Armatures: Use pliers for shaping and twisting wires. **Madonna:** Cut about 43″ of 18-gauge wire. Following the dimension pattern Fig. 1 on page 146, form oval for head from middle of wire, and twist together for neck (Fig. 3, p. 147). Cut 12″ piece of 18-gauge wire for the arms; center it at bottom of neck and twist one shoulder (Fig. 4); check with dimension pattern for accuracy, then twist other shoulder and measure again. Twist for waist (Fig. 5). Cut a 6″ piece of 18-gauge wire. Following dimension pattern Fig. 1, twist one hip wire together with one leg (Fig. 5); twist other side; check for accuracy against dimension pattern. If this twist comes out somewhat crooked, it will not matter.

Baby: Following the dimension pattern Fig. 2 and using 20-gauge wire, make armature in same manner as for Madonna, but without a waist or shoulders; cut arm wire 4″ long and hip wire 2″ long.

While working with pliers, make a little tool (Fig. 6) with a 9″ piece of 18-gauge wire that will be handy for handling pasted paper later on.

To Form Shapes: For paste, mix about ½ cup flour and about 3/8 cup water in a bowl until smooth and consistency of cake batter. Make fresh batches of paste as needed. Keep damp and dry cloths on hand to wipe hands; wash hands whenever necessary. Tear a few pieces of paper toweling into strips roughly 1″ x 5″; tear paper, do not cut it, because the ragged edges blend in better when pasted. Saturate paper towel strips thoroughly with paste.

Madonna: Tear a piece of newspaper roughly 15″ square and crumple it (do not fold or roll) loosely into a ball. Fasten it on the upper front of armature with a few paste-saturated strips of paper towel (see Fig. 7). Next put a wad of newspaper on the rear of the lower torso and anchor with paste-dipped strips. Fill in the waist-line with a small bit of crumpled newspaper, but keep waist very narrow; continue to cover the entire wire body with more crumpled newspaper and paste-dipped paper towel strips (Fig. 7). View body from all angles; if some part is too big, mash it down and put another paste-dipped strip of paper over it. If some part is too small, crumple more newspaper and add on with paste-dipped paper towel strips, modeling for a good shape. Do not make body too tightly compact as you go along, or it will not bend into position later. Crumple more newspaper around arm and leg wires; anchor and fasten to body with paste-dipped strips. Taper to very thin wrists and ankles as shown on page 146.

To make head, cut a piece of newspaper 12″ square; crumple into egg shape with slight shaping for chin on one side of tapered end. Place inside the wire loop and cover with paste-dipped paper towel strips. Fill in neck with newspaper and paste-dipped strips (see Fig. 7), keeping it quite slender. Keep turning body to view from all sides, and refer to figure illustration on page 146 for general feeling of form. When you have a satisfactory shape, check to see that all newspaper is covered with at least one layer of paper towel strips. After first layer of pasted paper has dried, smooth the face by shaving bad lumps off with razor blade and by pasting another strip of paper towel over it. Fill bad hollows with tiny crumples of paste-dipped paper towel and cover over with strips. Smooth the face and front of neck. Referring to Fig. 8, indicate features with pencil marks. For nose, make a very tiny wad of paste-saturated paper towel; stick in place and cover with bits of paste-dipped paper towel.

To make hands, cut ten 3″ pieces of 26-gauge wire. Tear paper towel into 1½″ square pieces; taper the width a bit so the fingers will be tapered at one end (see Fig. 9). Saturate the 1½″ pieces of paper with paste and roll around wire (Figs. 9 and 10). Exaggerate the length and slenderness of fingers, but do not make fingers spidery. With a little more paste, tuck in and taper ragged tip ends. Make ten fingers in this manner. Use the two slenderest fingers for the little fingers, the two fattest fingers for the thumbs. Lay four fingers together, making middle finger 1″ long; twist wires together at bottoms for wrist. Paste a small strip around lower portion, making palm 1″ long (Fig. 11). Add thumb at an angle (Fig. 12); twist thumb wire around other wires at wrist. Paste a small strip around thumb and palm (Fig. 13), and another small strip over space between thumb and index finger. Study figure illustration and Fig. 14 for positions of fingers; bend fingers and curl palm lengthwise. To fasten hands to wrists, slip wires of hand inside papier-mache of arm end. Fasten by twisting a piece of *continued on page 150*

continued on page 150

PAPIER-MACHE MADONNA

continued from page 149

fine wire around hand and arm wires (Fig. 15). Fill in wrists and cover with paste-dipped paper towel, anchoring hand to arm as shown in figure illustration.

To Make Seat: Using patterns, cut seat sides and top in one piece, and cut separate base out of lightweight cardboard; cut out along solid lines; score with razor blade and fold along dotted lines. Shape seat (see Fig. 16) with top and base in place and hold together with masking tape. Cover with irregular pieces of paste-dipped paper towel, being sure to have at least two layers over the cracks where sides of seat come together (Fig. 16). Use straight, flat part of seat as front. See photograph on page 146.

Bend the Madonna to sit on seat (see illustration on page 146 for position). Check with dimension pattern for bending hips and knees. Incline body to the side and forward, bending waist, neck, and shoulders. Bend arms halfway between shoulders and fingertips for elbows. Set one knee higher than the other. Study illustrations on pages 144 and 146, and bend figure to look as graceful and natural as possible. If papier-mache cracks as you bend it, that does not matter.

Baby: Use crumpled paper towel instead of newspaper to cover armature, and shape body, head, and limbs. Study the illustration, Fig. 17, to see how the plump tummy and hips and the narrow shoulders are exaggerated. Begin with first crumpled wad on tummy. Then do hips and legs, bending into final position as you mold (Fig. 17). Just indicate feet and hands by tapering. Make the face a little flat; do not bother with a nose. After the body has dried and stiffened, put a piece of pasted paper towel over top of head and push it around with wire tool into crinkles that look like hair. Mark features on face with pencil as for Madonna, following Fig. 8.

Clothing: Make one part at a time and put on the body before the pasted paper becomes dry. All clothing is made of three thicknesses. Cut first layer of newspaper, using pattern. Apply paste (with hands) to one side of newspaper shape and cover it with paper toweling. Tear towel paper to same shape as newspaper. Apply paste to other side of newspaper and cover with paper toweling; tear towel paper to same shape, but leave about 1" larger at edges marked on patterns with dotted line. Apply paste to this 1" and turn it over to make a hemmed edge. To make hem of skirt a little stronger, lay a piece of string along fold when turning up the 1".

To make sleeves, straighten out arms to put on sleeves. Follow the general directions for clothing above. Spread paste generously along the side and shoulder ''seams'' of the sleeve and overlap sides around arm. Position cuff and tie with string around wrist, about ¾" above edge. Remove string when dry. Finish adhering sleeve sides and shoulder. Fasten shoulder with extra strips of paper towel, pasting to body and to sleeve. Bend arms back into position, and arrange folds while paper is still damp.

For skirt, follow general directions for clothing above. After skirt is hemmed with string, straighten legs and try skirt on the Madonna, arranging gathers at waist, with seam in center back. Squeeze the skirt at waist to set the gathers. Remove skirt and lay flat. Apply paste around waist and hips of Madonna. Apply paste inside skirt around top and along back seam; lap back seam and press together to secure. Place Madonna inside skirt, feet first. Arrange gathers at waist and tie with string while drying. To drape the skirt, while it is still damp, rebend legs inside skirt to the seated position. Working with Madonna sitting on seat (but not pasted to it), arrange the skirt following illustration on page 144. The damp towel paper falls into beautiful shapes; you can arrange and rearrange until you are pleased with the effect. Be sure knees are far enough apart, the left lower than the right, so the blanket and Baby will be accommodated. See that the skirt is tucked close to the seat on both sides. Let dry overnight, so the skirt folds will stay where they have been placed.

Make blouse in three thicknesses as instructed above. Put paste around neck, on shoulders of blouse, and on Madonna. Paste blouse to Madonna, tucking it close around neck and tight at shoulder seams. Pat paste around top of skirt at waistline and inside lower edge of blouse. Pull blouse around underarms and paste points to back. Arrange blouse in pleasing folds, and gather lower edge over pasted waistline; squeeze tightly to set gathers.

For cowl, cut newspaper 2½" wide, 17" long, allowing 1" extra towel paper on one long side for hem. Make cowl following general instructions for clothing above and hem along one long side. Place damp cowl around head of Madonna, hemmed edge toward face, with one end at shoulder length and other end long, to drape around neck. Practice draping down each side of head and arrange into folds around neck to get lengths right. Remove cowl. Apply a generous amount of paste on head at top, back, and sides; down back of neck; and around shoulders. Paste on the cowl, being sure that the edges come together down the back of neck. Drape cowl on sides and arrange soft folds around neck as in illustration.

Cut mantle and make in three thicknesses, following general directions. Practice draping damp mantle, referring to illustration, with the Madonna on the seat. See that the mantle comes down close around the seat, so it can be pasted tightly to it. Remove mantle. Apply paste on Madonna body, head, shoulders, back, arms, and back of skirt. Paste on the mantle, beginning at top of head and with body resting on seat. When the folds are arranged to your satisfaction, put paste on the seat and paste the whole dressed body to it. When the Madonna and seat are dry and can be handled again, cover the entire underneath part of the figure and seat with three thicknesses of pasted paper, pasting carefully to bottom folds of skirt.

For blanket, use pattern and follow the general directions. Study illustration for draping. Place the most exaggerated corner of blanket in the Madonna's left hand, and arrange it with Baby in position. Paste blanket to lap and fingers, but leave Baby removable for painting.

Painting: When the figures are dry, give the Madonna and Baby one coat of flat white paint, using the No. 7 brush to reach inside the folds as far as possible. When the white paint is dry, use brown spray enamel on the deep interior folds of mantle and cowl; then spray the seat and base of figure brown.

Paint the dress red first. In a cup, mix some red and a little white paint. Use No. 7 brush for the small and inside areas. Use the wider brush for larger areas if you wish. Wipe the paint off the folds with a rag or toweling for an interesting effect, if desired.

Paint the cowl and blanket white. To paint flesh-colored areas, put a little white enamel into a cup, add a drop of red and stir; continue until you have a good flesh color. Be sure to paint under the chin and the neck as far down as you can inside the cowl, and paint the Madonna's hands. Paint the entire Baby flesh color. Let dry.

To paint the mantle, mix white with blue to soften. Paint outside and inside parts of mantle blue; let dry. When paint is dry, you can get an interesting effect by giving a light, quick spray of brown paint to the lower folds of the skirt and mantle, and up the folds of the back.

For the faces (see Fig. 8), put a little more red into the flesh color for the Baby's rosy knees, tummy and cheeks, and a spot for the nose, and the Madonna's cheeks; use a very small brush and fine, light strokes to make a blurry effect. For mouths, mix a drop of red with a touch of flesh color. Following Fig. 8 and referring to illustration on page 144, paint the mouths with tiny brush strokes: just a dot for the Baby; and for the Madonna, begin in the center, working out and very slightly up at the corners; keep it blurry. Paint Madonna's fingertips same red.

Spray a puddle of brown paint in a paper cup to use with a brush. Paint eyes, eyebrows, and hair brown. To make Madonna look downward, make the brush strokes more solid at the bottom of the eye ovals. For the Baby's hair, mix flesh color with a touch of brown paint used for eyes, brows, hair.

When all the paint is dry, glue the Baby to blanket, using all-purpose glue.

Variations: An El Greco painting inspired the Madonna on page 144, and our directions and illustration are for this particular style. If you prefer to follow another famous painting, use the basic procedures outlined, changing dimensions of armature, shaping, and positioning of the figure, as necessary.

To estimate changes required, work with a good color reproduction of the painting. Start with the basic armature (see Figs. 1-5, pages 146-147) and experiment with positioning it. If the figure you are copying requires longer or shorter arms and legs, cut off the ends of wire or add wire, if necessary. Form the shape with wads of newspaper, using thicker wads if the figure is fuller. Model with paste-dipped strips of paper toweling as directed. Use procedure for finishing and painting as outlined above, changing colors to conform to the illustration you are following.

JEWELED BIRDS

EQUIPMENT: Tracing paper. Pencil. Ruler, Scissors. Soft rag.

MATERIALS: Discarded light bulbs about 3½" long with 2¼" diameter. Styrofoam eggs about 1¾" x 2-3/8". Paper towels. Lightweight cardboard. All-purpose glue. Gold, white, and brown paint. Trims such as cord, braid, lace, rickrack, fine chains, beads, artificial jewels, sequins, etc.

DIRECTIONS: Trace patterns on page 152 for beak, wing, and tails; complete half-patterns indicated by dash lines.

For each bird, cut pointed end off styrofoam egg; place and glue egg on light bulb (Fig. 1) to form head and body of bird. Choose tail pattern in size and shape desired. Cut one tail of cardboard; fold at half-pattern line; snip front end as indicated and glue over stem of bulb (Fig. 2). Cut two beaks of cardboard; fold each at dotted lines. Using short ends as tabs, glue beaks on head as shown (Fig. 2), fitting one above the other for upper and lower beaks; leave beak slightly open. Cut two wings of cardboard, but do not glue on yet. Cut paper towels into ½" wide strips. Wrap and glue strips around head body, and tail (but not beak) to cover. Cover light bulb stem and underside of tail. Glue strips separately on wings to cover. Glue wing on each side of bird where shown. Glue on braid, rickrack, cord, and lace to decorate. Paint entire bird gold; let dry. Give an antique-like finish to bird by rubbing brown or white paint over bird lightly *continued on page 154*

continued on page 154

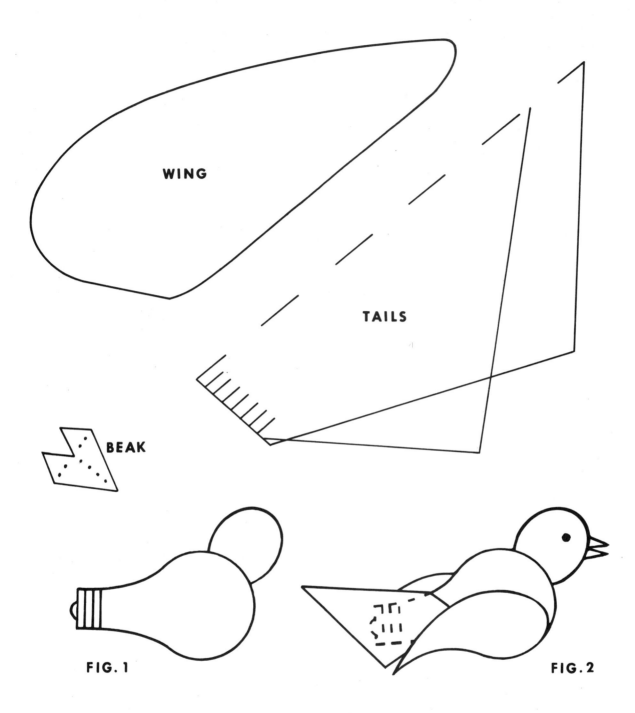

WING

TAILS

BEAK

FIG. 1

FIG. 2

A family of bejeweled birds have heirloom elegance. Nestled on a branch or suspended from a tree, they will gleam softly in the holiday lights. Bodies are made of light bulbs; heads are styrofoam; the wings and tail are cardboard. Tiny "jewels" and pieces of braid, cord, and lace lend Victorian opulence. See actual-size patterns above; Jeweled Birds, page 151.

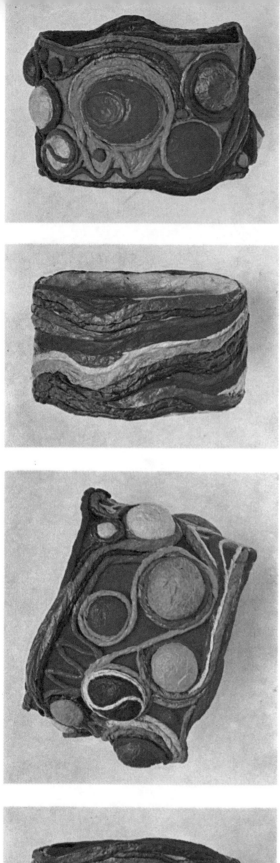

JEWELED BIRDS

continued from page 151

with soft rag. Wipe off any excess. For each eye, glue on sequin centered with seed bead where indicated by dot on Fig. 2. Glue on beads, sequins, chains, etc. to decorate bird.

GIANT JEWELRY

EQUIPMENT: Pencil. Scissors. Compass. Ruler. Tweezers. Small pointed paintbrush for glue. Crepe paper twister (optional). Tracing paper for patterns.

MATERIALS: Package of assorted colors of tissue paper. Thin, flexible cardboard. All-purpose glue. Clear lacquer. Lacquer thinner. Thin chains or cord for pendants. Masking tape.

GENERAL DIRECTIONS: Jewelry (except bracelets) is illustrated actual size; trace illustrations for patterns where desired, or, draw your own designs on tracing paper. Go over designs on back with a soft pencil.

Cut cardboard shapes, following individual directions. Brush lacquer on one side of cardboard shape; press a piece of tissue paper, larger than cardboard, onto lacquered side, turning edges of tissue over to back. Brush more lacquer on tissue. Adhere tissue to back with lacquer; trim edges even with cardboard. Trace design on front.

To make strips, cut tissue in varied widths from ¾" to 1½"; crumple strip well and then flatten out. Pull strip through twister, or twist strip by hand. Outline designs and make lines of inner designs with a thin line of glue; press twisted strips of various colors on lines of glue, using tweezers to place strips. To make raised circles and ovals, roll up a ball of tissue and cover smoothly with a small piece of same color; twist edges of piece together on back of ball; brush glue on back and let dry. Apply glue on background design where raised pieces will go; allow *continued on page 159*

Baroque jewelry is created ad lib with "strings" of colored tissue paper, to make fun put-ons for teenagers. The "gems" on the big pendants at right and on bold bracelets at left are formed by smoothing a layer of tissue paper over paper balls. The jewelry (except the bracelets) is illustrated actual size. Directions for the Giant Jewelry are given above.

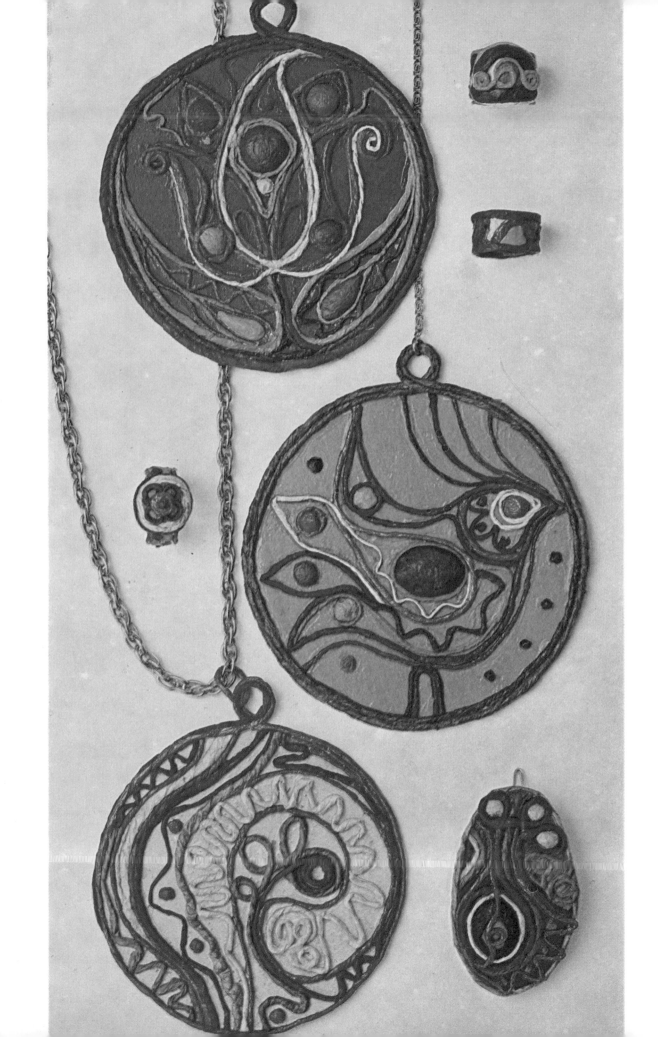

Simple, delightful designs transform white lampshades to enliven the room decor. Overlapping cutouts of tissue paper in varying shades have a translucent effect; some shapes are outlined in black cording for emphasis. Directions for the Tissue Lampshades on page 159.

SUN
2

1

1

1

3

3

4

3

2

3

2

2

2

158

GIANT JEWELRY

continued from page 154

to become tacky. Apply a little more glue and press on raised tissue piece. Before glue dries, press pieces down again.

Thin lacquer slightly and brush over entire piece, or dip small pieces in the thinned lacquer. Let dry.

Pendants: Draw a circle or oval of desired size on cardboard. Cover and decorate with tissue as instructed in General Directions. Make two or more twisted strips to fit around edge of pendant, allowing 2″ extra. Glue strips around front surface and edge of pendant, starting and ending at top. Form extra allowance of strips into a circle at top; glue ends at back. Coat with lacquer.

Bracelets and Rings: Cut cardboard strip the width desired and length to fit finger or wrist with a slight overlap; be sure bracelets are snug, but big enough to slip over hand. Shape strip into circle, overlap ends and tape. Cover inside and out with tissue paper; add a few extra strips of tissue over seam. Decorate and lacquer following General Directions.

TISSUE LAMPSHADES

EQUIPMENT: Tracing paper for patterns. Pencil. Ruler. Compass. Scissors. Thin cardboard or sturdy paper. Brush for glue. Cup or small bowl. Waxed paper.

MATERIALS: White inexpensive lampshades. Colored tissue papers. Polymer (by Liquid-tex) or use a little more than ½ cup of Elmer's Glue-All to ½ cup of water. Black cord-type string. Elmer's Glue-All.

GENERAL DIRECTIONS: Enlarge patterns on squares, page 158, by copying on paper ruled in 1″ squares. Trace the actual-size patterns; complete quarter-patterns indicated by dash lines. Cut each pattern out of cardboard or sturdy paper. For each motif, place cardboard pattern down on colored tissue paper and trace outline. Cut design out of tissue paper. (If cutting several of the same shape out of the same color paper, cut four at one time).

Brush a little polymer or glue solution on a

Lampshade patterns are on opposite page. Trace the actual-size patterns and complete quarter-patterns; enlarge house, tree, and sun patterns on 1″ squares.

small area of lampshade. Before it dries, place piece of tissue on moist area, being sure each part of tissue piece adheres well to lampshade. Then cover tissue with solution. Repeat this procedure until entire design on lampshade is finished. Then give entire shade an additional coat of solution.

To accent some designs and make parts of some designs, use string soaked in glue; put about three tablespoons of glue into bowl and place several 12″ pieces of string into glue. Squeeze glue and string together so glue penetrates well. Then run string through fingers to remove excess glue. Place string on waxed paper with pattern underneath; shape string along lines of pattern. Let string dry thoroughly in shape. Remove waxed paper and glue string in place.

Farm Scene: Cut narrow strips of light blue paper and cover entire shade as shown. Cut barn of red and black tissue paper, tree trunk of brown, tree top of green, apples of red, sun of yellow. Using patterns marked 1, cut three ducks of brown, two birds of blue, and two pigs of black. Cut a second tree without apples and cut grasslike strips of green paper. Referring to illustration, adhere pieces to lampshade following method above. Outline birds, ducks, tree tops, apples, and make pig's tail and duck's feet with string treated with glue.

Circle Design: Use pale and deep pink paper cut in 2½″ diameter circles. Using pale pink for first layer, adhere row of half-circles around top edge. Then make vertical rows of circles, in line with half-circles, using two or more circles for each row depending upon height of shade; finish with half-circle or part of circle. Repeat until shade is covered. Using deep pink paper circles, adhere second layer over areas between circles of first layer and overlapping as shown.

Flowers-with-Stems Design: For background, cut narrow strips of yellow paper and glue around lampshade to cover. Cut grasslike pieces of green paper; overlap and glue around bottom edge. Using patterns marked 2, cut sun of gold-color paper; use two gold-color circles for center; cut a variety of flowers in different colors and cut centers of different colors as illustrated. Make stems, outline flowers and centers with string.

Under-the-Sea Design: Cut narrow ragged strips of green and blue tissue paper. Adhere all around lampshade. Cut long and short grasslike pieces of green tissue and adhere to shade. Using patterns marked 3, make fish in varying sizes and shapes and snail of string. Use deep blue paper for eyes.

Free-Floating Flower Design: Using pattern marked 4, cut flowers of yellow, gold, and hot pink; overlap and glue as illustrated. Mark flower centers with 1¾″ diameter circles of string.

Create attractive, one-of-a-kind greeting cards with white notepaper and colored tissue. Cut circles and strips out of tissue paper in contrasting or related colors, cutting them free-hand for an uneven effect, if you like. Plan your design so that some shapes overlap, to add dimension and depth. Spray-glue the front of card, then press the cutout tissue shapes into place. Very easy!

Tie-Dye

The word "tie-dye" is a contemporary derivation
from "tie and dye." The origins of this technique
are uncertain, but proof that it is a very old
method of producing designs on fabric has been
found among artifacts in parts of the world
where the fabrics of early cultures are preserved.
Tie and dye is a resist method like batik; only here
it is the tied areas, instead of wax, that keep
the fabric from absorbing the dye bath. Also, still
called "tie-dye" is a technique of gathering the
fabric with a running or overcast stitch to follow a
preplanned design. Other effects are obtained by
tying various items into the fabric, such as
buttons—to produce circles, ovals, and squares.
The amount of dye that penetrates the cloth
depends upon how tightly or loosely the fabric has
been bound and how long it is left in the dye-bath.
A beautiful blending of colors can result from
tying and dipping, then tying new areas and
dipping again, as often as needed to shade from
light to dark or, for example, to shade from
the palest yellow through green to dark blue.
Even if you know how to mix colors, it is a good
idea to experiment first with scraps of cloth, for
although tie-dye is an easy craft, "fine art"
results, such as beautiful hangings or banners,
are possible with experience, patience, and care.

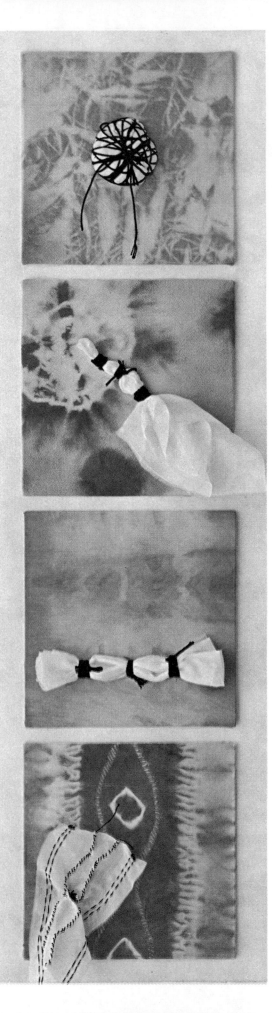

Marbling: Crumple and ball fabric so that one portion remains outside. Wrap the string across in all directions as shown to keep ball shape. Dip in dye, rinse, and untie. Shape into ball again but this time keep on outside the part that was inside. Dip in a second color.

Tying: Pick up center of proposed circle with a pin. Gather the fabric together tightly and tie with string. Make as many tyings spaced as necessary for number of concentric circles desired. Dip entire piece in dye or only up to last tying, keeping untied part out of dye.

Folding: Fold the fabric in half and in accordian pleats the desired width, the edges even. Folded piece may be given a twist and tied together in as many places as desired. Dip entire piece in dye—or dip center in one color, rinse, squeeze out; dip edges in another color.

Stitching: While fabric is flat, mark lines of design. Sew on lines with running stitch or use a close overcasting stitch (see outline of oval shape). Pull thread ends of all the stitching to gather the fabric tightly. Add center dot—see Tying. Dye, rinse, and squeeze out.

Ties in an endless variety of abstract designs can be created with different tiedyeing techniques. The ties (made with McCall's pattern #2971) were colored in liquid fabric dyes. At left, four techniques are shown. For Neckties, see page 166.

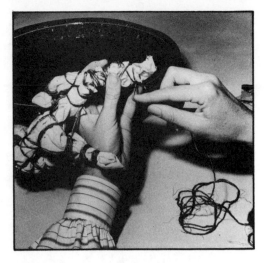

1. The wrapping and tying process is repeated at random all over the material.

2. Dyeing of the material: In this instance only some areas are being dipped.

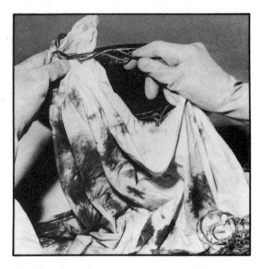

3. Untying the dyed areas, holding cloth so that dye does not stain the other areas.

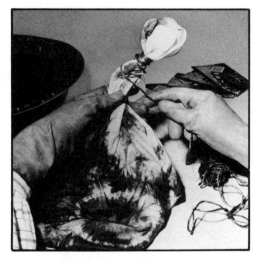

4. To obtain the multi-colored effect, material is tied and dyed a second time.

5. A single tied and dyed motif, shown as the fabric emerges from the dye bath.

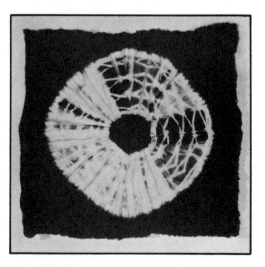

6. The same sample when opened. White areas show where cord "tied out" the dye.

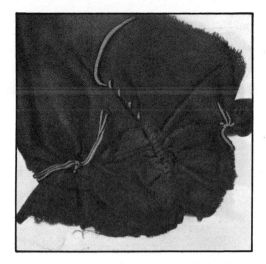

7. *A tied motif and finely stitched motif shown as cloth emerges from the dye.*

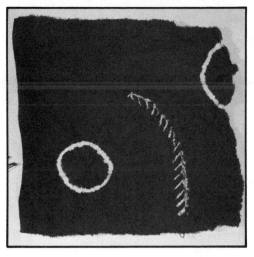

8. *The circle appears where fabric was tied, "herringbone" appears where sewn.*

9. *The doubled cloth was tied in one area, then closely pinned in another area.*

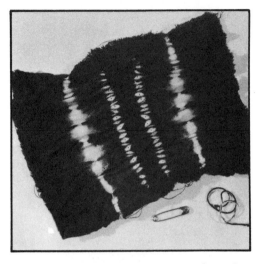

10. *This duplicate pattern results when the cloth is untied, unpinned, and opened.*

11. *No tying out was done on this sample; only stitch-resistant dyeing is shown.*

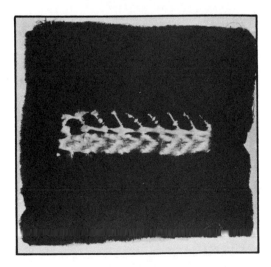

12. *The pattern appears bolder than above because of the coarser overcasting.*

HOW TO TIE-DYE

EQUIPMENT: Large enamel or stainless steel basin. Wooden spoon for stirring fabric in dye. Rubber gloves. Old towels. Heavy mercerized thread. Pale-colored chalk for marking designs.

MATERIALS: Thin, soft white cotton, rayon, or silk fabric. Liquid fabric dyes.

GENERAL DIRECTIONS: Wash fabric before dyeing to shrink and remove sizing. Follow directions on package for dyeing, rinsing, and obtaining permanent colors.

Tie-dyeing may be combined with stitch-resistant dyeing to obtain effects desired. When using both together on one piece, the stitching of designs is done first; in between, areas may be tied out as desired. To obtain a clear pattern when dyeing, the tying and stitching must be very tight and firm. Measure and cut fabric before stitching and tying; afterwards, material is too bunched up. Various tie-dyeing techniques are illustrated on pages 162, 164, and 165.

Tie-Dyeing Fabric: Pull up the fabric, tent fashion, where patterns are desired. Wrap thread or twine around and around as tightly as possible at desired distance from pulled up end of fabric: knot to secure. The fabric under the tied areas will remain white after dyeing. Marbles, pebbles, bottle tops, clothespins, or wooden blocks may be tied into the fabric to give centers to design.

Stitch-Resistant Dyeing: Trace design on fabric with chalk and stitch it in with running or overcast stitch, depending on effect desired. Have thread double in needle, or use string; pull thread taut to gather fabric into tight puckers. Stitched areas will remain white.

Dyeing Method: In dyeing thin fabric, it is not necessary to mix a large amount of dye solution, as the fabric takes the dye easily. Wet fabric before dyeing; squeeze out excess moisture in a towel. Test colors with scraps of fabric first. Bring dye to a boil; remove from heat (or follow directions on package).

After tying or stitching in designs, dip fabric in dye solution. Simmer in dye bath to obtain shade of color desired. For a deeper color at center, leave only that portion of fabric in dye until desired depth of color is obtained. Color should be slightly darker than desired color as dyed fabric will dry a little lighter. The process of tying and dyeing may be repeated until results are satisfactory. For a design of more than one color, start with lightest color and proceed to darker colors. Light colors will mix with other colors to form new tints: a darker color will usually cover a light color. However, to avoid muddy shades, do not mix opposite colors—for example, blue and orange or red and green.

Bleaching: Certain color combinations cannot be obtained on the same article without bleaching; dark tied or stitched-out designs against a lighter body are also impossible without bleaching. When such combinations or effects are desired, use color remover between dyeings, following the package directions.

To obtain a tied- or stitched-out design in color, rather than a white design against a colored background, dye fabric in desired color, tie or stitch out design and bleach fabric. One may start with an already colored fabric instead of dyeing it; then tie or stitch out design and bleach fabric. Before attempting this method, be sure original color is removable by home methods; test a sample with color remover in advance.

The process of tying out and stitching out colored designs and bleaching may be repeated so that other colors and designs are obtained on the fabric, but no more than two bleachings of a given fabric are recommended.

Finishing: Rinse in cold water. Squeeze out excess moisture from fabric; roll in towel. Let dry partially; untie. Remove threads and stitching. Shake out fabric; let dry thoroughly. Do not worry about any unevenness of dyeing; this is desirable. Press fabric carefully.

NECKTIES

See "How To Tie-Dye" above; Tie-dyeing techniques for neckties are illustrated on page 162.

Blue-Green Tie with Circles: This fabric is a combination of Tying and Marbling. The fabric was first marked off with alternating rows of dots

8" apart. The fabric was pulled up at each dot and tied three times (see Tying Sample). Next the fabric was balled (see Marbling Sample) with center of fabric length on outside. Fabric was dipped in green dye, rinsed and untied. Then it was reballed with edges of fabric on outside and dipped in blue dye. After rinsing and untying
continued on page 168

Seven bright scarves in subtle abstract and geometric designs are created by using the ancient technique of tie-dyeing. The patterns are made by tying or stitching fabric, which makes these areas resistant to dye. Experiment with various tying and stitching for different effects. The scarves shown here are in an assortment of styles — large and small squares, rectangles, and triangle. Directions for Scarves are on page 168.

NECKTIES
continued from page 166

ball, each tied circle was dipped in blue dye.

Orange and Red Tie: Points of fabric were pulled up and tied (see Tying Sample) in a hit-or-miss fashion. Then entire piece of fabric was dipped in yellow dye, rinsed and squeezed dry. Next each tied circle was dipped in red dye with rest of the fabric held back out of dye. Then it was rinsed, squeezed dry, and untied.

Blue-Green Tie with Stripes: The fabric was folded in pleats and tied (see Folding Sample). It was then dipped·in green dye; rinsed and squeezed out. The ends were then dipped in blue dye before unfolding. Fabric was untied and re-folded in half and half again in opposite direction from first folding. Then just the folded edges were dipped in blue dye.

Three-Color Tie: The stitching was done with fabric flat, first overcasting the middle wavy lines (see Stitching Sample). A point of fabric was pulled up at each wide space between overcast lines and tied. The straight lines between colors were stitched with running stitch, pulled up tightly and tied tightly. The overcast red stripes were dyed first, then the purple, then the green. Between each dyeing, the parts not being dyed were tied up, wrapped in strip of plastic wrap held in place with rubber bands. After each dyeing, rinse and squeeze out.

SCARVES

See "How To Tie-Dye" on page 166 and illustrations for various tie-dyeing techniques on pages 162, 164, and 165. Cut fabric in planned shape first—square, oblong, or triangular. Plan design on fabric. Experiment with various tying and stitching for different effects.

A round clothespin used in the center of an area and tied around the head, then cross-tied along length, will produce a small solid-color center and allow some areas of remainder to be dyed.

On oblong scarves, tie or stitch across fabric at intervals for striped effect. For clear color stripes, tie all of fabric except for stripes of lightest color; dip in dye; tie light areas and untie other areas for next color; dip in next lightest color, and continue in this way to darkest stripes.

For white and one-color dyeing of rings and circles, tie a small or large object in center of each area. Then tie or stitch at intervals to make larger rings and dip in dye.

For solid-color circles, stitch around each circle and dip each area in a different color dye; dip remainder in a darker color for background, carefully holding dyed circles out of dye.

Diagonal designs may be made by folding square of fabric in quarters, then tying diagonally across.

Roll narrow hems around scarves and slip-stitch with matching thread.

Weaving

The worldwide art of weaving is so old that, in
basic technique, nothing really new has come to it
for hundreds of years. However, new ideas in weaving
designs continue to develop, and the weaver has now
broken free from tradition to create contemporary
items such as three-dimensional decorator hangings.
While the origin of weaving is as old as man, during
the nineteenth century machine weaving took over
the making of cloth, and hand weaving nearly became
a lost art in this country, with the exception of a
few rural areas. Fortunately, weaving became a "fad"
in the teens and twenties and continued to be fairly
popular until today. Now, it is staging an exciting
comeback and is one of the world's favorite crafts.
The fundamentals of weaving are to interlace threads
to form a fabric. In this book a few easy ways of doing
this are shown—some using simple looms you make
yourself; others give a sampling of what can be done
on a little inkle loom or a flat frame loom. For a
weaver to become truly creative he must master the
fundamental techniques; he needs an awareness of the
character of his materials—the softness, the
stiffness, the brightness or dullness of various yarns.
Here you are invited to explore a craft that has new
cultural values—having once been an economic
necessity, weaving has turned into a creative art!

Rich cork textures form background for these simple weavings worked over pins; use a variety of yarns, cords, or grasses in vibrant patterns, add pompons for dimension. This craft is a fascinating one for the sophisticated artist, creative fun for a child. Cork weavings, page 176. To make pottery with slab and coil methods, see How To Make Ceramics, page 42.

Children's miniature tapestries are woven on looms made of small styrofoam trays with the centers removed; the loom is left in place to frame the finished piece. Round designs are worked in spiral weave; pictures may be done in single technique or combination of tapestry weave, wrapped weave, and Ghiordes knot. For Tray Tapestries, see page 176.

TAPESTRY WEAVE

SPIRAL WEAVE

WRAPPED WEAVE

GHIORDES KNOT (OR TURKEY WORK)

1   2   1   2

Patterns for Tray Tapestries are given above in their actual size.

Cream-colored panel is easy to weave on three small looms made from styrofoam trays (centers removed). Varying weights and textures of yarn are used. Each section of the 15" tapestry has a different pattern, combining Ghiordes knot, wrapped weaving technique. The panel is finished with dowels, a looped fringe. Directions for Tray Tapestries given on page 176.

CORK WEAVINGS

EQUIPMENT: Scissors. Large-eyed tapestry needle.

MATERIALS: Pieces of cork 1½" thick (mainly used for insulation) or wallboard may be used. A variety of yarns in desired colors. Straight pins.

DIRECTIONS: The background cork can be any size desired; the size and shape of the cork will determine the size and shape of the woven piece. The beginner should select a small piece of cork about 7" to 9". After background is selected, push pins into top surface of cork at ¼" intervals, in a line at top and at bottom. The farther apart the pins are placed, the more likely the warp yarns will be covered with weft yarns. The warp yarns are those which run vertically, on which the weaving is worked; the weft yarns are those which are woven horizontally over and under the warp. Insert pins so that heads slant away from area where weaving is to be done; do not push pins all the way into cork. Tie beginning yarn to the top pin at upper left-hand corner, then move warp down to lower left-hand corner; wrap warp around the two lower pins, then move warp to the top and wrap around next two upper pins. Repeat this action until you end at lower right-hand corner. Yarn should be taut.

Begin weaving process. Thread the needle with piece of yarn about one yard long. Do a darning weaving stitch across bottom of warp, going alternately under and over the warp yarns. After each row has been woven, push the weft down with your fingers. The tighter the weft is pushed, the more tightly woven the fabric will be. If a loose effect is desired, it is not necessary to pack down the weft. When weaving is done, push pins all the way in.

A variety of weaves can be achieved by winding warp around one pin instead of two, alternately weaving over two and under two warps, or in groups of three and one, two and one, etc. To make slits and holes, bring yarn back to side after reaching place where hole is desired. Then weave from other side; leave area unwoven.

You can work out many weavings; experiment with combinations, ideas and designs. You can use such unusual materials as grass, cord, or paper to weave into the warp. Pompons or other objects can be pinned or tacked on for accents.

To make pompon, wind yarn around piece of cardboard desired number of times (width of cardboard and number of windings is determined by size and thickness of pompon desired). Tie windings together tightly at one edge of cardboard. Cut through loops at opposite edge; trim.

TRAY TAPESTRIES

EQUIPMENT: Tracing paper. Pencil. Large-eyed needle. Scissors. Ruler. Single-edged razor blade. Masking tape.

MATERIALS: Odds and ends of yarns in medium and light weights. Plastic produce trays 5¼" square, 4½" x 8¼" and 5¾" x 8¼" oblongs. Thin white cord.

DIRECTIONS: The plastic trays are used as weaving looms and may be left in place after weaving is complete, as picture frames. Four weaving techniques were used: tapestry weave, wrapped weave, and Ghiordes knot for pictures, and spiral weave for the round designs. Pictures may be worked in just one technique or a combination.

To Warp the Loom: With razor blade and ruler, mark and cut out center of plastic trays: 3 1/8" square on small trays; 2" x 5¾" on narrow oblong tray; and 3½" x 6 1/8" on wide oblongs. Across top and bottom inner edges, mark dots 3/8" from edge, 1/8" apart. Thread needle with a long piece of white cord for warp threads; knot end. Insert needle from back at first dot, bring cord across loom to opposite dot and insert needle to back for first vertical warp thread. Insert needle from back to front at next dot and bring cord across to opposite dot. Continue stretching warp threads across, using all dots, and making an uneven number of warp threads. Warp threads should be taut, but not so tight as to pull frame out of shape; knot end on back.

To Plan Design: Follow designs and colors shown, or make your own, or ad-lib designs as you weave. For a planned design, trace patterns given, or draw your own to fit open space of plastic tray. Color areas of pattern and tape design to underside of tray. Following design, weave across warp threads in chosen technique.

Tapestry Weave: This is a flat weave, going over and under each warp thread. On each row, alternate weaving over and under each warp thread (see the detail on page 174). Side edges are free of plastic frame. For the slit technique, when changing colors or yarns, weave one color to edge of area and work back and forth to fill area. For next color, start weaving on next warp thread and work back and forth on that area, thus creating an open slit between colors. If you wish to join the areas of color, weave both colors at edge of area around the same warp thread.

Wrapped Weave: Weaving yarn is anchored at one side on back with a knot and worked across in both directions, going through plastic tray at end of rows on each side. Make rows as close as possible without breaking plastic edge. Following detail 1 (shown on page 174), work across warp threads, wrapping yarn around warp loosely; be careful not to pull warp threads while weaving. Work back across, following detail 2. Continue in this manner, beginning and ending threads at side edges when convenient or through back of weaving when designs are being done.

Ghiordes Knot: This loop knot can be made long or short and left in loop form, or the loops may be cut for a fringe effect. Work across warp threads with yarn as shown in details 1 and 2 (on page 174), holding the loop to keep from pulling through. Make rows of loops close together.

Spiral Weave: On open area of plastic frame, stretch warp threads across from all four sides at fairly equal distances, making an uneven number, so they converge at center (see the detail on page 174); dash lines show where warp thread is carried under plastic. With weaving yarn, start at center and weave over and under warp threads, around in a spiral outward. Weaving may be kept close or spaced if desired for lacy effect. Start new colors as desired by running yarn under weaving on back. For off-center designs, space warp threads unevenly as desired, making them converge in area or areas planned; weave around each converging center.

The Wrapped Weave may also be used for making spiral designs, instead of the plain weave.

Ladybug Design: This was done entirely in Tapestry Weave with slits at sides of adjoining colors. Ladybug antennae, legs, spots, and center line are straight embroidery stitches.

Forest Scene: This is entirely Tapestry Weave, with slits between colors at sides.

Dragonfly: This one was done completely in Wrapped Weave, worked loosely back and forth. Where colors meet, make one or two wraps of each color on the same warp thread to avoid slits. Tail end is straight embroidery stitches.

Dandelion: Background, leaves and stems are Tapestry Weave with slits. Flowers are Ghiordes Knots with cut loops.

Other designs in frames are Spiral Weave or ad-lib blocks of Tapestry Weave or Ghiordes Knots.

Hanging Panel (shown page 175): Made on three small trays. Warp each tray by running the threads ½" over edge of top and bottom cutout area. Weave about eight rows of cord in plain Tapestry Weave; this will be removed when the tapestry piece is finished so that there will be ½" loops of the warp showing; leave ½" of warp at bottom free. After weaving is finished, break away the plastic tray frame from the weaving. Overcast top and bottom edges of weaving with small stitches and fine thread. Attach woven tapestries to ¼" pieces of stained dowel sticks 4½" long, by running cord through the warp loops of tapestry and around dowel. Attach the top piece and bottom piece each, in one operation with center piece, going through warp loops of adjoining pieces and around a dowel. Loop fringe may be knotted to bottom warp threads and a braided cord tied to top dowel for hanging panel.

Weave each square of panel differently, using a combination of Tapestry Weave with slits to separate different yarns, Wrapped Weave, and Ghiordes Knots. Panel shown was done in cream-color yarns of different weights and textures.

POT HOLDERS

EQUIPMENT: Scissors. Pencil. Large-eyed blunt yarn needle. Glue.

MATERIALS: For Looms: Plastic lids from large coffee, shortening, or other can, ½" larger in diameter than desired size of pot holder. Corrugated paper. Plain white paper. Thumbtacks, 34 red, 2 white. **For Pot Holders:** Rayon and cotton rug yarn, one 70-yard skein each of two colors for one pot holder (one skein each of three colors will make five pot holders). Plastic rings.

DIRECTIONS: To Make Loom: Place plastic lid on corrugated paper; draw around it. Cut out circle 1/8" inside pencil line (so that circle will fit inside lid). Make two white paper circles the same. Glue one to corrugated circle. Insert in lid, paper side first. Fold second paper circle in half as a guide for marking half-circle; place on lid, insert white tack in lid at each end of fold. Insert red tacks around lid edge, ½" apart, using same number on each side (tack edges should be about 1/8" apart).

To Wind Loom: Leave 3" end of yarn and wind yarn once around one white tack. Bring yarn around opposite white tack, then down around tack at left of starting point. Then go up around tack at right of white tack opposite. Repeat back and forth in this manner, winding clockwise, until all tacks are wound. At last tack, bring yarn to center and fasten securely with a stitch or two inside the crossed windings. All tacks have a double strand of yarn except first one, which has a single strand. This is the starting point or beginning of row.

To Weave: Thread needle with two yards of matching or contrasting yarn. Begin row 1 by inserting needle under single strand of yarn on loom; then go over first strand of next pair and under second strand of same pair. Repeat until row is completed. For row 2, bring needle over single strand, then weave under and over next pair of strands; repeat to end of row. Repeat these two rows alternately, weaving loosely. (End of weaving yarn at beginning of row 1 can be woven in later.) Keep rows even and use needle as you weave to push stitches close to center. Refer to illustrations on page 179.

To complete, continue weaving as long as possible, then remove tacks and work a few more rows. To change colors at any point, tie yarn strand on at beginning of row only; tuck ends of yarn underneath worked part to weave in later. Weave in all ends on back as invisibly as possible. Catch ring on edge of pot holder when weaving last row.

FLOWER PICTURE

SIZE: 36″ square.

EQUIPMENT: Soft wood board for working surface. Pushpins. Long, blunt, large-eyed needle. Sewing needle. Scissors. Ruler. Pencil. Paper for patterns. Compass. Straight pins.

MATERIALS: Aunt Lydia's Heavy Rug Yarn, 70-yard skeins: 2 skeins #229 Watermelon; 1 skein #251 Red; 2 skeins # 296 Chartreuse; 1 skein #293 Fern Green; 1 skein #245 Brown; 1 skein #250 Lilac; 1 skein #232 Medium Pink; 2 skeins #247 Cerise; 2 skeins #246 Folly Pink; 1 skein White. Sewing thread to match yarn. Turquoise burlap 45″ square. Turquoise Indian Head fabric 45″ square. Artist's wooden canvas stretchers, 2 pairs 36″ long. Staples.

DIRECTIONS: Enlarge patterns on page 183 for leaves, stems, and bud by copying on paper ruled in 1″ squares; complete half-patterns for oval and pointed leaves. Cut out patterns. On leaves, stem piece, and bud patterns, placement of pushpins is shown by dots. For round flowers, draw circles on paper with compass in following diameters: 11″, 9″, 8½″, 7½″. To determine the placement of pushpins on round patterns, fold circle in half twice to form quarters, then fold again to form eighths. Open out and mark the eighth lines on edge. On 11″ circle, mark four evenly spaced lines between each eighth mark—40 marks around. On 8½″ and 7½″ circles, mark three evenly spaced lines between each eighth mark, 32 marks around. For 9″ circle, fold paper only into quarters; then mark eight evenly spaced lines between each quarter line—36 marks around.

To make loom, place each pattern on wooden board. Push a pin into board at each mark around outside of pattern.

Round Flowers: To make warp threads, leave a 3″ end of yarn, and wind yarn once around top center pushpin. Bring yarn down across pattern to opposite pin, go around pin and bring yarn up across pattern and around pin at right of starting pin. Bring yarn down across pattern and around pin to left of first bottom pin. Repeat in this manner clockwise around pattern until all pins are wound. To have an uneven number of warp threads on loom, do not tie end of yarn around beginning pin, but bring it to center and take three or four stitches over crossed windings; leave end.

To weave, thread needle with two yards of matching or contrasting yarn. Begin round one about an inch from center, by inserting needle under the single strand of warp on loom; then go over first strand of next pair and under second strand of same pair. Repeat over and under warp strands. For round two, bring needle over single strand, then weave under and over all strands around. Repeat these two rounds, weaving loosely

continued on page 180

Colorful pot holders are an engrossing project for children. Let them construct the simple loom needed — a plastic coffee-can lid circled with thumbtacks — and weave a series of pot holders; bulky rug yarn makes the work go quickly for a satisfying sense of accomplishment. The small illustration shows loom, winding and weaving steps. Pot Holders, page 177.

FLOWER PICTURE
continued from page 178

so warp strands are not pulled out of line. Pack rounds close together, but do not pull weaving yarn, or flower will cup when it is removed from loom. Keep rounds even and use needle to push them close together toward center. End of weaving yarn can be run in later. Continue weaving as close to pins as possible for plain round flowers; then remove weaving from board. Run end of yarn in on back. To change colors at any point (see middle illustration on page 182), tuck end of new yarn underneath worked part to weave in later. Weave around with new color to fill warp. Weave all ends in on back of flower and clip off excess.

Long-Petaled Flowers: Start same as plain round flower; weave to within 2" of end of warp. To make petals, start at right of single warp strand. Place an extra pin between next two pins. Take warp strands from the pins on each side and place them over extra pin (see bottom illustration on page 182). Weave over and under the four warp strands on extra pin; then back under and over strands. Repeat on these four strands for about 1" then weave over two strands and under two to taper petal. Weave over and under two strands to pin. Remove petal from pin; weave yarn on back of petal down to beginning of petal and work next petal the same. Repeat petals all around in this manner. For last petal, use two strands from one pin; thread end of single warp strand in needle, bring end down to center and run it in and out of weaving on back to make double warp on last pin. Use these four strands to make petal.

Short-Petaled Flowers: Weave same as round flower to within 1" of end of warp. To make petals, weave over and under two warp strands from one pin. Continue weaving back and forth over two strands to pin; run yarn down back of petal and continue weaving on next two warp strands. Repeat around to last single warp. Use end of single warp to make a double warp as for Long-Petaled Flowers, and finish last petal.

Leaves: Using patterns, tie warp yarn around bottom pin; bring yarn around first pin up on left, then back down around bottom pin. Bring yarn up and around second pin to left and down around bottom pin again. Continue in this manner (as shown by short dash lines on pattern) around all pins up to top and then down right side. At bottom, take a few stitches over crossed strands to hold. To weave, thread two yards of yarn in needle; begin at left or right side 1" up from bottom pin. Weave over and under two strands of warp in a semicircular row to opposite side. Then weave over and under two strands back again (see top illustration on page 182). Continue weaving up to top center pin, pushing rows down as for round

pieces. Weave end of yarn in on back.

Background: Assemble canvas stretchers to make a 36" square frame. Place Indian Head fabric over canvas stretchers; stretch fabric tautly over frame and staple on back. Place burlap over fabric on frame. Insert tacks into sides temporarily while stretching; be sure threads of burlap are straight vertically and horizontally. Bring excess fabric to back and staple to back of canvas stretchers. Follow Diagram, page 183, for flower arrangement.

Make No. 1 flower 11" in diameter. Use Red warp and weave with Red for 4" circle. Then change to Watermelon and weave for 9" circle; finish with Short Petals.

Make No. 2 flower 8½" diameter. Use Lilac warp and weave with Lilac to 2¾" circle. Change to Cerise yarn and weave round flower.

Make No. 3 flower 8½" diameter. Use White warp; weave with White yarn to 3½" circle. Change to Folly Pink yarn and weave for 1"; finish with Long Petals.

Make No. 4 flower 7½" diameter. Use Lilac yarn for warp and weave with Lilac yarn for 3¼" circle. Change to Watermelon yarn and weave a round flower.

Make No. 5 flower 7½" diameter. Use Folly Pink yarn for warp and weave with Folly Pink to 3¼" circle. Change to Medium Pink yarn and weave round flower.

Make No. 6 flower 9" diameter. Use Red yarn for warp and weave with Red to 3½" cirlcle. Change to Cerise yarn and weave to 4¾" circle; finish with Long Petals.

Make No. 7 flower 8½" diameter. Use White yarn for warp and weave with White to 4" circle. Change to Folly Pink and weave round flower.

Make No. 8 flower 8½" diameter. Use Watermelon yarn for warp and weave with Watermelon yarn to 3¼" diameter circle. Change to Lilac yarn and weave to 5" circle; finish with Long Petals.

Make leaves No. 9 in pointed shape. Use Chartreuse yarn for warp and weaving.

Make leaves No. 10 in oval shape. Use Fern Green yarn for warp and weaving.

For bud No. 11, use pattern and make in two parts. Place warp threads horizontally across lower portion and vertically across upper portion (short dash lines on pattern, starting at x's). For lower portion use Folly Pink for warp and weaving. For upper portion, use Red for warp and weaving. Weave pieces together with Red yarn.

For stems No. 12, use pattern. Starting at x, place brown warp threads across base from side to side and across each stem from side to side as shown by short dash lines on pattern. With brown yarn, weave up and down length of stems into base. Make three more stems each 7" long.

Finishing: Place stems, leaves, and flowers on
continued on page 185

Eight giant blooms in dramatic hues are boldly stylized, give striking three-dimensional effect to a 36"-square picture. No special loom is needed; the flowers, stems, and leaves are woven separately over pushpins, then bouquet is appliquéd to a colorful burlap background, mounted on a canvas stretcher frame. The directions for Flower Picture start on page 178.

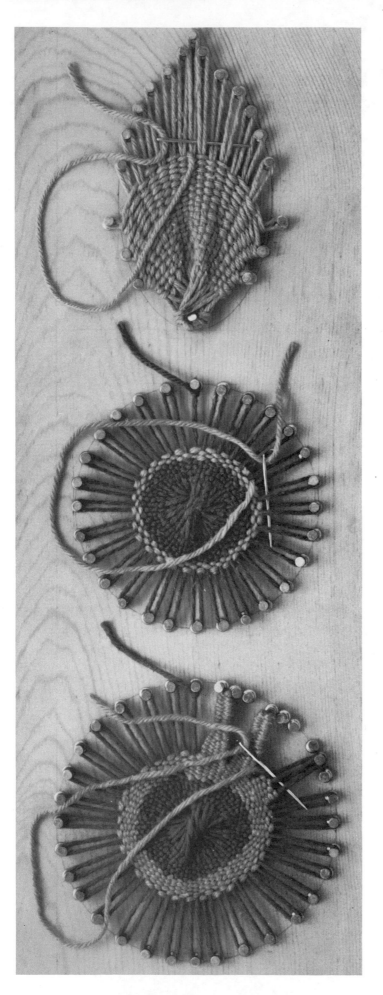

Weaving method is simple — pushpins are inserted into the soft board, then strung with rug yarn for the warp. Weave flowers in solid circles or with petaled edges for variety; use oval shape at top to form the leaves.

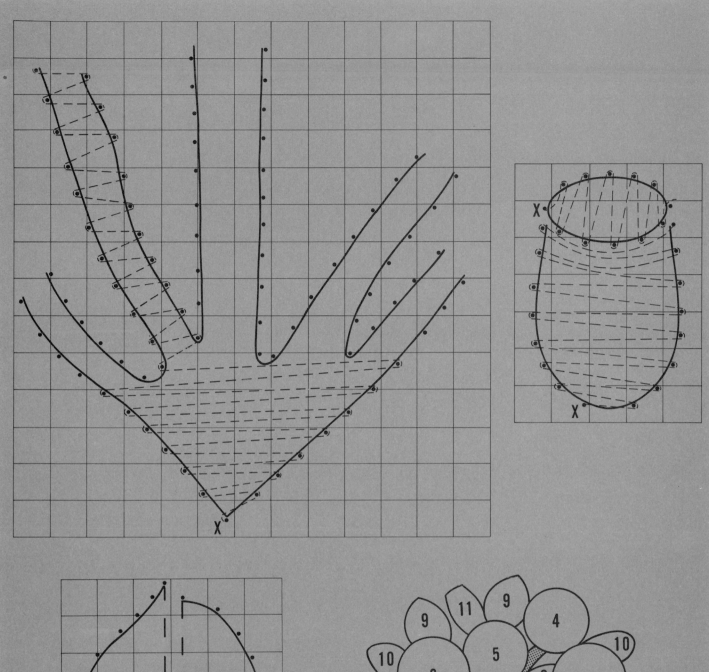

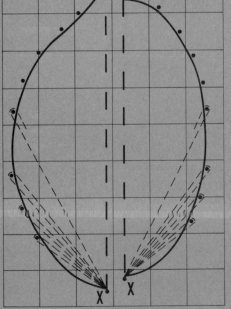

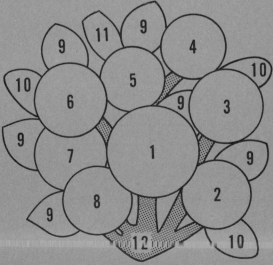

Flower Picture patterns for leaves, stem, and bud; to copy on paper ruled in 1″ squares. Diagram shows placement of pieces.

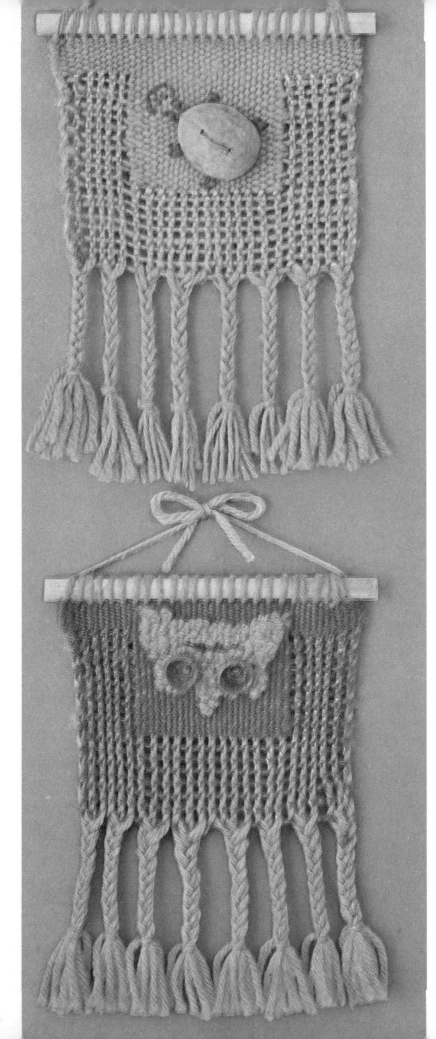

Nature's creatures inspire decoration for two charming little weavings. Hangings are fashioned on looms made from wooden picture frames, worked with knitting worsted and finished by braiding and tasseling warp ends and hanging from 6" dowels. See Little Hangings, opposite.

FLOWER PICTURE

continued from page 180

stretched burlap, following placement on diagram. Pin in position while arranging. With matching thread, sew each piece to stretched double fabric with straight stitches. Sew along both edges of stems. Sew leaves in place along both sides of center. Sew flowers in place, leaving petals and outer edge of round flowers free.

LITTLE HANGINGS

EQUIPMENT: Wooden picture frame 8″ x 9″. Brads ½″ long. Pencil. Ruler Hammer. Scissors. Steel crochet hook, No. 4. Comb. Rubber-tipped bobby pin. Drill with ¹⁄₁₆″ bit. Large-eyed and sewing needles. Tracing paper. Sandpaper.

MATERIALS: Dowel ⅜″ diameter, 6″ long for each. Small amounts of knitting worsted, 4-ply, in contrasting colors. Sewing thread. One-half walnut shell. Two acorn caps.

GENERAL DIRECTIONS: To make loom: With ruler, center and mark off 6½″ along top of picture frame, leaving a margin at sides. Mark off ¼″ divisions along 6½″ at top and bottom. Hammer a brad into frame at each mark. Leaving about 12″ of yarn at beginning and end, string yarn tightly around each brad as in Fig. 1. Begin at top of frame and end at top of frame. Secure ends by winding them around other brads. This is called the warp. The yarn which will be woven under and over the warp is called the weft. Be careful, when weaving, not to pull weft yarns too tightly. Push woven yarn together as closely as possible by pushing rows up with comb.

For weft, wind about seven yards of yarn around a book; remove from book and place a bobby pin through weft bundle at one end to hold. Start the first row of work ¼″ below top of hanging to leave room for insertion of dowel. Leave about 6″ of weft yarn at beginning to be worked in later. With bobby pin leading, weave weft bundle alternately over and under each warp strand for 14 rows. Keep unwinding yarn from weft bundle as needed.

The next type of weave is called leno. To work it, cross the second warp strand over the first, then insert weft. Do this with the first 12 strands and last 12 strands (six pairs each) of warp and work plain weave as above (under and over each warp thread) in center area. Work three rows of plain weave for each row of leno. Continue until you have woven 12 rows of leno combined with plain weave in center. Now weave eight rows of plain leno. Leaving 6″ of weft yarn after last row, cut off extra yarn.

Trace patterns for turtle and owl; complete half-pattern indicated by dash lines. Decorate each hanging as indicated below in individual directions.

After decorating, cut warp threads across at bottom to make them 5½″ long from last row of leno weave. Remove work from frame. Braid warp yarns together, using six strands in three pairs for each braid; however, the center two braids and last braid will have seven strands each because of the extra 6″ of weft you will incorporate in the last braid. Tie each braid with a matching piece of yarn; trim.

Sand dowel ends. Insert dowel through loops at top. To make hanger, tie warp ends at top together.

TURTLE: Drill two holes in center of half walnut shell. Sew shell through holes to center area of hanging, allowing room for stitching. Following illustration and pattern, embroider head and four legs in backstitch.

OWL: Using pattern, mark outline of owl head on hanging. Fill in owl head area with short Turkey work loops (also known as Ghiordes Knot; see detail on page 174), leaving shaded areas unfilled. Drill hole in center of each acorn cap. Knot sewing thread and insert through hole in cap from concave to convex side; sew to head for eye. Repeat for other eye.

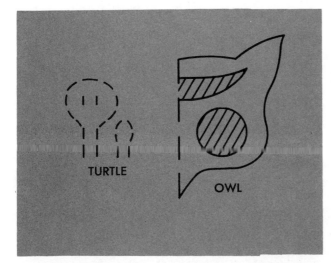

Actual-size patterns to embroider Little Hangings.

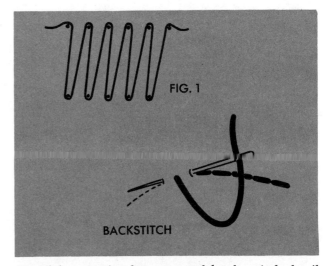

Detail for warping loom around brads; stitch detail.

WEAVING SAMPLER

SIZE: 1 yd. x 3½ yds.

EQUIPMENT: Inkle loom. Flat frame loom 15" x 20". Tape measure. Scissors. Large blunt needle. Sewing needle. Large crochet hook. Paper for sun pattern. Ruler. Pencil. Hammer. Small, flat paintbrush. Fork.

MATERIALS: Yarns: Aunt Lydia's Heavy Rug Yarn for warp; Bear Brand yarn, various types, for weft (see individual directions for colors and types of yarn). Sewing thread to match yarns. **For Sun:** Heavy cardboard circle, 12" diameter; wooden dowels ¼" diameter, 14 feet. **For Background:** White duck 36" wide, 3½ yards. Spray starch. Clear pine, four pieces 1" x 2", 36" long. Wood stain. Eight small nails. All-purpose glue. Two screw eyes. Picture wire for hanging.

GENERAL DIRECTIONS: Each piece is woven separately, lined, and assembled later on the white duck background. The long pieces are made on the inkle loom, the remainder on a simple frame loom.

Follow instructions that come with looms for warping the loom. Use Aunt Lydia's Heavy Rug Yarn for the warp on all pieces, in colors given in individual directions. See Fig. 1, page 190, for identifying woven pieces and for arranging them.

For weaving, follow individual directions for patterns, type and color of yarn. Wind weft yarn (weaving yarn) on a shuttle and follow the directions that come with loom for weaving.

Many of the pieces are plain, or tabby, weave, or start with two rows of tabby weave for the heading. Tabby is weaving with the weft yarn, over one warp thread and under one warp thread across; for return row, weave over and under alternate warp threads. When weaving back and forth, be careful to leave weft yarn loose enough at sides of warp so that warp will stay vertically straight and not become pulled in at sides.

Tapestry weave (see detail on page 174) is the same as tabby, but weft threads are packed close together so that no warp shows.

To follow the weaving charts (page 190) for other patterns, weave over a warp thread for each black square shown on chart, and under a warp thread for each blank square. Each row of squares represents one weft across.

On the frame loom, pack the first 1" of weaving very tightly so that the warp loops will be filled when the piece is removed from loom. Remove finished woven piece and use a large needle to push the weft yarn evenly in place on the warp end loops. To fill frame fully at opposite end, after weaving about two-thirds of the way, start at opposite end of loom and weave rows, working toward center to meet previous weaving. Weave yarn ends in on back. After weaving is removed from loom, use sewing thread to stitch through warp threads behind weaving to secure ends across top and bottom edges.

On inkle loom, be sure to keep warp threads evenly spaced throughout, and measure the width continuously while weaving. Use a fork as a beater to push weaving strands close together. To finish woven piece, trim warp threads at each end to 1½" and run in on back of weaving, or leave longer ends for fringe.

Piece 1: Made on inkle loom with rug yarn #250 Lilac for warp, and Bear Brand Winsom, Jubilee Jade #324 for weft.

Warp loom with 17 threads, making them 5¾" wide. Weave in plain tabby for 26". Trim and run warp ends in on back.

Piece 2: Made on frame loom with rug yarn #219A Light Jade for warp, and Bear Brand Winsom, Jubilee Jade #324 for weft.

Warp loom with 35 threads (11¼" wide) and weave in plain tabby for 4¼". Cut off warp threads on top edge, leaving 1½" long for fringe.

Piece 3: Made on frame loom with rug yarn #296 Chartreuse for warp, and Bear Brand Supra Mohair, Kelly Green #8 for weft.

Warp loom with 9 threads (3" wide) and weave in tabby, loosely packed (8-9 threads to 1") for 12". Cut off warp threads on top edge, leaving fringe 2" long.

Piece 4: Made on frame loom with rug yarn #296 Chartreuse for warp, and Bear Brand Supra Mohair, Kelly Green #8 for weft.

Warp loom with 11 threads (4" wide). Weave in tabby with double mohair yarn, closely packed for 11". Cut off warp threads on top edge, leaving fringe 3¼" long.

Piece 5: Made on inkle loom with rug yarn #296 Chartreuse for warp, and Bear Brand Wool and Shetland, Lime Twist #233 for weft.

Warp loom with 5 threads (2" wide) and weave 28½" in tabby. Trim warp threads in on top edge and run in on back. On other end, cut warp threads off leaving fringe 4" long.

Pieces 6A and 6B: Made on frame loom with rug yarn #229 Watermelon for warp, and Bear Brand DeLuxe Knitting Worsted, Dusty Rose #338 for weft.

Make both pieces the same on frame loom. Warp loom for each with 11 threads (3½" wide) and weave in checker pattern following Fig. 6. Start with two rows of tabby, then weave across following diagram; the 22 rows of diagram are one complete pattern. Repeat pattern completely again, then repeat first nine rows; end with two rows of tabby (4" long). Cut warp threads on one edge, leaving fringe 2" long.

Piece 7: Made on frame loom with rug yarn #250 Lilac for warp, and Bear Brand Winsom, Jubilee Jade #324 for weft.

Warp loom with six threads (1¾" wide). Start with two rows of tabby weave. Then weave rib pattern, following Fig. 8 across; repeat pattern to make piece 12″ long. Cut off warp threads on top edge, leaving 6″ long fringe.

Piece 8: Made on frame loom with rug yarn #250 Lilac for warp, and Bear Brand Winsom, Jubilee Jade #324 for weft.

Warp loom with five threads (1¾″ wide). Start with two rows of tabby; then follow Fig. 9 for overshot weaving pattern, repeating pattern for 18¾″ (entire length of loom). For fringe at one end, run in ends of five 8″ pieces of rug yarn.

Piece 9: Made on inkle loom with rug yarn #229 Watermelon for warp, and Bear Brand Win-Sport, Rosy Pink, #338 for weft.

Warp loom with 12 threads of rug yarn (3¾″ wide). Use weft thread double throughout, and pack rows loosely. Start piece with two rows of tabby weave from left to right, then back to left. Start weaving twill pattern from left to right following Fig. 11, repeating each row across. Repeat the four rows of pattern to make piece 32″ long. Weave in ends of warp threads on one end; cut warp threads on other end, leaving 4″ fringe.

Piece 10: Made on frame loom with rug yarn #250 Lilac for warp, and Bear Brand Wool and Shetland Wool, Pickle Pepper #349 for weft.

Warp loom with 12 threads of rug yarn (3½″ wide); use weft yarn double throughout and pack yarn loosely. Start weaving with two rows of tabby from left to right, then back to left. Start weaving herringbone pattern from left to right, following Fig. 12; repeat the four rows of pattern to make piece 11½″ long. Cut off warp threads at one edge, leaving fringe 2″ long.

Piece 11: Made on frame loom with rug yarn #229 Watermelon for warp, and Bear Brand DeLuxe Knitting Worsted, Dusty Rose, #338 for weft.

Warp loom with 21 threads of rug yarn (7″ wide). Start piece with three rows of tabby from right to left, left to right, then back to left. Have all warp threads flat for doing the Soumak stitch. Start Soumak stitch (See Fig. 2A) from left to right, going over three warp threads and back under two; repeat across. Make second row from right to left (see Fig. 2B). Then work five rows of tabby, and make two more rows of Soumak. Continue alternating tabby and Soumak for 7¼″, making 10 groups; end with three rows of tabby. Cut off warp threads on one end, leaving 1″ fringe.

Piece 12: Made on inkle loom with rug yarn #219A Light Jade for warp, and Bear Brand Wool and Shetland, Pickle Pepper #349 for weft.

Warp loom with 12 threads of rug yarn (4″ wide). Weave 18 rows of tabby; leave ½″ space on warp and weave two rows of tabby; leave ½″ space and weave 10 rows of tabby; leave ½″ space and weave 2 rows of tabby. Repeat from beginning, making open weave piece 28¾″ long. Cut and weave warp ends in on one edge; cut

warp ends on other edge, leaving 4″ fringe.

Piece 13: Made on inkle loom with rug yarn #296 Chartreuse for warp, and Bear Brand Wool and Shetland Lime Twist #233 and Pickle Pepper #349 for weft.

Warp loom with 9 threads (3¼″ wide). Weave two rows of tabby with Lime Twist, from left to right then back to left. Begin overshot square pattern only (arrowed section), Fig. 10, using Pickle Pepper; work over three warp threads in direction of arrows for six rows. Then work next set of six in opposite direction. Weave overshot square pattern for about 7″. Then with Lime Twist, weave in tabby all the way across warp, going under overshot pattern on each row. Continue weaving tabby to fill around checker pattern. Weave strip in this manner for 27″. Cut warp ends on one edge and weave into back. Cut warp ends on other edge, leaving 4″ fringe.

Piece 14: Made on frame loom with rug yarn #219A Light Jade for warp, Bear Brand Wool and Shetland, Lime Twist #233 for weft overlay, and Supra Mohair, Kelly Green #8 for brocade.

Warp entire loom (35 threads) with rug yarn. With Lime Twist, weave two rows tabby; following Fig. 13 for overlay pattern, weave across first row disregarding arrow lines. Using Kelly Green for brocade areas, weave over and under same warp threads of first five threads. With a separate strand of Kelly Green weave each brocade pattern between overlay patterns, as indicated by arrow lines on diagram. Weave second row of overlay pattern with Lime Twist. Weave brocade patterns back with Kelly Green. Continue for seven rows. Weave five rows of tabby with Kelly Green.

Repeat overlay-brocade and five rows of tabby for 15½″, ending with five rows of tabby (14 patterns). Leave a space on warp threads at right, the equivalent of two patterns (about 2″) and 9″ wide. Continue weaving pattern up left side for two repeats; then weave all the way across to fill loom.

Piece 15: Made on frame loom with rug yarn #229 Watermelon for warp, and Bear Brand Win-Sport, Rosy Pink #338 for weft.

Warp entire loom (35 threads) with rug yarn. Weave 1″ of tabby tightly packed. Divide warp threads into groups of 7 for slit tapestry; to hold the groups separate, tie a piece of yarn loosely around each group. Weave plain, back and forth on each group, attaching separate weft yarn for each group, see Fig. 3; weave for 20 rows (2½″). Remove dividing ties. Divide warp threads again into groups of 5, 2, 2, 3, 2, 2, 3, 2, 2, 3, 2, 2, 5 and tie each group. Weave each group separately for 20 rows. Divide warp strands again into groups of 5, 4, 3, 4, 3, 4, 3, 5; weave each group separately for 6¾″. Finish top half same as
continued on page 188

bottom, reversing the sequence, to fill entire loom.

Piece 16: Made on frame loom with rug yarn #229 Watermelon for warp, and Bear Brand Win-Sport, Rosy Pink #338 and DeLuxe Knitting Worsted Dusty Rose #338 for weft.

Warp entire loom (35 threads) with rug yarn. With knitting worsted, weave 1″ of tabby tightly packed (2″ finished when removed from loom). Following Fig. 7, continue weaving tabby, leaving spaces on warp threads the sizes indicated (vertical lines in spaces indicate warp threads). On right-hand column of spaces, weave tabby over middle warp threads as indicated by heavy outline, using Win-Sport yarn. Fig. 7 is half of piece; repeat in reverse to top of loom; weave 1″ of tabby tightly packed.

Using Win-Sport yarn, work flossa on warp threads of left-hand spaces. To do flossa, wind yarn around a 2″ wide length of cardboard and cut strands along one edge, making 4″ long pieces of yarn. Knot each strand around warp thread, Fig. 4, using a crochet hook to draw strand ends through loop; pull ends to tighten knot. On 2¼″ spaces, place about 16 knots on each warp thread and also on the two side warps over edge of tabby weave. On the 2″ spaces, place about 12 knots on each warp and at edge of tabby.

Piece 17: The sun is made on frame loom with rug yarn #226 Orange for warp; Bear Brand DeLuxe Knitting Worsted, Apricot Brandy #91 for background circle, Orange #56 for rays and center circle; Bucilla Strawtex Pumpkin #49 and Orange #19 for flossa fringe on center of sun.

Warp entire loom (35 threads) with rug yarn. Enlarge sun pattern on page 190 by copying on paper ruled in 1″ squares. Retrace quarter-pattern, flopping it over and matching dash lines, to make complete circle. Tape pattern to underside of loom, right side up, to follow when weaving. Weave center circle in plain tabby, loosely packed. Weave remainder of sun, using Apricot for background and Orange for rays. Dark vertical lines on pattern indicate slits in weave (Fig. 3, separating colors). The straight diagonal lines of rays are joined on the same warp thread (Fig. 5) when changing colors from ray to background.

When tapestry weaving is complete, the center circle is filled with flossa, using Strawtex in Pumpkin and Orange; make flossa fringe as for Piece 16. Outline circle with a round of Pumpkin, knotting pieces about ¼″ apart. Fill in center with Orange flossa.

Cut warp ends around top and bottom of circle and weave ends into back; tack securely with thread. Glue sun to cardboard circle.

continued on page 194

Modern sampler, planned to give beginner experience in ancient art of weaving, makes a fascinating wall collage. The eighteen individual patterns are woven on inkle and flat-frame looms, then assembled on a 36″ x 89″ panel. The "fabrics" are worked in interesting blends of colors and textures in a variety of yarns. Directions for Weaving Sampler on page 186.

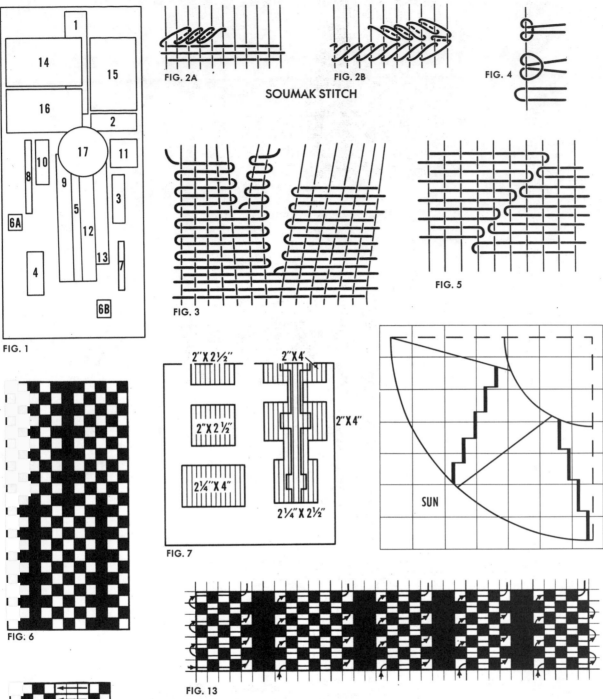

SOUMAK STITCH

FIG. 2A   FIG. 2B   FIG. 4

FIG. 1

FIG. 3

FIG. 5

2" X 2½"   2" X 4'

2" X 2½"

2" X 4"

2¼" X 4"

2¼" X 2½"

SUN

FIG. 7

FIG: 6

FIG. 13

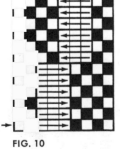

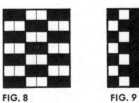

FIG. 10   FIG. 8   FIG. 9

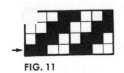

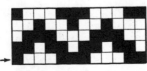

FIG. 11   FIG. 12

Ten swatches, shown actual size, give a sampling of the variety possible in handweaving. Areas of light and shade, as well as color combinations, are an important part of the finished design. Swatches in the first row, left to right, are woven on 7"-wide inkle loom; swatches in second and third rows are worked on a frame loom, 15" x 20". The patterns shown are:

A—Rib Weave   F—Checker Pattern
B—Plain Weave   G—Brocade
C—Overshot Pattern   H—Open Weave
D—Soumak   I—Overshot Square
E—Herringbone Twill J—Twill

Inkle loom weaving produces an infinite variety of narrow strips. Use singly or group for a wall hanging; tie or add buckle for belt. Strips illustrated here are in plain tabby or modifications of tabby weave; different textures, harmonious colors add interest. Woven Belts and Strips, page 194.

WEAVING SAMPLER
continued from page 188

Cut 32 pieces of dowel 5″ long. For each dowel, cut 6 pieces of Orange Strawtex 4″ long. Fold each piece in half; place around one end of dowel and tape in place. Wrap each dowel with one layer of knitting worsted to cover, alternating Orange and Apricot Brandy as shown and covering ends of Strawtex; knot and glue ends. On back of cardboard sun, space the dowels evenly around edge, leaving 3½″ of dowel extending. Glue and tape dowels in place. Punch two holes through center of cardboard sun, ½″ apart, for attaching to background.

Finishing: For background, cut piece of duck 36″ wide, 2½ yards long. Stain the four pieces of pine and let dry. At each end of duck background, glue the duck between two pieces of pine. Nail the pine pieces together from the back with four small nails evenly spaced across.

Steam-block each woven piece (except Sun), by pinning out to shape on a padded surface, making sure corners are square; steam lightly and let dry.

For each woven piece (except Sun), cut a piece of duck fabric 1/8″ smaller all around than weaving. Spray starch on each piece and press smooth. With matching thread and running stitch, sew each woven piece to matching duck piece all around edges. Tack through center wherever necessary to keep flat. On open work pieces, sew edges of openings to duck. Arrange lined pieces on duck background, following Fig. 1. Sew each piece in place, tacking where necessary. Attach Sun by tying through duck and holes in cardboard with rug yarn. For hanging, attach screw eyes at each side on back of top pine piece and stretch picture wire between.

WOVEN BELTS AND STRIPS

EQUIPMENT: Inkle loom. Scissors. Ruler or measuring tape. Blunt tapestry needle.

MATERIALS: See individual directions for yarns.

GENERAL DIRECTIONS: Warp loom following directions that come with it. To begin, weave three or four rows of heavy scrap yarn, to be removed later. Width of work is given at beginning of individual directions; make sure that this width is maintained throughout the weaving process. Trim all beginning and last ends of weft threads to 1″ unless otherwise specified; when work is completed, run ends in on back. Steam-press.

BROWN, RUST, AND GOLD: Materials: One skein each rust, brown, and dark gold heather-type fine yarn.

Directions: Warp loom, using following sequence: 4 brown, 2 rust, 6 brown, 2 rust, 6 brown, 2 rust, 4 brown. Width of hanging is 3½″.

Weaving is plain tabby or tapestry (see detail on page 174), using different color yarn for weft for each new pattern. Patterns of unwoven warp threads are interspersed among the plain weave. Certain threads are left unwoven by continually passing under them with weft thread, row after row, for as many rows as desired.

Basic patterns, which may be varied as desired, are given below. For example, vary number of warp threads remaining unwoven. Vary number of rows and color in which patterns are woven. Be sure to leave ample number of rows of plain tabby weave between patterns. Begin and end weaving with several rows of plain weave in each color.

Pattern A: Using rust as weft, weave six rows of plain weave across all warp threads. Weave six more rows, leaving four brown threads unwoven on each side; pass shuttle under brown threads and over rust threads of bottom layer. Weave seven rows plain across all warp threads, using brown for weft.

Pattern B: Using gold for weft, weave for 1½″, leaving six threads on each side unwoven and passing shuttle over brown and under rust of bottom layer.

Pattern C: Using gold for weft, weave for 1¾″, passing shuttle under twelve brown center threads of bottom layer.

Pattern D: Using brown for weft, weave for 1″, passing shuttle over brown threads and under rust threads of bottom layer. Using rust for weft, weave six rows, passing shuttle over all six rust threads and under all center brown threads. Repeat first 1″ of pattern, using brown for weft.

Pattern E: Using rust for weft, weave seven rows plain across all warp threads. Using gold, weave plain for about ¾″ on six threads at each side, leaving center fourteen threads unwoven. Using rust for weft, weave seven rows plain across all warp threads.

Pattern F: Using brown for weft, weave six rows, passing over brown and under rust threads of bottom layer. Using rust, weave three rows plain. Using brown, weave eight rows, passing over brown and under rust threads of bottom layer. Using rust, weave three rows plain. Using brown, weave ten rows, passing shuttle over brown and under rust threads of bottom layer. * Using rust, weave thirteen rows, leaving two threads on each side unwoven, and passing shuttle over brown and under rust threads of bottom layer.* Weave four rows plain across all except rust warp threads. Repeat from * to *. Weave four rows plain across all except rust threads. Repeat from * to *.

Pattern G: Using gold for weft, weave twelve rows plain. Using rust, pass shuttle over rust and under brown threads of bottom layer for five rows. Using gold, weave four rows plain across all warp threads. Repeat four rows plain weave four times, using rust, gold, rust, gold for weft. Using rust, pass shuttle over rust and under brown threads of bottom layer for four rows. Using gold, weave four rows plain across all warp threads.

Pattern H: Using brown as weft, weave two rows plain across all warp threads. Weave eight rows, passing shuttle over brown and under rust threads of bottom layer. Weave two rows plain across all warp threads. Weave thirteen rows, passing shuttle over brown and under rust of bottom layer.

Finishing: Remove weaving from loom. **Top:** Divide threads into groups according to color. Tie an overhand knot (see page 76) with each group of brown close to weaving; tie two more overhand knots 1½" apart. Bring two outside pairs of rust threads to center, passing them over brown groups, and, treating each pair as one thread, begin a braid 1" from edge of weaving. Continue braiding for about 6". Tie an overhand knot with each center brown group near end of braid. Tie an overhand knot with rust thread around remaining threads 1" from braid. Tie rust thread into hanging loop; trim ends to 1".

Bottom: Trim fringe to 5"; form arc with bottom rust weft thread by pulling gently.

ORANGE, RUST, AND OLIVE: Materials: Knitting worsted: one skein each rust and orange. Rug yarn: one skein olive. One metal house number 0, 4" long at widest point (available at hardware stores). Glue.

Directions: Warp loom, using 21 threads of orange yarn, making width 3". Belt is woven in stripes of plain tabby weave, using orange and olive for weft, and a variation of tabby weave, using rust weft.

Using olive for weft, begin from right side, making sure outside warp threads are down. Weave seven rows plain.

Rust pattern: Using rust for weft, weave ten rows as follows: Rows 1, 3, 5, 7, 9: plain weave. Rows 2, 4, 6, 8, 10: (outside warp threads must be down) pass shuttle over first outside warp thread of bottom layer, under next bottom warp thread, over the next; continue in this manner across warp threads, ending by passing shuttle over last thread of bottom layer. Beat weft tightly into place.

Using orange for weft, weave five rows plain, beating weft ends tightly into place. Rust pattern: ten rows. Orange: ¾". Olive: seven rows, beating weft ends loosely into place. Rust: nine rows plain. Orange: four rows plain. Rust: nine rows plain. Continue weaving, repeating arrangement above or designing your own arrangement, for length desired; length of original is 28".

Finishing: Remove weaving from loom. Trim one end to 9"; divide ends into six pairs with a group of three at each side and at center. Knot ends of groups with an overhand knot (see page 76) close to last row of weaving. Repeat with other end. Wrap number 0 with rust yarn; conceal ends by tucking in and gluing in place. Thread fringe of one end through covered number from front to back; divide ends into four groups. Pull two center groups around side of number and through space between weaving and number at center, from back to front. Bring outside groups around sides and tie each with an inside group using an overhand knot.

LAVENDER AND BLUE: Materials: One skein each lavender and blue knitting worsted. For hanging, one blue painted dowel 4½" x 3/8".

Directions: Warp loom using following sequence: 10 lavender, 9 blue, 10 lavender. Piece is 3¾" wide and about 60" long, without fringe. Design is composed of plain tabby weave, interspersed with patterns of unwoven warp threads. Basic patterns are given below. If desired, patterns can be varied; for example: vary number of center and side warp threads left unwoven. Vary number of rows and color in which pattern is woven. Vary the number of times pattern is repeated in sequence. Begin and end weaving with several rows plain weave, using blue for weft.

Pattern A: Weave eleven rows, using lavender for weft. **Odd-numbered rows:** (Outside warp threads are in down position.) Plain weave. **Even-numbered rows:** Pass shuttle under first 2 warp threads, over next 2, under next 2, over 3, under 2, over 2, under 2 threads of top layer.

Pattern B: Using blue for weft, weave seventeen rows. **Odd-numbered rows:** (Outside threads are up.) Pass shuttle under first 3 warp threads, over next 2, under next 5, over next 2, under last 3 threads of top layer. **Even-numbered rows:** Pass shuttle under first 3, over next 2, under 4, over 2, under last 3 warp threads of top layer.

Pattern C: Using lavender for weft, weave 29 rows, passing shuttle over all lavender and under all blue warp threads of bottom layer.

Pattern D: Using lavender for weft, weave nine rows. **Odd-numbered rows:** (Outside warp threads are up.) Pass shuttle over all lavender and under all blue threads of top layer. **Even-numbered rows:** Weave plain. Using blue for weft, weave seven rows, passing shuttle under all lavender and over all blue warp threads of top layer for odd-numbered rows and weaving plain for even-numbered rows. Repeat first part of pattern, using lavender for weft.

Pattern E: Using lavender for weft, weave five rows plain on nine blue center threads. Using blue for weft, weave ten rows plain on nine blue threads. Repeat first part of pattern, using laven-
continued on page 198

Colorful narrow strips can be woven on inkle loom by adult or child, combined and appliquéd in many ways to make handsome gifts. These three pillows show methods of creating a design; ends may be turned under or over, strips sewn on diagonally. The fringed pillows are 13¼" square; the diagonal pillow is 14¾" x 7½". See Woven Band Pillows, page 199.

der for weft.

Pattern F: Using blue for weft, weave 22 rows, leaving six threads on each side unwoven. **Odd-numbered rows:** (Outside threads are in down position.) Pass shuttle over first 2 threads, under next 4, over last 2 threads of top layer. **Even-numbered rows:** Weave plain, leaving six threads on each side unwoven. Using lavender for weft, weave five rows plain on nine blue threads. Using blue for weft, repeat first part of pattern for nine rows. Weave five rows plain on blue threads using lavender for weft. Using blue for weft, repeat first part of pattern for sixteen rows.

Pattern G: Using lavender for weft, weave six rows plain. * Weave 12 rows, passing shuttle over lavender and under blue threads of bottom layer. Leave outside lavender threads unwoven for ½". Repeat from * three times. Weave 13 rows, passing shuttle over lavender and under blue warp threads of bottom layer. Weave six rows plain across all warp threads. Using lavender for weft, weave 15 rows plain on unwoven blue center threads four times, about ½" apart.

Pattern H: Using blue for weft, * weave six rows, passing shuttle over first 2, under next 3, over all blue, under next 3, over last 2 warp threads of bottom layer.* Weave four rows across all warp threads. Repeat from * to *. Weave four rows across all warp threads. Repeat * to * for twenty rows.

Pattern I: a) Using blue for weft, weave six rows, leaving 4 threads at each side unwoven. Weave nine rows on center blue threads, leaving all lavender threads unwoven. Beat weft very tightly into place. Repeat first part of the pattern. **b)** Using lavender for weft, weave 12 rows. **Odd-numbered rows:** (Outside threads are down.) Pass shuttle over first 2, under next 3, over next 5, under 3, over last 2 warp threads of bottom layer. **Even-numbered rows:** Pass shuttle over first 2, under next 3, over 4, under next 3, over last 2 warp threads of bottom layer. **c)** Weave 16 rows, using lavender for weft and leaving 4 threads at each side unwoven. Begin close to blue weft. First row: (outside threads are down) Weave plain tabby; this row should curve upwards at center, **Remainder of odd-numbered rows:** Pass shuttle over lavender and under blue threads of bottom layer.

Even-numbered rows: Pass shuttle over first 3, under next 4, over last 3 threads of bottom layer. Sixteenth row should curve downward at center, almost touching first row.

Repeat b, c, b, omitting last row from last b repeat.

Pattern J: * Using blue for weft, weave fourteen rows across all warp threads. **Odd-numbered rows:** (Outside threads are down.) Pass shuttle over first 2, under next 3, over blue threads, under next 3, over last 2 threads of bottom layer. **Even-numbered rows:** Weave same as odd-numbered rows. * Weave two rows plain across all threads. Using lavender for weft, weave four rows, leaving four threads at each side unwoven. Pass shuttle over first 3, under all blue, over last 3 threads of bottom layer. Beat so last two rows of blue weft curve downward when woven on lavender warp and upward at center. Weave two rows plain across all warp threads, using blue for weft and beating weft so the two rows curve upwards when woven on lavender warp and downwards at center. Repeat from * to *

Pattern K: Using blue as warp, weave five rows. **Odd-numbered rows:** (Outside warp threads are in down position.) Pass shuttle under first 2, over next 3, under 4, over 3, under last 2 threads of top layer. **Even-numbered rows:** Pass shuttle under 3, over 2, under 5, over 3, under last 2 threads of top layer. * Weave seven rows plain across all warp threads, passing shuttle under blue threads for all rows. Repeat * to *, curving downward to weave close to first weaving on center blue threads. Weave eight rows on blue center threads, leaving all lavender threads unwoven, using blue for weft.

Finishing Belt: Remove weaving from loom. Cut ends to 6"; divide into groups of five and tie knot with each group close to last row of weaving.

Wall Hanging: Finish as for belt. Fold fringe of one end over dowel, ends to back, and tie ends of groups to beginning of groups close to weaving with short lengths of blue yarn at back. Cut an 8" long piece of blue yarn; fold in half; tie one end to each end of dowel for hanging loop.

RED, ORANGE, AND BLACK: Materials: Lily Carpet Warp (Crochet Cotton): one skein each red, orange, and black.

Directions: Warp loom using the following sequence: 2 red, 1 orange (4 times); 2 red, 2 orange; 1 red, 2 orange (6 times); 7 red; 1 black, 2 red (6 times); 1 black. Repeat red, orange sequence in reverse. Make width 3".

Using red for weft, weave across warp threads according to loom directions. Take care to pull weft thread through warp threads tightly enough so weft thread is visible at side edges only.

Weave first six rows in a plain tabby weave.

Pattern: Pattern involves going under certain black warp threads with the weft thread, rather than over them as would normally occur in the course of weaving a tabby weave. Remainder of warp threads, including other black threads, are woven normally. Row 7: Weft thread (shuttle) under black warp threads five, six and seven. Row 8: Four, five, six. Row 9: Three, four, five. Row 10: Two, three, four. Row 11: One, two, three. Row 12: One, two. Row 13: One, two, three. Row 14: Two, three, four. Row 15: Three, four, five. Row 16: Four, five, six. Row 17: Five, six, seven. Row 18: Six, seven.

Repeat pattern 24 times. Tie black warp threads together with an overhand knot (see page 76) close to work. Continue weaving for about 2″, adjusting for the absence of black warp threads by dividing 14 center red threads into seven pairs and treating each pair as a single warp thread.

Finishing: Remove weaving from loom. Divide warp threads and weft thread at each end into groups for braids as follows: Beginning end will have 101 warp threads plus 1 weft thread (102 threads). Divide into 28 groups of three threads with nine groups of two distributed evenly among them. Other end will have 94 warp threads plus one weft thread (95 threads). Divide threads into 31 groups of three with one group of two at center. Using three groups of threads, make 3″ long braids at each end. Tie pairs of braids together by wrapping one thread from each pair of braids around remaining threads of pair several times, tucking it in wrapped portion; trim ends to 2″.

GREEN, TURQUOISE, AND OLIVE: Materials: Turquoise and olive rug yarn, green boucle dress yarn: one skein each. Round plastic buckle with tongue removed. 3″ outside diameter, 1¾″ crossbar.

Directions: Warp loom, using following sequence: 2 olive, 2 green, 2 olive, 5 turquoise, 2 olive, 2 green, 2 olive, making it 2″ wide. Work is tightly woven throughout.

Pattern: Using olive for weft, weave seven rows plain. Using green for weft: * when three turquoise warp threads are up, weave plain; when down, pass shuttle over green and olive threads as usual, but under three turquoise for ¾″ *. Weave one row when three turquoise threads are down, passing shuttle through normally for plain weave. Repeat * to *.

Repeat plain weave and pattern seventeen times (belt should measure 34″), ending with seven rows plain weave and using olive for weft.

Remove fabric from loom; knot ends close to last row with an overhand knot (see page 76), knotting adjacent strands of same color together (seven knots). Trim fringe to 6″ at other end; divide ends into pairs and tie an overhand knot close to last row with each pair. Wrap buckle with olive yarn, concealing ends by tucking in and gluing in place. Fold fringeless end of belt around crossbar of buckle and sew in place with green yarn. Trim ends close to work.

WOVEN BAND PILLOWS

EQUIPMENT: Inkle loom (for weaving strips). Scissors. Sewing needle. Tape measure. Straight
continued on page 200

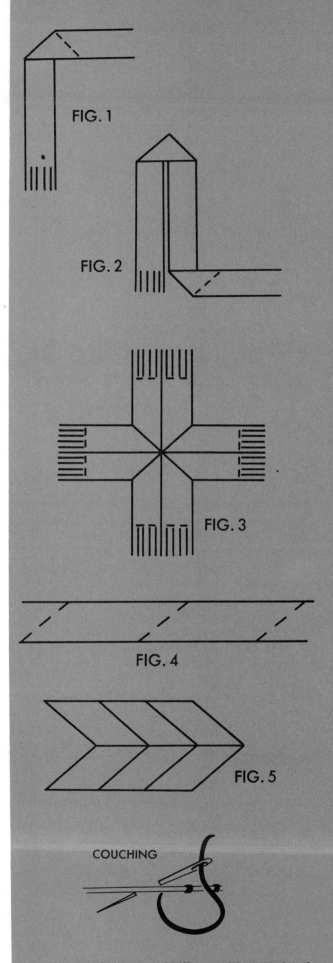

Designs for Woven Band Pillows, with stitch detail.

WOVEN BAND PILLOWS
continued from page 199

pins. Masking tape.

MATERIALS: Knitting worsted in colors shown or as desired. Knife-edge kapok pillow forms, 14" square and 7½" x 15½" oblong. Felt or upholstery fabric to cover pillow form, 15" x 30". Sewing thread.

GENERAL DIRECTIONS: Following directions that come with inkle loom, warp loom, using color sequences in individual directions. Weave across warp threads according to loom directions, taking care to pull weaving yarn (weft) throught the warp threads tightly enough so weft thread is visible only at side edges. Weave band the length given in individual directions. Remove weaving from loom.

For pillow cover, cut two pieces of felt or fabric for each: 14½" square for the square pillows and 7¾" x 15¾" for oblong pillow. Pin woven bands to piece of fabric for pillow top according to individual directions; details are on page 199. Sew bands in place by slip-stitching with thread to match edge of band. With right sides of front and back pillow pieces together, sew around three sides with 3/8" seams. Turn right side out. Insert pillow form and slip-stitch remaining side closed. (Pillow cover is slightly smaller than inner pillow for a snug fit.)

Square Gold Pillow: Warp the loom with knitting worsted, placing colors in following sequence: 4 blue, 1 green, 1 blue, 1 green, 1 blue; 4 green, 1 red, 1 green, 1 red, 1 green; 4 red, 1 green, 1 red, 1 green, 1 red; 4 green, 1 blue, 1 green, 1 blue, 1 green; 4 blue. Weave with blue yarn. This band is 2" wide; weave 60" long.

Fold band on pillow top according to Fig. 1 and Fig. 2. Leave 2" for fringe at lower left beginning, and make first fold over band 9½" up from edge of fringe, following Fig. 1. Fold band under and down (dash line, Fig. 1). Make next fold over band at bottom, Fig. 2, with point even with edge of fringe. Fold under (dash line, Fig. 2) and up. Continue, making two points at top and bottom and ending with a 2" fringe at top right. Sew touching edges of bands together. Slip-stitch in place and finish, following General Directions.

Square Green Pillow: Warp loom with knitting worsted, placing colors in following sequence, in three groups: 1st group—6 black (1 pink, 1 black) 2 times; (1 black, 1 pink) 3 times; 1 black; (1 black, 1 pink) 2 times; 2 black; 2nd group—6 pink, (1 chartreuse, 1 pink) 2 times; (1 pink, 1 chartreuse) 3 times; 1 pink; (1 pink, 1 chartreuse) 2 times; 2 pink; 3rd group—6 chartreuse, (1 black, 1 chartreuse) 2 times; (1 chartreuse, 1 black) 3 times; 1 chartreuse; (1 chartreuse, 1 black) 2 times; 2 chartreuse. Weave with black yarn.

This band is 3" wide; weave 64" long, including a 2" fringe at each end. Cut into four equal pieces (including fringes). Fold each piece in half into a point as shown in Figs. 1 and 2, with ends even. Fringe unfringed ends of each piece 2" deep. Sew center edges together. Steam-press each piece. Pin pieces on pillow top with overlap of folded point down, and points meeting at center, Fig. 3. Slip-stitch points together. Slip-stitch entire piece to pillow top. Across each section at top of fringe, couch two strands of black yarn (dash lines, Fig. 3).

Oblong Pillow: Warp loom with knitting worsted, placing colors in following sequence: (4 black, 4 turquoise) 3 times; (1 black, 1 turquoise) 11 times; 1 black. Weave with black yarn. This band is 2½" wide; weave 45" long.

From completed band, cut six sections at a 45° angle, each 7¼" long (see dash lines in Fig. 4); secure edges before cutting with masking tape, allowing ¼" on each side of cut free. Pin the six pieces diagonally together, matching weaving designs, as shown in Fig. 5. Slip-stitch side edges of pieces together. Sew along center seam with about ¼" seam allowance. Steam-press center seam flat, and slip-stitch piece to pillow top. Sew pillow front and back together, sewing in weaving.

Other Crafts

Each previous chapter has concentrated on one craft technique, giving the craftsman several ideas for developing ability in that medium. Following are a variety of items, each in a different technique to add dimension to this book and to hopefully inspire craftsmen to develop more handcraft skills. Make the designs featured to learn the procedure and then — originate your own wall plaque of tacks, nails, and wire — create a bold decoration for the patio from packing-crate lumber — experiment with coping-saw carving — play with seeds and make fun designs — crush and dye the common eggshell to use for mosaics — twist wire and add tissue to form jewelry — find scraps of wood and print their shapes on fabric or paper for pictures and hangings. Many of the craft items in this section were created by men; however these techniques do not require extra strength and are easy for women. No power tools are needed — just wire cutters, pliers, a small hand drill, and a hammer and saw — plus the usual household items such as a ruler and scissors.

SHINING ROOSTER

SIZE: About 18″ square.

EQUIPMENT: Paper for pattern. Pencil. Ruler. Tracing paper. Coping saw. Sandpaper. Brush for stain. Tack hammer.

MATERIALS: Plywood 3/8″ thick, 18″ square. Walnut stain. Fine-pointed felt-tipped ink marking pen. Wire nails 1¼″ long, gold-color finish. Shingle nails 1½″ long, galvanized, zinc-coated. Finishing nails 1¾″ and 1¼″ long. Brass escutcheon pins 5/8″ long. Wire brads ½″ long. Corrugated metal fasteners about 1″ long. Tacks, blue-black finish, about 7/8″ long; copper about ½″ long. Silver-finish, round-headed thumbtacks. Electrical wiring staples with blue and silver-color finish. Upholstery nails (commonly called tacks): smooth-head with nickel finish, and one with gilt finish; hammered-head and flowered-head with brass-color finish. Metal washer about ½″ diameter. Fine wire in both silver and gold-color finish. Small piece of aluminum tooling foil. All-purpose glue. Strong wire for hanging.

DIRECTIONS: Enlarge rooster pattern on page 204 by copying on paper ruled in 1″ squares. Trace pattern. Place tracing, penciled side down, on wood; go over tracing on wrong side to transfer outline and area lines to wood. Cut rooster outline out of wood. Sand edges smooth. Go over penciled area lines with pen. Stain wood following directions on can; let dry.

Following illustration and pattern for placement of nails and tacks, carefully hammer nails and tacks in place, working areas in order given below. Hammer nails in just deep enough for them to stay in place. Be careful that points do not project on back. Hammer upholstery nails and thumbtacks all the way in unless otherwise directed.

For eye, hold metal washer in place with gilt-finish upholstery nail; hammer a few escutcheon pins and wire brads around washer.

In area A, hammer flowered-head nails and thumbtacks alternately at each dot. Where lines intersect and at ends of lines, hammer an escutcheon pin; bring gold-color wire along lines in one direction and silver-color wire in other direction, wrapping around pins.

Outline area B and border line between A and C with escutcheon pins. At each dot, place a hammered-head upholstery nail; hammer wire brads around dot to fill scrolls; outline scrolls with escutcheon pins.

In area C, hammer wire brads and copper tacks along all diamond lines.

In area D, hammer flowered-head upholstery nails in curved lines from top to bottom; hammer escutcheon pins between.

In area E, place curved rows of corrugated fasteners from top to bottom of area; hold each fastener in place with three escutcheon pins hammered between corrugations on both sides.

In area F, hammer a nickel upholstery nail at each dot; hammer escutcheon pins around each nail.

In area G, hammer blue and silver-finish staples to fill area, alternating colors, placing blue staples horizontally and silver staples vertically.

On feet area H, hammer a wire brad at each dot. Wrap silver-color wire around brads to outline area, and criss-cross area.

In areas J, hammer blue-color tacks close together to fill, and slant tacks out toward edges.

In area K, hammer blue-color tacks in straight to fill area.

In area L, hammer gold-color wire nails closely, slanting them outward.

In area M, hammer shingle nails to fill area, some straight and some slanted.

In area N, hammer 1¼″ finishing nails closely to fill area, slanting them all slightly outward, except in small area next to area G; slant these toward area G.

In areas P, hammer finishing nails 1¾″ long to fill area; slant nails at bottom of center area down toward feet.

For beak, cut a 1″ square out of aluminum; bend over wooden beak area and glue to secure.

For hanging, make loop of strong wire by twisting ends together securely. Staple loop to back of rooster in position to hang straight.

JUMBO SUNBURST

SIZE: 44″ in diameter.

EQUIPMENT: Paper for pattern. Thin cardboard. Pencil. Ruler. Scissors. Thin nail, string, and pencil for compass. Saw. Hammer. Flat paintbrushes. Nail set. Coarse sandpaper.

MATERIALS: Wood: packing-crate lumber, 63 ft. of 6″ boards (read through directions before purchasing wood to determine total number and lengths of boards): 1″ x 2″ pieces of lumber—one 40″ long, two 32″, one 20″, and two 18″ long. Poster paint: blue, yellow, and orange. Finishing nails. Plastic wood.

DIRECTIONS: Enlarge patterns for face and rays on page 204 by copying on paper ruled in 2″ squares; complete half-patterns indicated by long dash lines. Mark face pieces and each ray on thin cardboard and cut out for patterns.

Lay eight 46″-long boards together vertically. For braces, nail 40″-strip of wood across center back and two 32″ strips above and below and equidistant from center. To mark circle on boards, hammer a nail at center of boards, tie string to nail and tie a sharp pencil to string 22″ away from nail. Using this as a compass, swing

continued on page 208

Wooden rooster is brilliant with hardware feathers! Using a coping saw, rooster is cut from 18″ square of plywood and then stained dark brown. With a variety of tacks and nails, plus thin wire, an opulent texture is created producing the effect of a richly plumed three-dimensional bird. Pattern, page 204, gives cutout line and defines areas for placing the decoration as illustrated. See directions opposite.

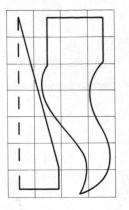
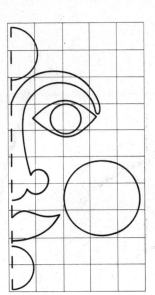

Patterns above and right are for Jumbo Sunburst;
trace rays and face on paper ruled in 2" squares.

Below, pattern for Rooster; trace on 1" squares.

Gigantic sun in warm orange and yellow will brighten the patio or bring sunshine to a modern indoor setting. This stylized sunburst, 44" in diameter, has an interesting rustic texture as it is constructed of packing-crate lumber! The sunrays are nailed to a stained background, then a bright face and features are added, giving the plaque dimension. Charts are on opposite page; directions are on page 202.

Fanciful wood birds to perch alone or in a grouping: an unusual craft idea. Intriguing sculpture, which we call "coping saw carving," is made of three layers of wood. The entire outline of bird is cut for center layer; the side pieces give body thickness. Layers are glued, then finished by distressing wood or painting bird in bright colors. Birds on individual stands make an interesting decorator accent. On opposite page, the birds decorate a unique room divider—a pine door and a ready-made planter. All the birds may be made in three sizes, from 5¾" to 15½" long. To make the Decorator Birds, see page 208.

a circle 44″ in diameter. With saw, cut off boards to form circle. To form head, lay four 24″ long boards together vertically; for braces, nail 20″ strip across center back and two 18″ above and below equidistant from center. Mark 22″ diameter circle on wood. With saw, round off boards to form circle.

Place cardboard face pieces and rays on pieces of 6″ board; go around outline with pencil to mark on wood. Repeat each ray shape eight times. Cut out all pieces with saw. Sand all edges.

Thin poster paint with water so that it will only stain the wood and the grain will show through. Paint 44″ background circle blue; 22″ head circle, triangular rays, and pupils yellow; paint wavy rays, nose-brow pieces, outer eyes, mouth, cheeks and chin and forehead circles orange; let dry.

To assemble, mark eight equidistant points around outer edge of blue circle. Nail a triangular ray on front of blue circle with point outward and at edge of circle as shown; repeat around at each marked point. Place wavy rays, all going in same direction, overlapping and between triangular rays as shown; nail in place. Nail features in place on head circle. Center head circle on background circle over rays and nail. Countersink all nails which show on front; fill holes with plastic wood; sand flat and touch up with thinned paint.

DECORATIVE BIRDS

EQUIPMENT: Pencil. Ruler. Paper for patterns. Carbon paper. Jigsaw or coping saw. Fine and medium sandpaper. Drill with 3/16″, ¼″, and 5/8″ bits. Paintbrushes: small flat and fine-pointed. Small and large paper punches. **For Antiquing and Distressing Wood:** Chain; matt knife or gouging tool; awl; soft rag.

MATERIALS: Wood: (**Note:** Each bird can be made in three different sizes. Each bird is made up of three pieces of wood. The thickness of wood required for each size is given; judge wood size by enlarged pattern pieces.) For large birds, 7/8″ thick white pine; for medium birds, ½″ thick white pine or ¼″ thick solid-core plywood; for small birds, 1/8″ thick veneer. Pine wood for stands: 4″ x 7″ x 2″ thick for large birds; 2¼″ x 4½″ x ¾″ thick for medium and small birds. Dowels: 5/8″ diameter for large birds; ¼″ diameter for medium birds, in desired lengths. Metal rods 3/16″ diameter for small birds in desired lengths. Wooden or plastic beads, if desired, for decoration and eyes, and wire to fit beads. Wood glue. **For Painted Birds:** Poster paints and heavy bond paper. **For Distressed Wood Birds:** Walnut stain and paste wax (optional). **For Antiqued Birds:** Ebony glaze (or walnut stain) from antiquing kit.

DIRECTIONS: Enlarge the bird patterns given below to the size desired by copying on paper ruled in 1″ (small), 1½″ (medium), or 2″ (large) squares; one bird is also given actual-size (small) *continued on page 210*

Enlarge patterns for the Decorative Birds to size desired by copying on 1″ squares (small), 1½″ (medium), or 2″ (large). The bird on the opposite page is shown actual size (small).

x

right. Using carbon paper, transfer bird patterns to pieces of wood. Cut entire outline of bird out of one piece of wood. On this piece only, mark holes to be drilled in center of bottom edges and heads (if adding bead decoration or bead eyes) where indicated by X's on pattern. Cut two more of the same bird, without extensions, following short dash lines on patterns. Glue the three bird pieces together with complete bird in center. Round off corners and sand entire bird and stand smooth with medium, then fine sandpaper. Drill holes in bottom of birds and center of stands: use 5/8″ bit, 1″ deep for large; ¼″ bit, ½″ deep for medium; 3/16″ bit, ¼″ deep for small. Whittle ends of dowels if necessary so they will fit well into holes. Paint all stands black; paint all dowels gold, except for distressed wood bird and antiqued bird.

Painted Birds: Paint entire bird one color as shown or as desired; let dry. A second coat may be necessary to make color even. Paint decorations on each bird on both sides with lines, dots, and circles as shown, or make your own designs; medium and large circles may be punched out of bond paper, painted, and glued on bird.

To decorate with beads, use colored glass beads, or paint wooden beads and drill holes for wire (you will need small bits or hammer and nail to make hole). Glue wire in holes; glue beads on ends of wires. Large beads may be glued on tips of tail feathers.

When bird is finished, glue dowel in bird and in stand. Spray with clear lacquer; let dry thoroughly.

Antiqued Birds: To give bird antiqued look, as for brown and yellow bird, tone down poster paint by painting with ebony glaze or walnut stain and then wiping with soft rag. Eye is a yellow wooden bead, red glass bead, and tiny blue seed bead on wire glued in head.

Distressed Wood Bird: First beat plain pine wood bird with chain to make soft dents; stab at it with matt knife or gouging tool; then stab at it with awl to make worm holes. Sand bird lightly. Stain bird with walnut stain. If desired, use paste wax to bring out natural patina in wood and buff to soft luster. Eye is 1″ diameter brass plate with brown bead hammered into it on bird. Stain dowel and finish as for painted birds.

SEED-ART PLAQUES

EQUIPMENT: Tracing paper. Pencil. Toothpicks. Small, pointed paintbrush. Ruler. Scissors. Small bowl. Slotted spoon. Paper towels. Waxed

paper. Carbon paper.

MATERIALS: Heavy cardboard for backing. Colored construction paper. Elmer's Glue-All. Seeds as indicated for individual pictures. Food coloring. Black ink. Picture frames as desired. Heavy black thread.

GENERAL DIRECTIONS: Measure and cut cardboard to fit in picture frame. Cut colored construction paper the same size, and glue on cardboard.

Trace designs from actual-size illustrations on these pages. Using carbon paper, lightly retrace main areas of designs onto construction-paper background. Spread glue on one area of design at a time, and press seeds in place to fill area. For neat appearance in filling areas, first outline the space with a row of seeds, then fill successive rows to middle. In placing small seeds, you may find it helpful to use toothpicks with a tiny dab of glue on tip, to pick up each seed and place it.

To dye rice, mix a little vegetable coloring with water in a bowl. Drop small amounts of white rice at a time into dye. The rice will quickly reach a bright shade. Remove rice from dye with slotted spoon and spread on paper towel to blot; then place dyed rice on waxed paper to dry thoroughly.

Cat: Glue on two dried baby lima beans for feet, two lima beans for cheeks, a dried lentil for nose, and two black-eyed peas for eyes. Cover remaining area of body, head, and tail thickly with glue; sprinkle poppy seeds thickly over entire cat, let set a few seconds, then shake off loose seeds. Cover lima bean feet with glue and cover with poppy seeds. Cut six pieces of black thread from ¾″ to 1″ long, and glue to cheeks for whiskers. Tie a short piece of narrow blue ribbon into a bow and glue to neck.

Mouse, Peas-in-Pod, and Flower: Dye a small amount of rice green; dye a few grains of rice red.

Fill entire pea pod with green rice, and make stem of green rice. Glue on dried green peas in a line along center; glue on four dill seeds at stem end of pod. Glue a large dried lima bean above

continued on page 212

Ordinary seeds can inspire you to create these amusing plaques — actual size, they can be traced for patterns. Vegetable coloring is used to dye the rice red for apple and flower — green for pea pod, and yellow for worm's feet. Poppy-seed cat has lima bean cheeks and a lentil nose. Glue all to cardboard and construction paper backing; directions on page 210.

pea pod for mouse body, two yellow corn kernels for ears, a peppercorn for nose, and white rice for legs with dill seeds for feet. Draw eye and mouth with black ink. Cut ½″ pieces of black thread for whiskers, and glue in place. Cut 3½″ piece of black thread for tail, and glue in place as shown, with an apple seed at end.

For flower, glue a lentil at center, apple seeds radiating from center with dill seeds between, and three red-dyed rice grains at tip of each apple seed.

Ear of Corn: For cob area, fill with yellow corn kernels. Fill both sides of husk area up to tips with white rice. Make tips of husks with dried dill seeds.

Apple Slice and Worm: Dye a small amount of rice red and a few grains yellow. Fill in bottom area of apple with red rice for skin; fill in top section with white rice, using three real apple seeds for core.

For worm, make body of yellow corn, legs of yellow-dyed rice. For head, glue two dried baby lima beans at end of body, one above the other. Glue two black-eyed peas on head for eyes, and a peppercorn for nose. Cut short pieces of black thread; glue in place for antennae and tail.

EGGSHELL MOSAICS

EQUIPMENT: Glass jars, various sizes. Tweezers: Metal spoon. Tracing paper. Carbon paper. Scissors. Pencil. Small pointed paintbrush.

MATERIALS: Eggshells. Liquid fabric dyes or food coloring (colors given under individual directions). Elmer's Glue-All. Clear acrylic enamel spray. For additional materials, see individual directions.

GENERAL DIRECTIONS: Save eggshells from cooking. Rinse them in water and remove thin membrane that may have adhered to interior. (Membrane pulls off easily.) Shells from four large eggs cover area about 6″ x 11″.

To Prepare Surfaces: Paint or paper item (see individual directions); dry thoroughly. Copy or enlarge designs, below, on tracing paper; transfer to surface by going over lines of design with carbon underneath.

To Dye Eggshells: Use a different jar for each color, pint or quart size depending on quantity of shells to be dyed. Mix dye with hot water ac-
continued on page 214

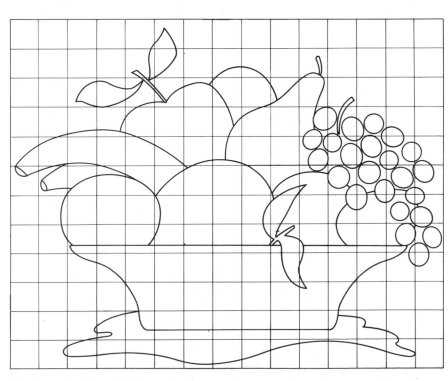

Patterns for Eggshell Mosaics; trace flowers; enlarge bowl on 1″ squares.

The ancient art of matching small pieces of stone, glass, etc., to form a mosaic design can be experienced with dyed eggshells! Pieces of colored shells are glued to a painted or papered surface. Note the vibrant marbelized effect in a bowl of fruit against white fiberboard, in the 16″ x 20½″ picture above. Paper tray with natural eggshells and bright flowers becomes a snack server. See Eggshell Mosaics, left.

EGGSHELL MOSAICS
continued from page 212

cording to directions on bottle, then immerse egg-shells in dye-bath and stir with metal spoon until desired shade is reached. Rinse shells in cold water; set aside to dry. **Note:** Since eggshells range from white to brown, dye will cover them in varying shades, adding to the interest.

To Apply Eggshells: Break up eggshells into irregular pieces, varying from about 1¼" in diameter to bits the size of a pinhead. Apply larger pieces first. With small paintbrush, cover back of shell with film of glue; place in position with tweezers. Press shells firmly until they are flat and glue adheres; the pressure produces a crackled finish. For tiny pieces, just dip into glue and apply where needed to fill in small areas. When glue has dried thoroughly, spray with clear enamel.

TRAY: Additional Materials: Two paper trays, 10¼" x 5¼" (the kind used for packaging meat). Orange spray paint. Green and orange dyes. Four ¾" felt disks.

To Make: For a sturdy tray, glue one tray inside the other; then wet edges thoroughly with water and apply glue between them, squeezing the two edges together until they adhere to each other. Place a weight on center of doubled tray to hold its shape while drying. When dry, spray with several coats of orange paint.

Using actual-size flower patterns above, trace flowers and transfer to tray. Glue on eggshells, making two orange flowers with dark green centers, two light green flowers with orange centers, a dark green flower with white center. Add a few dark green bits scattered over background. Fill background with various shades of undyed eggshells. Spray with clear enamel. Glue four felt disks to bottom corners of tray.

PICTURE: Additional Materials: White fiberboard, 16" x 20½". Dyes: red, green, purple, yellow, blue. Lattice strips, 1" x ¼": two 16" long, two 21-1/8" long. Small nails. Hammer. Dark green paint. Paintbrush. Gold braid, 2¼ yards.

To Make: Enlarge design for bowl of fruit above by copying on paper ruled in 1" squares; transfer design to fiberboard. Glue on eggshells, using following colors: red for apples, yellow for lemons and bananas, light green for pear, purple for plum and grapes, medium blue for eggplant, light blue for bowl, dark green for leaves, stems, shadow. When glue is dry, spray with clear enamel.

To Make Frame: Fit lattice strips closely around outside of fiberboard; nail together at corners; paint dark green. Run a line of glue around edges of fiberboard and place frame over it with frame extending to front as shadow box. To finish, glue gold braid along inner frame.

WHIMSICAL JEWELRY

EQUIPMENT: Tracing paper. Pencil. Round-nosed pliers. Wire cutters. Scissors. Fine, pointed paintbrush.

MATERIALS: Thin copper wire. Colored tissue paper. Elmer's Glue-All. Acrylic paint. Colorless nail polish. Earring backs. Fine chains.

DIRECTIONS: Trace actual-size illustrations of shapes and designs of jewelry. Form a small loop in the middle of a length of wire; twist wire below loop. With pliers, shape wire to form design, following tracing. Make sure wire lies flat. Cut off excess wire after design is complete, making sure end is inconspicuous.

With finger, rub a thin layer of glue on wire shape; while glue is still moist, carefully press wire down on double piece of colored tissue. Let dry to adhere well. With scissors, cut off excess paper. Coat both sides of jewelry (tissue and wire) with nail polish. Let dry and coat again. If desired, leave plain or pencil in design, following tracing, and paint, following illustration. Outline some designs with black paint as shown. When paint is dry, attach loop of each earring to earring back; insert chain through each pendant.

SCRAP WOOD PRINTING

EQUIPMENT: Brayer. Palette knife. Glass or other non-absorbent surface for rolling inks. Brush for cleaning loose dirt from wood blocks. Newspapers. Kerosene. Rags or paper towels. Pencil. Crayons.

MATERIALS: Oil-base block printing inks (or textile paints*). Linseed oil, light machine oil, or printing ink reducer to thin inks. Wrapping paper, colored construction paper, or cotton fabric (percale, linen-like cotton, etc.), according to use to which prints will be put. Scrap wood in various sizes, shapes, grains: poor-grade plywood, sand-blasted wood, weathered boards, etc. Thin strips of wood, dowel rods, etc., for adding *continued on page 218*

A variety of wire and tissue-paper jewelry provides whimsical, colorful accessories. This is a creative craft for all ages — the ideas and designs appropriate to this technique are unlimited. Realistic, abstract or amusing details can be added with acrylic paint after the tissue is coated with colorless nail polish and dried. Directions are given above.

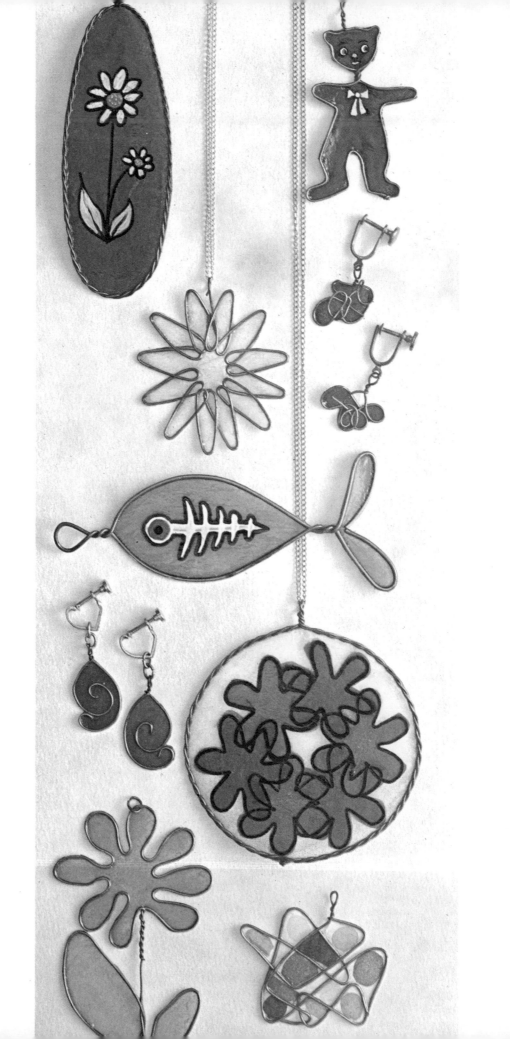

215

Bits of weathered wood provide blocks for printing on paper or fabrics. The stamped rough-wood impressions create designs that can be humorous, fanciful, rustic, or sophisticated. A peaceful duck floats on water of azure and purple, overprinting the first brown background impression. Duck print, made on construction paper, is matted and framed. Scrap Wood Printing on page 214.

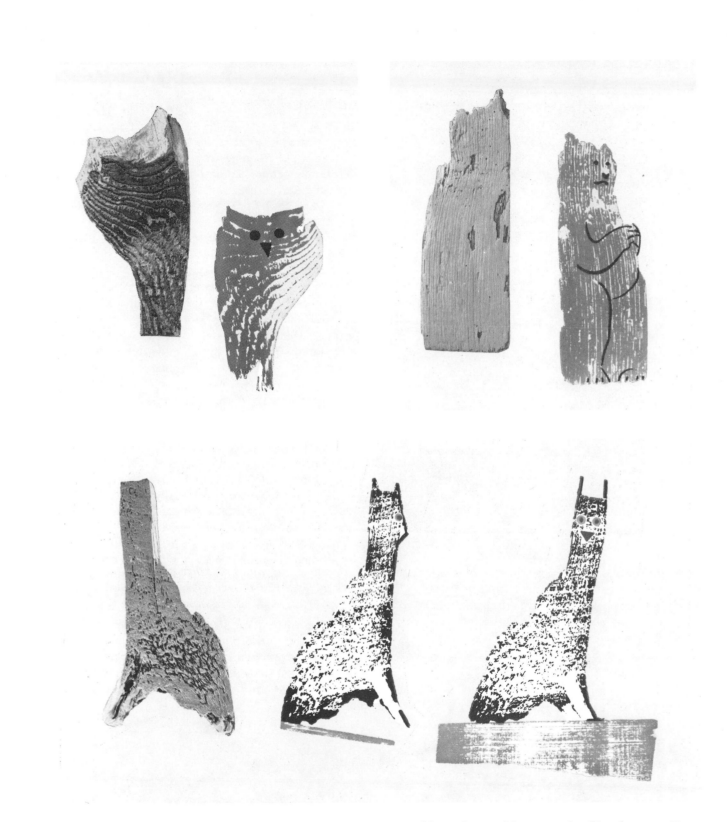

Illustrations at left and above show the evolution of block printing with wood scraps. Duck print: eye is stamped on duck with dowel; beak printed with narrow wood strip. Above, wood blocks form curvilinear owl.

An oblong shape, with crayon detailing, becomes Papa Bear. Majestic cat, created from a random form, is given two treatments—profile and full face; with a plank print, cat is seated on fence. See page 214.

SCRAP WOOD PRINTING
continued from page 214

details to the designs.

(*Note: Textile paints may be used instead of printing inks. Mix according to manufacturer's directions, spread with palette knife on rolling surface, and allow to dry out a bit before using. When paint can be rolled with brayer without skidding, use in same way as inks; experiment to determine proper consistency. Set according to manufacturer's directions.)

SELECTING BLOCKS FOR PRINTING: Since observation of blocks is not a reliable index as to the printed result, make trial prints first, printing them on scrap paper and following directions below. Bits of wood you might be tempted to discard often make the most interesting prints. Big, strongly grained boards are difficult to handle and usually require more thought than small scraps, which may suggest forms that are easily elaborated. The prints illustrated were all made from wood picked up at an abandoned farm and used with no reworking.

After making several trial prints of each block, inspect them in various positions and begin adding details; these may be sketched in pencil or crayon to help crystallize impressions. Most of the blocks used in the samples illustrated suggested natural forms and were developed as such. One could just as easily create abstract patterns by concentrating on color and distribution instead of pictorial interest.

When you are satisfied with the results of your experimental prints, plan their use, color, and placement; print as directed below.

GENERAL DIRECTIONS FOR PRINTING: Mix inks to obtain desired colors. If ink seems stiff, thin with a drop or two of linseed oil, light machine oil, or printing ink reducer; inks from freshly opened tubes are of proper consistency. Dip brayer into ink and roll brayer back and forth on glass until ink has a smooth texture and makes a snapping sound.

Brush wood block clean of loose dust or dirt.

Illustration left shows how duck design repeated on fabric makes interesting hanging. See page 214.

On opposite page, one block print turned upside down is either a whale or a road runner. Printed on construction paper, framed prints are mounted against silvery weathered board "mats." Directions, p. 214.

Apply ink to block with brayer, moving brayer back and forth over surface in all directions until block is well covered.

Place material to be printed on an inch-thick pad of newspapers on floor. Place block, inked side down, on material and step on it with full weight, being careful not to shift position of block once set in place. Step all over block to be sure contact with entire surface has been established. If print is too light, use more ink and/or more pressure on subsequent prints. Repeat as desired, re-inking block before each printing. Be sure to clean ink from block and let dry before attempting to print block in a different color.

Blocks too small to have ink rolled on may be inked by tapping against brayer.

To print fabric, cut it to size rather than attempting to print long lengths. Plan placement for repeat patterns on paper large enough to show pattern. If you wish to mark guide lines on fabric as an aid in placing patterns, use tailor's chalk, which will wash out. For sharp ink impressions, dampen fabric before printing. Lay dampened fabric on bed of newspaper, smooth out wrinkles, square up cloth, and print.

When prints are dry, add the simple details needed to complete them by inking thin blocks of wood for straight lines, dowel tips for circles, etc., and overprinting original motifs. If more elaboration is necessary than is practical to print on, crayon details may be added when print is to be used for a picture, as for Papa Bear shown; when print is to be used for a fabric, add details with textile paints.

Clean blocks and all equipment with kerosene and rags or paper towels.

Allow fabric prints to dry for several days; to set colors, press fabric on the wrong side.

INDEX